HW 10-1

SEEKING
SICILY

SEEKING
SICILY

A Cultural Journey Through Myth and
Reality in the Heart of the Mediterranean

John Keahey

THOMAS DUNNE BOOKS
St. Martin's Press
New York

Note: The recipes in this book are from two sources: Renée Restivo, founder of Soul of Sicily, and *Sicily: Culinary Crossroads* by Giuseppe Coria. Restivo's organization is a cultural association based in Noto, Sicily. It offers cooking programs to visitors and opens doors to the culture, art, literature, food, and wine of southeastern Sicily. Programs share local traditions and ingredients: www.soulofsicily.com. Coria (1930–2003) was a Sicilian gastronome, culinary historian, folklorist, and vintner. He collected authentic recipes from family notebooks, interviews, and historical records from as far back as Sicily's Greek period. Oronzo Editions published his book and other Italian cookbooks: www.oronzoeditions.com.

THOMAS DUNNE BOOKS.
An imprint of St. Martin's Press.

SEEKING SICILY. Copyright © 2011 by John Keahey. All rights reserved. Printed in the United States of America. For information, address St. Martin's Press, 175 Fifth Avenue, New York, N.Y. 10010.

www.stmartins.com

Book design by Phil Mazzone

Map by Ken Gross

Library of Congress Cataloging-in-Publication Data

Keahey, John.
    Seeking Sicily: a cultural journey through myth and reality in the heart of the Mediterranean / John Keahey.—1st ed.
        p. cm.
    Includes bibliographical references and index.
    ISBN 978-0-312-59705-4
    1. Sicily (Italy)—Description and travel.   2. Keahey, John—Travel—Italy—Sicily.   3. Sicily (Italy)—Social life and customs.   4. National characteristics, Sicilian.   5. Sicily (Italy)—Intellectual life.   I. Title.
    DG864.3.K43 2011
    945'.8—dc23

                                                                        2011026786

10   9   8   7   6   5   4   3   2

To the memory of my teacher Bessie Mae Savage Baker.

Long ago, when I was sixteen, she encouraged me to take her journalism class, opening the door to the rest of my life.

CONTENTS

PREFACE

M<small>OST SUMMER</small> afternoons when I was six or seven, and for many years beyond, I would walk two miles from my southwest Idaho home to the Carnegie Library in downtown Nampa. I would grasp the large door handle with its beautifully rubbed patina, pull open the heavy leaded-glass portal surrounded by wonderfully smooth and polished-oak frames, turn to my left, and head downstairs along a narrow stairway, its creaking treads worn into shallow depressions.

There, in a long, narrow room that served as the library's children's section, I would sit for hours at a large table poring through stacks of stereo cards imprinted with mysterious, sepia-toned double images, slipping one at a time into the frame of a stereoscopic holder. Through the eyepiece, I could see— magically I thought—the double photograph now as one startling, sharply focused 3-D image.

I absorbed thousands of these images of Chicago, New York, San Francisco, Rome or Paris, and vivid scenes of the European countryside. I discovered the Empire State Building, the Roman Colosseum, the Eiffel Tower. But what I luxuriated in were the foreign scenes of peasant farmers—men, women, and children—threshing wheat or picking grapes that were piled high in baskets strapped tight onto sturdy backs, or images showing large milk cans being hauled in the back of donkey-drawn carts.

These photographs, which I viewed in the days long before my family got its first television and for years afterward, were my introduction to the world far beyond my neighborhood of neat two-bedroom, postwar houses. The scenes, probably dating back to the late nineteenth and early twentieth centuries, are how I visualized Europe, and in particular Italy, well into adulthood.

When I eventually got to Rome, Florence, and then Sicily in 1986 at age forty, I saw nothing like those pictures. There were no donkey-pulled carts with drivers chewing on the stems of stubby pipes, no families gathering and bundling wheat by hand. Instead, there were tractors like the ones farmers used in the countryside around my hometown, and long, straight rows of corn and potato fields, and flowing acres of golden wheat punctuated here and there by mechanized combines. There were a few elderly women wearing black, but that was about it. During those first two weeks in Sicily, I found myself driving down well-paved roads, surrounded not by donkey carts but by Fiats.

It didn't take long to realize that the images I had absorbed in that quiet library basement of my boyhood were gone forever.

Now, thankfully, this much-abused peasant class is gone. Tourists flock to Sicilian farms in agritouristic droves to help pick grapes or harvest lemons, oranges, or olives, and to eat hearty food prepared by Sicilian families who supplement their incomes off the land by hosting visitors from Germany or Great Britain or the United States—all willing to pay significant money to try to reconnect to the earth of their ancestors. But most of these visitors, who stay for only a few days or perhaps a week, don't take the time to understand what it was like in these once malaria-ridden plains and valleys just a few generations earlier.

I discovered that there was a better way to find out what it was really like way back then, at a time before or during the taking of those stereoscopic images. It happened one day when, absently thumbing through books on a bookstore shelf, I came across a Penguin Classic edition of Giovanni Verga's *Cavalleria Rusticana and Other Stories*. Like a hand leaping out of the pages, the stories grabbed me, reminding me of those sepia images discovered in childhood. Once again I could visualize reapers heading to or from their fields on foot, sometimes traveling so far that, during the harvest, they had to sleep out in the open in the fields or in tiny huts, eating like soldiers in an army: "biscuit in the morning and bread and bitter oranges at nine o'clock and midday, and homemade pasta in the evening . . . served from kneading troughs as big as washtubs."

I began to live vicariously in another time. Nineteenth-century Verga led me to Luigi Pirandello, whose writings spanned both centuries, then on to twentieth-century Leonardo Sciascia, perhaps the greatest Sicilian writer of them all. They taught me about a world unlike anything on the peninsula of nearby Italy that I had experienced during all my years of traveling there. Through the pages of story after story, novel after novel, essay after essay, they whispered to me that Sicily, in the entire Mediterranean world, is truly unique, that in many ways it is like a puzzle made up of thousands of tiny pieces and is almost impossible to put together completely. But each piece, standing alone, is complicated, complex, and rich.

I have gone to Sicily several times since 1986. Most recently, for this project, I made four trips in one year: March and July 2009 alone, November 2009 with my son Brad, and early March 2010 with photographer and documentary filmmaker Steve McCurdy. My idea was to see the island in various seasons, and the final visit in late March was to witness Easter, a major event for most Sicilians.

The goal in writing this book is to develop a better understanding of Sicilians and their unique culture, which is demonstrably separate from Italy itself, through conversations with these Mediterranean islanders and by studying their writers, their myths, and a history that spans more than three thousand years. This history is a key to everything else. One foreign power after another has trampled over this land—northern Italians were the final conquerors—adding to and co-opting unique aspects of the island's character. This is a people who never had control of their own destiny.

I don't know if I can do this strange, magnificent, brooding island justice. But if I can look at it through these various eyes and compare that to what I have personally witnessed, maybe I can begin—just barely—to understand a land that has been scourged by so many and lovingly embraced by a few.

CHRONOLOGY

B.C.

8000–7000—Evidence has been uncovered of the earliest occupation in Sicily by humans, particularly in caves around present-day Scopello and Palermo.

2000–1100—Three major groups of people settle on the island, coming from areas around the Mediterranean. They are the Sicani, who first went to the western part. Different sources give different guesses about who came next, but the Sicels and the Elymians arrived in due course. The Elymians settled in the west, forcing the Sicani to the island's center, and the Sicels settled in the east.

1000—Phoenician merchants begin landing along the island's coastal areas, ending up primarily in the west after the Greeks arrived. Legend has it that in 814 the Phoenicians had established a colony at Carthage in North Africa from which the Carthaginian Empire developed.

Ca. 800—Greek merchants begin arriving in Sicily, establishing outposts. Carthage also creates way stations, particularly in the west.

735—The Greeks start colonizing the island. The first is Naxos, near Taormina, between Catania and Messina. Eventually numerous colonies are established as far west as Selinous (established in 630), now referred to as Selinunte.

Ca. 500–280—Syracusae, today's Siracusa, grows into the most powerful Greek city on Sicily. The Greeks are firmly entrenched on the island's eastern half. Carthaginians dominate the western half. Earlier peoples are absorbed into the newer cultures.

264–212—Rome and Carthage fight the first of three Punic wars. Rome wins, eventually taking over the island from the Greeks as well and turning it, in 227, into its first province, primarily to serve as a wheat-growing area. Siracusani resist Rome but are finally defeated in 212; Archimedes, a resident of Syracusae, is killed by a Roman soldier.

A.D.

410–535—As the Roman Empire in the West disintegrates, Sicily is controlled for a time by Germanic Vandals, until 476, and other foreign rulers, such as the Ostrogoths, until 535.

535—Sicily once again comes under Greek control, but these are Byzantine Greeks centered in Constantinople.

827–1061—The Arabs fight to take the island from the Byzantines. They bring in emigrants from all over the Muslim world, particularly North Africa, and these people begin to blend in with, and become, Sicilians.

1061–1190—The Normans, as mercenaries, land in Sicily and begin a decades-long battle to take over the entire island. What follows is a succession of Norman rulers, including Great Count Roger I and his son Roger II, who becomes the first king of Sicily (1130–1154), after serving as count (1105–1130) from age nine, and also ruler over Norman possessions in southern Italy.

1194—Sicily falls into the hands of the Germanic Hohenstaufen dynasty when Constance—daughter of Roger II, ruler of Sicily for four years after the death of William II, and one of the last in the Norman line—marries Henry VI, who becomes Holy Roman Emperor. Henry is crowned in Palermo. His son becomes Frederick II, one of the most able and progressive of Sicily's early rulers following the Arab period. Frederick is born in a tent in Jesi, midway down the Italian peninsula, while Constance was en route to Henry's coronation.

1250—Frederick II dies, followed by minor, ineffective successors.

1266—The pope names the Frenchman Charles I to the throne, a move bitterly resented by Sicilians. He is from the House of Anjou, also known as the Angevins.

1282—A revolt, known as the Sicilian Vespers, erupts on Easter Monday on the outskirts of Palermo at the church of Santo Spirito. Sicilians launch a revolution against the French in an attempt to force them out, killing most of the French on the island. The Angevin ruler, Charles I, sends an army to put down the rebels. When the revolt gets too big for Sicilians to handle by themselves, they call on the Spaniard Peter III of Aragon for help. He defeats the French, effectively halting Charles I's expansionist dreams for the eastern Mediterranean. In 1283, Peter takes control of the island, leaving it in Spanish hands for most of the next 575 years.

1302—The War of the Vespers officially ends at the Sicilian village of Caltabellotta. The French ruler Charles I and the pope agree that the Spanish ruler Peter's third son will be recognized as king, but under the designation "king of Trinacria" during his lifetime rather than as king of Sicily.

1479—The Spanish Inquisition is launched in Spain, eventually spreading throughout the Spanish world, including Sicily. Ultimately, Jews are expelled from Sicily.

1693—Much of eastern Sicily is devastated by an earthquake. Noto is leveled and later rebuilt at another location. Caltagirone and numerous other towns and villages are badly damaged.

1713–1720—The House of Savoy, lodged in what today is southeast France and northern Italy, gains control of Sicily and Victor Amadeus II becomes king. This is short-lived because Sicily is traded to Austria for the island of Sardinia.

1734—Another Spanish dynasty, the Bourbons, takes over Sicily and Naples.

1782—The Spanish Inquisition is abolished in Sicily.

1812—Sicily briefly gains independence from Naples but is still under the Bourbons. In 1816, the king reneges on his promise of autonomy and combines Sicily and Naples once more.

1848—A revolution breaks out, Palermo and Messina are bombed, and Palermo surrenders to the Bourbons.

1860–61—Northern Italians, led by Giuseppe Garibaldi, take control of the island from the Bourbons and eventually take southern Italy, too, unifying the nation from north to south. An 1861 vote shows overwhelming support of Sicilians to become a part of Italy. Italy comes under Vittorio Emanuele II, head of the House of Savoy.

1866—A brief revolution breaks out as a response to Sicilian belief that the 1861 election was fraudulent. Palermo is bombed by Italian ships, and the revolt is put down after three days.

1908—A massive earthquake destroys much of southern Calabria and the northeast of Sicily, including the city of Messina. The two areas lose as many as one hundred thousand people.

1922—Mussolini comes to power and launches a movement to force Sicilians to speak only Italian. He also clamps down on the Mafia, heavily diluting its power until the Allies in World War II use Mafia leaders to regain control of towns and villages when the Germans are driven out in 1943.

1946—Italy, in an attempt to quell a bloody separatist movement, names Sicily as one of its five autonomous regions.

1948—Italians vote to toss out the monarchy. Italy becomes a republic.

Mid-1980s—Hundreds of mafiosi stand trial in Palermo and most are convicted.

1992—Anti-Mafia Judge Giovanni Falcone, a key figure in those trials, is murdered on May 23 along with his wife and three bodyguards. A Mafia bomb explodes underneath a highway at Capaci, northwest of Palermo, as his motorcade passes by. On July 19, his friend from childhood and fellow judge Paolo Borsellino, along with five bodyguards, is killed in Palermo when a bomb goes off as he gets out of a car in front of his mother's house. Massive anti-Mafia demonstrations break out in Palermo.

Present era—Most Mafia leaders have been arrested, along with their associates, and billions of dollars in assets have been confiscated and turned over for public use. No Sicilian deceives him or herself by believing that the Mafia will disappear anytime soon.

SEEKING
SICILY

ONE

"A Leopard in Very Bad Trim"

Don Fabrizio could not know it then, but a great deal
of the slackness and acquiescence for which the people
of the South were to be criticized during the next decades was due to the stupid annulment of the first
expression of liberty ever offered them.

—Giuseppe di Lampedusa,
The Leopard (1960)

IN SICILY, 'no' often becomes 'yes'!"

So proclaims Claudio Cutrona as we scramble down scaffolding erected against a nondescript building just a few blocks
from the port of Palermo. It is a bright March morning in
2010 under a cloudless sky near the heart of Palermo's old
town. The day before, Claudio, my host at a bed-and-breakfast
tucked nearby in a narrow medieval-era street of the Vucciria,
had obtained permission from a group of painters to let us
climb their scaffolding. From that perch, we could look down
into the ruined grounds of the neighboring compound that
holds the busted-up remains of the fabled Palazzo Lampedusa.

The palazzo, in much gentler times, had been the home since his birth there in 1897 of Giuseppe di Lampedusa, author of the great Sicilian masterpiece, *Il gattopardo* (*The Leopard*), a novel that is a must-read for anyone who wants insight into Sicilians and how they became who they are, separate both culturally and emotionally from the rest of Italy.

Locked doorways and stone walls, perhaps fifteen feet high, had closed off the 1,600-square-yard compound for the past sixty-seven years. An Allied bomb, dropped on April 5, 1943, and aimed at German and Italian ships in the nearby Port of Palermo, missed its target, blasting the palazzo apart, turning its western wing to chunks of stone and shattered plaster; its eastern wing, still standing, was peeled open like a can of beans, exposing rooms, some with ceiling frescoes and huge carved-stone fireplaces, to decades of rain and wind.

Briefly, in the years immediately following the war, brick-making equipment had been set up in the rubble, complete with a tin roof held up on hastily poured concrete pillars. It served to help rebuild portions of bomb-damaged central Palermo. But that manufacturing site, too, was abandoned and the compound was closed off.

Now this space, with its jumble of stones and large trees, palms and hardwoods springing out of the destruction, is inexplicably full of workers. From the scaffold, we watch them cut up the woody vegetation and haul it away.

Claudio, from his perch, shouts down, asking one of the men piling up great chunks of freshly cut tree limbs if we can come in. His curt response: "No! It is too dangerous."

Then, the man in charge, an architect who joins the workers during this discussion, shouts up, asking Claudio why we want to come inside. Told that an American writer, an admirer of Giuseppe Tomasi, prince of Lampedusa, and his great Sicilian novel, is with him, the young architect doesn't hesitate. "Yes! Of course," he says. "Come around the wall and enter through the small doorway from Via Bara all'Olivella."

The bombs that laid waste in 1943 to much of central Palermo and this once magnificent palazzo were preparing the way for the Allied invasion of Sicily. Some of the destruction was not Allied-caused, however. German sappers set explosives throughout the city center in preparation for their army's departure. The island had been under the control of Axis troops of Germans and Italians. The Allied invasion, launched from newly conquered North Africa, began at the island's south shore the night of July 9. On July 22, American general George Patton's army, after slogging its way in a northwestern sweep from Gela and Licata, entered Palermo against light resistance, the Germans by then far to the east.

Sicilians, digging out of the rubble of war, generally welcomed the Allied invaders just as they had initially welcomed Garibaldi and his red-shirted army of one thousand–plus northern Italians eighty-three years before. They were eager to get out from under German and fascist domination. That, plus many of the U.S. soldiers were first- and second-generation Sicilian-Americans whose families had immigrated to America decades earlier.

Sicilians, I suspect, also saw this twentieth-century war as a chance to declare their independence from Italy, a once grand but now unrealistic idea that had faded over the decades. Sicilian separatists, along with their neighbors in Sardinia to the north-west, eventually were silenced with the Italian government's offer to make the islands into autonomous, self-governing regions. Today, there may be some self-governing, but Rome still calls most of the shots.

The battle for Sicily ended August 17, 1943, when what was left of the German army, some sixty thousand troops, skipped across the Strait of Messina onto the toe of southern Italy. Italy surrendered on September 3 and became an ally of the Americans and British. Allied troops did not take Rome until June 1944, and it took nearly another brutal, bloody year before Italy was completely reclaimed.

We scramble down the scaffolding and retrace our steps along the east wall of the palazzo, the most intact part of the building. Our pathway along this edge goes through what used to be the narrow garden of the Oratory of Saint Zita, a building still located on the other side of the open space. The garden is now gone; it is simply a patch of dirt where vehicles for the workers were parked.

Lampedusa's mother's dressing room had been on the third floor on this side of the once glorious palace. Lampedusa, in autobiographical writings, tells us that her room had two balconies overlooking the garden and offering a view that remained ripe in Giuseppe's memory until his death in 1957, just months before *Il gattopardo* was published. Today, those balconies, and the nine others that dominated the front of the palace along Via Lampedusa, are gone.

I am excited to be invited inside. The location of the palazzo had come to my attention the previous November. Via Lampedusa, a narrow street that, a hundred years before, knew the clatter of horse-drawn carriages used by the wealthy and ancient Lampedusa clan, was closed off at both ends, as were the large wooden gates leading into the compound. Around the corner, a small doorway led through the protective stone wall along Via Bara all'Olivella. It also was shuttered and locked. Peeking through a crack, I could see only junglelike foliage and tumbled masonry.

Via Lampedusa was blocked off because just across the street the Bank of Sicily was renovating the Branciforte Palace, also a sixteenth-century structure. It will become a museum hosting painting and sculpture exhibits. Its restoration architect, Gae Aulenti, created the Musée d'Orsay in Paris out of a former train station.

During that first visit in November 2009, a construction worker had let me through the gate closing off the street so I could see the front wall of the sealed-off Palazzo Lampedusa compound. He had stood with me as I looked over the ruined, crumbling façade of this once great building.

Shrugging, he said simply: *"Nessuno. Abbandonato per molti anni. Si è rovinato, perduto."* (No one. Abandoned for many years. It is ruined, lost.)

Now just four months later, we are greeted warmly at that small door through the wall, held wide open by Gabriele Graziano and Alice Franzitta, two thirtysomething Palermitani who introduce themselves as architects. We step into the bombed-out area, gingerly dodging workmen hauling out the great chunks of freshly toppled trees.

This place had a small role in *The Leopard* (printed in English in 1960). It is a novel, a bit of historical fiction manufactured by Giuseppe di Lampedusa. He based it loosely on his grandfather, Giulio Tomasi (1815–1885), called in the book by the name Don Fabrizio Corbera, prince of Salina.

The book, a blockbuster when it was published posthumously in Italian, was made into a 1963 film by Luchino Visconti. It starred Burt Lancaster as the prince and Claudia Cardinale as Angelica, the bride-to-be of Fabrizio's nephew, Tancredi, played by Alain Delon. It tells the story of an aristocratic Bourbon family and the impact Garibaldi's invasion of Sicily in the name of Italian Unification had on its members.

In the book and film, Tancredi convinces his uncle of the need for Garibaldi to overthrow the island's Bourbon rulers and bring Sicily into Italy. He speaks the oft-repeated lines that seem to sum up a classic Sicilian attitude: "Unless we ourselves take a hand now, they'll foist a republic on us. If we want things to stay as they are, things will have to change. D'you understand?"

Now, standing here in the midst of this long-hidden, bombed-out place, I discover that my timing is remarkable. Gabriele and Alice tell us that the workers began to clear out the trees and the rubble just one week earlier. Soon the rest of the ruined structure will be torn down, leveling a three-story building whose foundations were laid in 1480, and expanded upon in 1505, before being acquired by the Lampedusa family in 1788.

"It is impossible to save any of it for restoration," Gabriele said sadly.

The two architects, along with another colleague, Sabina Padrut, have been given a remarkable opportunity: the rebuilding of Palazzo Lampedusa.

"Of course," Gabriele says, "we cannot replicate the interior. But the exterior will be as it originally was, before the bombing. The property is owned by thirty people. They created a foundation, and we will build apartments for each of the owners."

There will actually be thirty-one units, he says. The extra one may, or may not, be for sale when the project is complete in five years. I have to remember: This is Sicily, where nothing seems to get done according to schedule.

Short of that reality, this is exciting news. Many buildings in Palermo have been rebuilt over the decades following the war; many others are in desperate need of restoration. Some, in the port area and in the medieval market section of the Vucciria in one of the city's oldest areas, are still in ruins, untouched since the aerial bombardment of World War II. Even in the heart of the city, some of the buildings along busy thoroughfares are abandoned. And many balconies on both occupied and unoccupied buildings are closed off and shrouded in heavy netting to keep pieces of stone and rusted iron railing from falling onto passersby below.

Giuseppe di Lampedusa, who wrote *The Leopard* late in life, in the opening chapter of an autobiography he started but never finished, "Places of My Infancy," offers a good description of his family's palace on Via Lampedusa. If the architects are true to their word—and I have no doubt that they are—they have a solid literary blueprint to follow.

Giuseppe and his parents lived in one wing, the one on the east end; his paternal grandparents occupied the other wing;

bachelor uncles lived on the second floor. There were "three courtyards, four terraces, garden, huge staircases, halls, corridors, stables, rooms on the mezzanine for servants and offices—a real kingdom for a boy alone, a kingdom either empty or sparsely populated by figures unanimously well-disposed."

Lampedusa was inclined, in later life, not to call it a palace. He preferred Casa Lampedusa, the "house" of Lampedusa, believing the word "palace" had been debased in modern Italy.

As for the façade that the architects promise to replicate, Lampedusa said it had "no particular architectural merit." It was made of white stone. The borders around the windows were "sulfur yellow, in purest Sicilian style of the seventeenth and eighteenth centuries." The front along Via Lampedusa ran for seventy yards, he wrote, with wide gates near each corner, and across an upper floor were strung nine balconies.

This palace was the family's townhome in the 1860s when the novel takes place. Of course, the Lampedusa descendants, including the author's family, occupied it nearly full-time during the twentieth century; Giuseppe last slept in it just two months before it was ripped asunder by the Allied bomb.

Most of the book's events take place in two other Lampedusa palaces owned by the family of the fictional prince: one is a palazzo on the northern outskirts of Palermo on the Piana dei Colli, today a scene for concerts and art exhibitions. This palace occupies the opening scenes in both the book and the film with the family kneeling in prayer during a private Mass. The other principal site for both book and movie is the fictional

Donnafugata in southwest Sicily, based on the ancestral country estate of Lampedusa's mother.

As for the house in Palermo, the site of the architects' ambitious restoration project, it is referred to in the movie only as
a place where the prince stashes his carriage when he rides
into town, accompanied by his personal priest, to meet with a
prostitute—after he drops the priest at his order's monastery.
And when Garibaldi's Red Shirts are about to enter Palermo,
the prince sends his eldest son, Paolo, from the palace on Piana dei Colli to occupy the townhome, saying the structure, if
it were empty, would be a tempting prize for an invader.

At the book's end, in a section not replicated in the film,
the dying prince is returning from Naples, where he has seen
physicians for his deteriorating health. The family decides to
put him up in a Palermo hotel rather than the nearby palazzo
because "the house was not in order . . . it was used only for
occasional luncheons by the sea; there wasn't even a bed in it."

While in a room in that hotel, the Hotel Trinacria, which
was a real place in the late 1800s and early twentieth century,
the prince observes himself in a mirror. "He recognized his
own suit more than himself: very tall and emaciated, with
sunken cheeks and three days' growth of beard . . . A leopard
in very bad trim. Why, he wondered, did God not want anyone to die with his own face on?"

Giuseppe di Lampedusa, before the bomb, had imagined
himself dying in the family's Palermo home, in the same room
he had occupied since childhood, just a few feet from where
his mother gave birth to him. Her room was "very lovely, its
ceiling scattered with flowers and branches of old coloured

stucco, in a design gentle and corporeal as a piece of music by Mozart."

I saw a photograph in March 2010, taken by the architects, of that ceiling painting. Neither Giuseppe nor the prince made it home, each dying in strange places, alone with their memories.

Reading *The Leopard* was a significant step in attempting to understand Sicily and Sicilians. Through the dialogue of the characters, principally the prince of Salina and his nephew, Tancredi, Giuseppe di Lampedusa progressively reveals how Sicilians are the way they are and how they differ from mainland Italians.

The prince is a man of the privileged upper class that has flourished for generations under the Bourbon rulers based in Naples. He senses that change is coming and works to adapt to it so his and his family's way of life will continue. He has taken Tancredi, the son of a sister, under his wing and, it seems, has much more feeling for him as a son than as his nephew. Tancredi is a cynic in the true Italian sense of the word: one who readily adapts to changing circumstances and who can shift loyalties when it's convenient. He joins Garibaldi and the red-shirted One Thousand to free Sicily from Bourbon rule. Then, when it works to his advantage, he abandons Garibaldi, who has fallen from favor among the Piedmontese. Tancredi joins the royalist army of Vittorio Emanuele II, king of Piedmont, Savoy, and Sardinia, who became the first king of a united Italy in March 1861.

There are telling lines in the novel that reveal much about the secretive Sicilians of the mid- to late nineteenth century: "[I]n this secret island, where houses are barred and peasants refuse to admit they even know the way to their own village in clear view on a hillock within a few minutes' walk from here . . ."

The most important part of the book is the dialogue between the prince and Cavaliere Aimone Chevalley di Monterzuolo, who as a government official in the newly unified nation invites Don Fabrizio to be a senator in Parliament. The prince, tired and sensing his days are numbered, turns him down. He cites the centuries that Sicily has been ruled by others of differing religions and languages.

The newest conquerors at the time, northern Italians, certainly did not speak Sicilian. Through all this sweep of history and rule by foreigners, Sicilians accommodated themselves to this reality. Now this accommodation, and the inability to participate fully in government, has become ingrained in Sicilian souls. Since the time that Garabaldi and his Red Shirts landed at Marsala, "too many things have been done without [Sicilians] being consulted for you to be able now to ask a member of the old governing class to help develop things and carry them through. . . . We're as white as you are, Chevalley, and as the Queen of England; and yet for two thousand and five hundred years we've been a colony. I don't say that in complaint; it's our fault. But even so we're worn-out and exhausted."

Despite Chevalley's pleas that things are different now—after all, Sicily is part of a unified nation—Don Fabrizio will not budge. He and his fellow Sicilians want only sleep. ". . . they will always hate anyone who tries to wake them, even in order to bring the most wonderful gifts; and I must say, between ourselves, I have strong doubts whether the new Kingdom will have many gifts for us in its luggage."

These were prophetic words on the part of Don Fabrizio. Northern Italians did not offer much to the South, except the draft to fight Italy's wars. The South became a source of labor; industry was largely kept in the North. In recent times, some industry has moved south; Fiat established a major auto-manufacturing plant on the coast east of Palermo. However, in the late first decade of the twenty-first century, when the company faced economic troubles, it was the plant in Sicily and the thousands of jobs it represented that was targeted for shutdown.

Of course, Giuseppe di Lampedusa had nearly a hundred years of experiences from his own lifetime to know how to give meaning wisely to the prince's words. Nevertheless, the prince's concluding words to Chevalley, describing the physical environment Sicilians labor in, capture what writers Giovanni Verga, Luigi Pirandello, Leonardo Sciascia, and others wrote about so brilliantly.

> [T]his climate which inflicts us with six feverish months at a temperature of a hundred and four; count them, Chevalley, count them: May, June, July, August, September, October; six times thirty days of sun sheer down on our heads; this summer of ours which is as long and glum as a Russian winter and against which we struggle with less success; you don't know it yet, but fire could be said to snow down

on us as on the accursed cities of the Bible; if a Sicilian worked hard in any of those months he would expend energy enough for three; then water is either lacking altogether or has to be carried from so far that every drop is paid for by a drop of sweat; and then the rains, which are always tempestuous and set dry river beds to frenzy, drown beasts and men on the very spot where two weeks before both had been dying of thirst.

To break this spell of ingrained Sicilian temperament is nearly impossible. "The crust is formed."

Today, summers remain beastly hot, but air-conditioning is everywhere. Ubiquitous automobiles replace the donkey and led to footpaths between villages becoming paved roads. Irrigation systems keep fields green and vibrant. Markets are full of products. But, Fiat aside, Sicily and its sister regions in southern Italy face still double-digit unemployment and likely will for decades to come.

Life is certainly better today than during the lifetime of the prince, when he and his family lived in robust comfort while the peasants that worked his farms, vineyards, orchards, and olive groves suffered and starved. Many of those former peasants, like Don Calogero Sedàra, whose daughter, Angelica, married Tancredi—a marriage between the social classes that before Garibaldi arrived would have been unheard of—became the new upper middle class. It was Don Calogero, instead of Don Fabrizio, who ended up as senator in the Italian Parliament.

The Sicily I found in the late twentieth and early twenty-first centuries obviously has much improved on the prince's preferred feudal world. But the repression by three thousand years of conquerors and the inability to control its own destiny—along with the resistant soil and the Sicilian blood that repeatedly stained it—are part of who the people are as much as the Greeks and the Arabs.

Lampedusa's gift of *The Leopard* was the beginning to this understanding.

TWO

Palermo

[T]he Abbot ventured out of the house. He had himself driven in a carriage through the city. It was one of those iridescent Palermo mornings, the clouds a shelving deep blue and russet. He rejoiced in the sun, the air, the warm Norman stone, the red Arabic cupolas, the aroma of seaweed and lemon in the market. . . .

—Leonardo Sciascia,
The Council of Egypt (1963)

AN IMAGE stands out from my first days wandering the heart of Palermo: a scrawny, long-legged dog, its thinning clumps of dark gray hair mottled with what appear to be crusted-over sores. This droopy, tail-dragging creature is crossing traffic-packed Via Roma, a main north-south artery where, on a March 2009 afternoon, the cars, buses, and screaming motorcycles and scooters are making up an unceasing daylong parade that begins in the early morning and lasts until late evening. The dog's head is down; he appears oblivious to the dangers along

its path leading to who knows where. Cars start to creep forward as the mutt approaches; one driver sees it and jerks the
car to a stop just in time. The creature reaches the narrow
sidewalk packed with people waiting for a bus, makes its way
around the tangle of human legs, and disappears down a cross
street, never once lifting its head, its nose almost scraping the
pavement.

The noise and confusion, found in this city of 150,000
people crammed in a crescent between the sea and the mountains, must be wearing, making Palermitani appear just as
oblivious as they push through crowds on narrow sidewalks
that line narrow streets, or as they move forward in automobiles, a few feet at a time.

They think nothing of stepping off the sidewalk without a
glance backward to see who, or what, might be coming, and
out into the street to move around an obstacle: a signpost placed
squarely in the middle of a three-foot-wide sidewalk, or a pe-
destrian ahead moving a bit too slowly, or the rusting frame-
work of a scaffold that might have been sitting in place for years
awaiting a renovation that never seems to happen.

I think of the American author Mary McCarthy who, writing about Florence in the mid-twentieth century, described
the dangers from Florentine traffic when one steps off the narrow sidewalks in order to look at the upper levels of medieval
buildings. In Florence, many of the streets are a bit narrower
than in Palermo. This city at least allows you to look down
slightly wider boulevards at buildings perhaps not as tall or as
stony gray as those in the Tuscan capital without taking the
chance of being nailed by a tiny Fiat or a scooter screaming its
bone-chilling whine.

If you stand and look too long, you soon realize you are blocking those behind you, forcing them onto the street's edge where they can be clipped by fast-moving cars—or Vespas built more for speed than the pure transportation function of their 1950s counterparts.

We can't escape it; it is a grinding reality, and it's one of the images that most visitors carry home, along with memories of the art, the food, the passion, and the soul exhibited by Italians, Sicilians, and Calabrese. I, for one, occasionally dart into the calming, cooling climes of a nearby church to get respite from the clamor.

Palermo is a rough-appearing place. That doesn't mean one should feel unsafe here; I never did. It's more of a visual thing. Palermo's buildings, like those in Florence, exude both the roughness of the region's stone and the aesthetics of a long succession of invaders. This city's buildings do not reflect the gentle apricot colors of Rome that glow in the warm Italian sun. There are few soft colors here to contrast with the shifting blues and grays of the sea just a few hundred meters to the north.

Palermo instead is made up of harsh, gray stones that, to me, suggest the colder northern climes of the Normans who, centuries ago, left western France for the southern Mediterranean and, beginning one thousand years ago in the eleventh century, forever chiseled their mark onto Sicily and southern Italy. These descendants of the Vikings mixed together their architectural sensibilities with those of the Arabs whom they overtook around the mid-eleventh century.

While the ruling class of Muslims left, many of its people remained. And their writing, poetry, and craftsmanship were sought after by the Normans and their immediate successors for a few hundred years more.

Middle Easterners and North Africans had intermingled with the Sicilians who were a combination of Greek, Carthaginian and, perhaps, a few Romans—not to mention the remnants of the indigenous peoples the colonizing Greeks absorbed into their culture during the seventh through third centuries B.C.

It's a complicated history on this island, the Mediterranean's largest and most contested from ancient times onward. The Arabs, who came in the ninth century A.D., had in turn chased out the Byzantine Greeks—the successors to Rome and the earlier Carthaginians. These North African invaders had succeeded the original Greek colonists and the indigenous peoples the Greeks found here—the long-lost Sicels, Sicani, and Elymians whose DNA is carried by modern islanders.

All this human stew from the melting pot called Sicily seems to come together in one place in Palermo: the centuries-old marketplace of the Vucciria, the city's warren of twisting streets, most no wider than footpaths that snake among clusters of medieval buildings and then suddenly open into tiny squares and piazzas. Street names are unique here. Travel writer Aldo Buzzi caused me to look for the street of the Land of Flies, Via Terra delle Mosche, and the street of the Flying Chairs, Via delle Sedie Volanti. If a car makes it into here—and they certainly do—it cannot pass another coming from the opposite direction. One must wait or back out and try another route. Usually this is done with little argument. One driver, typically the one closest to an escape route, makes eye contact with the other, acknowledges with a slight shrug his willingness to move, and then does so. As the two drivers pass, they will nod and go on with their day, accepting that life is full of delays and compromises.

Buzzi also describes a scene that I was able to witness during my first research visit, in March 2009: the periodic grilling in the Vucciria's food market of lamb entrails "roasted on a spit with onions and parsley," called *stigghiole*. His description of the "azure smoke and exquisite aroma" was just like I saw with my Palermo friend Conchita Vecchio, who brought me here to taste the delicacy. It wasn't as bad as I had anticipated. Years earlier I had consumed, while dining with friends in Calabria, a stew of heavily spiced organ meat—liver, heart, spleen, and who knows what else. I was no stranger to the exotic dishes of the South.

If visitors are familiar with the well-scrubbed villages of, say, Tuscany, where fruit, vegetable, and meat sellers line up in orderly rows against a backdrop of the freshly plastered and painted walls of recently restored buildings, then they would be amazed at the contrast here. Vucciria's meat, fish, produce, and fruit sellers appear in what can only be described as well-orchestrated disarray. They are loosely strung along the edges of the narrow streets, cluttering their spaces with piles of trimmings from the huge heads of broccoli that, in March, dominate vegetable displays. Stacks of cardboard boxes and worn wooden crates that once held Sicilian blood oranges from the eastern edge of the island, near Catania, or the imported bananas, or the tiny strawberries, also are casually tossed in among the fruit and vegetables now strewn helter-skelter on low, rough tables.

The streets, paved in blocks chiseled out of some nearby quarry, are slimy with refuse. One or two scrawny, ownerless dogs trot up and down the street, pawing through the leavings looking for, and finding, scraps. Feral cats, with scars and torn ears—one I saw was missing an eye and the other was nearly festered shut—are either curled up on top of a parked car's still-warm hood or on the pavement next to the fish seller's stand, munching on a castaway gift from the sea.

For parts of three days I walked among this melee of food, taking in the spectacle of disorder: the low-slung tables groaning under the weight of the fruits of the earth and sliced cuts of lamb, veal, beef, chicken. Occasionally I saw a hanging skinned hare, a cow's head stripped of its skin, exposing a thin layer of meat below, a pair of calves' heads, also skinned and neatly arrayed in a meat-seller's glass-lined refrigerated case.

Then, on my third night, I watched over it all from above as I ate dinner at a place incongruently called Trattoria Shanghai, a small family-run operation on the upper level of a medieval building. The ground-floor entrance took me through an unpainted, dented, splintered doorway. A set of narrow, twisting stairs carried me up a roughly plastered corridor with decades-old paint peeling from the walls.

Reaching the first level, I entered a kitchen area where a small television, perched precariously on a narrow counter along one wall, was presenting the news. A man, obviously part of the family that ran the trattoria that doubled as their home, sat at the table, munching from a plate of spaghetti crowned with a hint of red sauce and sprinkled with a heavy dose of finely slivered cheese. His back was to me; my presence went unnoticed for a few moments. I stood, wondering whether I had barged into a family's private quarters.

Then a young woman, wrapped in a dark coat against the chill of the early-March evening, appeared from out of a side doorway and motioned me toward the terrace outside.

There were a few scattered tables covered in clean red-and-white-checked cloths. They were set out next to a rickety iron railing roughly painted dark red. The view was stunning: the market, with its vegetable, fruit, and meat sellers, was arrayed below me, their ranks beginning in the tiny Piazza Caracciolo and flowing up along the narrow street of Discesa Maccheronai. Behind me, on the narrow street below, was blasting a loud American rendition of "Summer Nights" from the musical *Grease*. I looked over the terrace's edge and saw a group of local teenagers dancing to the music, laughing loudly, and having a wonderful time.

The young woman who had led me to the terrace reappeared with a simple, stained menu, and the first thing I saw was the low prices: €3 or €4 each for an antipasto, *primo*, or *secondo*. I chose antipasto of cheese and salami, a first dish of spaghetti *pomodoro*, and a second dish of *salsiccia*, or sausage.

Over the course of an hour, the dishes were delivered in slow succession; there seemed no reason to hurry here. Each was cooked to perfection—the antipasto just right with a few thick slices of tongue-tingling salami, a half dozen or so rich, flavorful dark-green olives, and two slices of milky mozzarella drizzled with just a hint of herb-enhanced olive oil. The pasta was perfectly al dente, and the tomato sauce lightly layered throughout, keeping to the true Sicilian culinary tradition where pasta should be the most important element and the sauce only secondary.

I did not know what to expect for the *secondo*—the *salsiccia*—but a long roll, perhaps about twelve inches and as thick as a thumb, was set down before me. The sausage was shaped into a semicircle surrounding a wedge of lime that, when I sprinkled the juice onto the meat, drew out flavors I had never before experienced.

While devouring all this, I noticed the tables around me filling with men in suits and ties and well-dressed women in fur coats. They appeared to be regulars at this rough little family restaurant, its walls in need of paint and its incongruous oriental name belying the pure Sicilian food and the unforgettable view of an ancient Sicilian marketplace.

Meanwhile, in the piazza, a slice of Sicilian life passed by: a market that has happened in this same spot, day after day—except Sundays—year after year, decade after decade, century after century.

It is July 2009, the second of four visits to Palermo and just four months following that culinary experience at the Shanghai. For this particular trip, I had decided to stay in the famed Hotel Des Palmes, one of the city's best and oldest. This was where many of the intrigues of Sicilian politics were carried out, where treaties were agreed upon over cognac and cigars, where famous people stayed. General George Patton reportedly lingered here for a few days after leading his American army south to north across the island, taking Palermo in the heat of summer 1943. Richard Wagner, just a year before his death in 1883, had written most of his final opera, *Parsifal,* in his room at Des Palmes. And it is where the nineteenth-century French writer Guy de Maupassant, star-struck by the fact his idol Wagner had lodged here while writing his finest opera, stayed before setting out on his journey via horseback around Sicily.

It is a grand, modernized hotel and not overly expensive by the much more exalted standards of Paris or Rome. I once looked at its location on an 1880 Baedeker travel map—drawn before Via Roma was plowed through the city in the late 1890s. Baedeker liked the hotel's beautiful garden. On my visit 129 years later, there was no such garden. The nineteenth-century map shows why. The building then had three multistory wings: a back and two sides. In the middle was an open space, obviously the spot for a garden. Today that spot is filled in, making the Des Palmes one large, blocky structure.

After a series of interviews and much wandering about, I was leaving for a journey eastward across the island. My rental car was delivered. The doorman helped me load luggage and offered a pleasant farewell. The streets along the port leading out of the center toward the Catania-Palermo autostrada were remarkably clean of the debris I had plowed through just eight hours earlier.

The night before, friends and I had snaked our way through tens of thousands of revelers celebrating the annual procession, down Via Vittorio Emanuele, of the city's patron saint, Santa Rosalia. She had lived as a hermit in a cave near the city and died in the mid-twelfth century. Her remains were found nearly five hundred years later and were carried through the city. A plague then in full swing, killing hundreds, perhaps thousands, suddenly ended. Rosalia got the credit, and every July 14 her gold-gilded statue is carried from the cathedral to the port.

Palermitani, even those who do not claim to be religious, revere their city's patron saint. It seemed that all of Palermo turned out for her procession. Everywhere along this mile-long stretch of city street was packed, the masses spilling into side streets.

There is no such thing as crowd control in Sicily. Processions, whether in the smallest villages or the largest cities, push their way through crowds of people who move slowly, ever so slowly, out of the way. And this particular one takes place in July, Sicily's hottest, stickiest month.

Traditionally, the statue was drawn by oxen. When I saw the procession in 2009, she was ensconced in a large boatlike structure that hid a motor vehicle. Rosalia not only delivered Palermo from the plague, but also she gets credit for everything that works, from good marriages and recovery from life-threatening diseases to protection from earthquakes. No one blames her when things go bad.

Palermitani take the annual affair seriously. Thousands walk with the procession all the way. Thousands more jam the streets, waiting for the giant float to pass slowly, grindingly by.

The handcrafted boat float was exceptional. It featured, arrayed around its deck, young bodysuited women who moved in slow rhythm, like mythical sirens calling to sailors on the sea. They kept going for the several hours it took the statue-laden craft to make its relatively short trip from the cathedral to the harbor's edge.

In the procession were two giant clusters of helium-filled balloons—one white, the other black. The balloons were held in place by several large ropes controlled by men who could play out the ropes and let the balloons rise slowly above the height of the two- and three-story buildings. Incredibly, hanging from each cluster was a single dangling trapeze with a young woman sitting on the bar. As the balloons rose, she would twist and turn high in the air, tumbling down, almost in slow motion, her arms entwined in the stout ropes.

The ropes held, and the balloons stayed inflated and tight in their respective clusters until the very end, when they and the ship carrying the saint had safely passed under the arch that marks the northern end of Via Vittorio Emanuele and the entrance into Piazzetta San Spirito near the harbor shore. There the trapeze artists disembarked and the balloons were suddenly set free. They sailed up, up into the early-morning sky—it was now one A.M.—and disappeared over the Tyrrhenian Sea.

After it was all over and the last of the fireworks had died out, we moved with a great flowing multicolored river of humanity along Via Cala and into the Vucciria en route to homes or vehicles parked far, far away.

We had to plow through mounds of trash generated by the sweaty, thirsty, and hungry festivalgoers. Shards of broken beer bottles lay everywhere; soggy mounds of stomped-on food collected underfoot; paper—bales and bales of it—jammed gutters or was strewn along the street, the narrow sidewalks, and the flowerbeds like clumps of wrinkled snow.

The next morning I am leaving Palermo for Catania on the island's east coast. Driving along Via Cala just eight hours later and under the torturously hot July sun, I find the city surprisingly free of automobiles; the streets where we had trudged through garbage are now, unbelievably, swept clean.

Sanitation workers, who just a month earlier had been on strike and who let Palermo swelter for weeks amid tons of stinking, piled-high garbage, had worked through the predawn hours. It seemed to be another miracle the Palermitani can give credit to their beloved saint.

THREE

The Cart Painter

In centuries past, these works of art [carts] were everywhere in Sicily. The few that remain, and the few
which are created each year, seem to represent more
than another era. They symbolize a way of life, and
the fact that Sicily's unique medieval history has never
been far from the popular mind.
                                    —*Best of Sicily*

GIOVANNI VERGA wrote a short story that hints at what roads
were like in inland Sicily in the mid-nineteenth century. They
weren't roads at all but mere tracks that, for centuries across
the rolling hills, humans, mules, and donkeys hammered out
of the dirt. When the Romans were here, they maintained the
roads left by their predecessors, the Sicilian Greeks. It is said
that they built fifty-three thousand miles of roads throughout
their empire. However, despite their road-building prowess elsewhere, they appear not to have done much in Sicily, the Roman breadbasket.

The Romans eventually left, and others who had no sense

of how to maintain these byways came and went. The roads, where carts were easily used by the earliest colonists, once again degenerated into paths. This forced folks to abandon carts for several hundred years, relying on foot power, mules, donkeys, or horses.

In good weather, roads were passable; in bad weather, impassible, and people stayed put, unable to move even short distances. The peasant walked because his mule or donkey was used for carrying goods and harvested crops. The well-to-do sometimes rode on horseback, the women lying down or seated on litters attached to poles strung between sure-footed mules, one or two in the front and rear.

Verga's story "So Much for the King," contained in a slim volume entitled *Little Novels of Sicily*, focuses on Cosimo, a litter driver who is summoned to transport the king's wife between Caltagirone and Catania. The royal couple, based in Naples, is in Sicily to see firsthand the island's need for roads. Cosimo successfully transports the queen and returns to his home and stables where, years later, his mules are confiscated in the name of that king because Cosimo could not pay his debts. The improved roads that resulted from that royal visit destroyed his ability to make a living with his litter.

The advent of better roads in the sixteenth century made way, once again, for wheeled carts, or *carretti*. The mules now could pull them.

Transportation became more efficient through the early nineteenth century. The Regia Strada, or royal highway, connected Palermo and Messina and, in the 1830s, was one of the earliest roads in post-Roman times to connect major Sicilian cities. Reports from early travelers indicated it could take five days to make the journey that now takes a few hours along a superhighway and through dozens of tunnels bored into coastal mountains that dip down to the sea.

Various early nineteenth-century writers journeying to the island reported seeing litters and small carts, giving us the first descriptions of their adornment.

An American, Henry Tuckerman, writing in the 1830s, said a litter he saw near the temple of Segesta in western Sicily "was rudely painted with the effigies of saints and martyrs." Late nineteenth-century writer Baron Gonzalve de Nervo reported seeing, on the north coast near Palermo, a small cart painted blue with images of the Virgin and saints on the side panels. His was an early description of the horses, which he said had colored plumes on their heads and wore harnesses with designs in copper or gilded heads of nails.

Marcella Croce and Moira F. Harris have written *History on the Road: The Painted Carts of Sicily*. In it we learn how carts differed from one part of the island to the other, based upon their function and the type of environment in which they were used. For example, carts that hauled salt around the western Sicilian port of Trapani had higher wheels and did not have decorative iron axles because of the salty water they drove through. Other carts were named by type: The *tirraloru* carried sand, gravel, or dirt. The *vinarulo* hauled grapes or wine barrels; the *frumentaru* hauled wheat.

And the style of painting differed as well: In the eastern part of the island, around Catania, paintings are framed in squares; around Palermo, they appear on trapezoidal panels.

———

The black-and-white photograph, its high-contrast image beautifully composed, jumped out at me from the page of Enzo Sellerio's book *A Photographer in Sicily*. A shirtless boy, perhaps eight, maybe ten, with tousled hair, knee-length shorts, and appearing to be barefoot, is clinging to the back of a horse-drawn carriage, the type used today to haul tourists around Palermo. The boy's legs are draped around the axle casing, his hands gripping an iron rod high across the back. The carriage driver, seemingly oblivious as he pays attention to his horse, sits in the front, his back to the camera.

I happened upon that photograph several months after my first trip to Palermo in March 2009, and it reminded me instantly of my visit with Franco Bertolino, who claims to be the last of the traditional Sicilian cart painters. The caption under Sellerio's photo reads simply: "Palermo 1960." That is the year before Bertolino, forty-eight when we meet, was born in a small stone house opposite the west end of the cathedral on the edge of Piazza Sett'Angeli.

I ask Franco how he learned the art practiced by his father and, on both sides of the family, by his grandfathers. This tall, handsome, thin-featured man, who exudes passion about his dying craft, tells me he had not been a willing student.

"I absolutely did not want to hear or learn any of this," he says, his arm gesturing around a stone-floored room full of paintings on large sheets of heavy paper and canvas, as well as on wooden panels that would one day make up a Sicilian cart. "Because when we were young, we wanted to go out, play, have fun. We had the habit of—you know the horse and buggy, the tourist ones?—well, we would get behind these buggies and hang on as the horses were moving"—like the small boy in Sellerio's photograph.

It was apparently a well-established tradition for little boys to do this. This would have been before most Sicilian youngsters had televisions to watch in this postwar city that, two decades after Italy's surrender, was still struggling out of the rubble of Allied bombing.

"Today, young people have scooters, they have discos; we didn't have anything," Franco tells me that warm afternoon. "So we chased after the carriages and hung on for a ride. We would tease and insult the driver in Palermitano [the local dialect]. We would insult the name of his father," he says, laughing to cover up a hint of embarrassment. The driver couldn't stop in the middle of the road, and he would take his frustration out on the young boy hanging out of sight on the rear of the carriage by flicking his whip backward, mostly missing its mark.

"One day he couldn't take it anymore; he came to my dad and told him what I was up to." His father caught him in the act one afternoon and, enraged at his son's misbehavior and disrespect for the hardworking carriage driver, grabbed a wood-handled umbrella and started to beat him around the legs. "I fell on the floor," Franco says. "I couldn't walk."

For one month, while his legs healed, his father forced Franco to sit on a chair in the corner of the workshop where he and the boy's grandfather worked to create and paint Sicilian carts.

"I was forced to actually see how my father and grandfather worked here. I sat and observed. There was nothing else to do. My father told me, 'Learn the craft while you are sitting there.' And I did. So it's been thirty-eight years that I have been doing this job. I came off that chair and started painting."

The years passed. His grandfather and father passed on, as did other craftsmen. Franco's advantage was that as a child and young apprentice in the shop, he was surrounded by family members who practiced the cart art in a variety of styles and disciplines. While his father and both grandfathers were cart painters, other family members on his mother's side were in charge of making the iron parts. On his father's side were woodworkers as well as painters. He got to watch them all; now, as the lone survivor of the craft in his family, he does it all: cart building, wheel making, ironworking, painting. Mostly painting and making small models for collectors and tourists, he says, because no one wants a full-size cart anymore. They might want an old one repaired, touched up, or a part replaced.

Franco acknowledges that he knows of a young woman in Catania—two hours away by car and a world apart from Palermo—who paints carts. As he puts it: "It's a girl who graduated from fine arts academy. Her technique is different from the traditional technique that I use.

"You see, the images that I reproduce, they are fuller images. There are more characters in my work compared to what others are doing. They might have two 'puppets' in one square. I paint entire scenes" that might contain many figures. "I use actual pigments; she might use oil-based paints." Therefore, he says, his colors are bolder and stand out in a dramatic way.

"The actual cart is full and rich in imagery and rich in character. I concentrate on the decorations, on the arms, the costumes, or I concentrate more on more colors for the art it-self. But I guarantee you that the style today is the style that was used two hundred years ago."

He chuckles as I point out something to him that I saw in one of his puppet-show backdrops: six fingers on a knight's hand gripping a sword. "There is no perfection in art." He smiles. I get the impression he slips in that kind of anatomical mistake every once in a while as a sort of trademark. Or maybe he does these scenes so quickly he loses track of how many fingers he puts on a knight's hand. He keeps the truth a mystery.

Now Franco's tone is one of resignation.

"No one's going to continue it," he tells me. "Even if there is someone who actually takes it upon himself to continue this tradition, there is not the technique anymore. No one teaches what our ancestors taught us. All that will be left are the historic carts, and then what will happen?" he asks. "My generation and the generation before me won't be around to actually tend to the carts," to keep the colors vibrant, the iron pieces from crumbling.

Franco looks around the room, now full of small-scale versions of carts to sell to collectors or to the infrequent tourists who stumble across his unadvertised workshop down a narrow side street. To make ends meet, he also creates and paints small figurines, outfitted in traditional peasant garb, that sit in the small models of carts. In an adjoining room, tipped backward on their shafts, is a jumble of carts—older, historic ones that he owns. Other carts line his narrow street, also tipped back to show off the ironwork and designs of the axles.

He finds it hard to believe that his ancestors, just one or two generations ago, lived and worked in this tiny shop's space.

"In this room, we used to have the mother, the children, the horse, the cart." The families, of course, eventually moved into nearby homes. "For hygienic reasons," he chuckles, "you can't keep the horse in the house. Up to five years ago, we kept the horses here for the parades. The room was called the *cartorio*."

He pauses as a sense of sadness, of nostalgia, sweeps over his features. "A lot of things are being lost; slowly everything will come to an end."

Perhaps that will happen sooner rather than later. Franco is battling the city and the cathedral over ownership of the workshop that once housed two or three generations of cart makers and painters. His family, decades ago, put up this particular building, squatting on cathedral-owned land. Nothing was done about it until recently, when the church and the city wanted it back to build a multistory building there.

Several months after my first visit and in the midst of his court battle (which he lost and has under appeal—it could take years to resolve, given the slow way things happen in Sicily), the tin roof collapsed. Franco was forced to move all of his carts, large and miniature, and his puppet-show scenery, paints, brushes, and tools into other buildings he owns farther along the narrow street.

On top of that, he was sent a bill for more than €30,000: back "rent" for decades of squatting on that tiny strip of land, plus €6,000 for the other side's attorney fees. When I visit him a year later, he hasn't paid. "It's under appeal." He shrugs when asked how long that would take.

Meanwhile, during a late March 2010 afternoon, he sits with family members in an open doorway down the street from the condemned building that once housed three generations of cart builders, their horses, their workshop, and carts. Behind him, on shelves, are rows of the miniature carts and figures, all for sale. There are no customers.

As I turn to leave, Franco leans a ladder against the side of the building, climbs up, and hooks one dangling bare wire against another dangling bare wire. Christmas-like lights come on, lighting the street and a small sign indicating a cart painter's shop is there, open for business.

In the old days, according to cart historians Croce and Harris, and as Franco described, each part of the cart had its own craftsman: the cart maker would select "walnut for the box, beams, and wheel rims; beech for the shafts; and ash for the spokes," wrote the cart historians. Metalsmiths, or *fabbri*, created the wrought-iron designs above the axles, best seen when the cart, like those in Franco's shop, is tipped backward. Then, the painters took over, creating scenes from mythology and history. In their book, for example, the authors show paintings on the side panels of one cart that feature scenes from "Cavalleria Rusticana," the nineteenth-century Giovanni Verga story that was made into the well-loved Sicilian opera.

Some of these carts still exist, owned by collectors, museums, or others who care for the carts passed down in their families through generations. Occasionally, for parades, some are brought out of storage; horses are brought in from the fields and dressed in their finery (which in the old days was created by still another group of craftsmen). But the parades are becoming fewer and less frequent.

Says Franco: "We only do the displays on request now, per-haps in the different quarters of the city or a particular neigh-borhood. They might want two or three carts. When they have Santa Rosalia's *festa*, there might be ten or more." In this case, Franco provides all the carts from his own collection.

"I will get the old-timers, the *carrettieri*, to drive them."

Three days following that first visit with Franco in March 2009, I am driving along a narrow highway southwest of Palermo, just inland from the west coast. The day is bright, clear—a glorious day for a ride through the countryside. I stop for a cof-fee and a cream-filled *cornetto* at a roadside stand. As I stand there, looking across a broad field of wildflowers, the sound of horse hooves rises in the distance. Around the corner comes a gaily painted Sicilian cart pulled by a single horse. The driver is wearing a brown leather jacket and Sicilian-style wool cap pulled tight across his forehead. He clucks as he flicks the leather reins against the horse's broad, glistening brown back that anchors a tall red plume, like one described by Baron Gon-zalve de Nervo nearly two centuries ago.

I get back into the car, follow behind the cart for a few min-utes, and then pass it, getting far ahead. I pull over, grab my camera, wait, and, as the cart passes by, snap a series of photo-graphs. The driver keeps his gaze straight ahead. He and his brightly painted cart fade into the distance. Other than the ones in Franco's shop, it is the only cart I see during four trips to the island.

FOUR

Racalmuto

I tried to tell something about the life of a town I love, and I hope to have given the sense of how far this life is from freedom and from justice, that is, from reason.

> —Leonardo Sciascia, on plaque overlooking the village of his birth, translated from the Italian by Anna Camaiti Hostert

My first view in March 2009 of Racalmuto, home of Sicilian writer Leonardo Sciascia and famed opera *tenore* Salvatore Puma, was through the back door. That's the way in for most folks traveling along the highway between Agrigento and Caltanissetta. My B and B, Tra i frutti (Among the Fruit), is situated in an orchard down the hill and just off the highway. The directions to the village from my hostess, Paola Prandi, were simple: Cross the highway on the bridge, travel up the hill and over the crest, and drop down into the village.

To the uninitiated visitor, Racalmuto can appear complicated. I was there nearly a week before I got comfortable and felt that I knew my way around. The streets, laid out on a steep hillside more than a thousand years ago to accommodate foot traffic and donkeys, are narrow and twisting. It seemed I was always getting lost trying to find the main street, say, or the theater, or the piazza.

Now, after a few visits, I feel as if I have always been there. I know I can zip up and down those streets in my small rental car and, if I meet someone coming in the opposite direction, they will smile accommodatingly as we slowly, inch by inch, jockey around each other.

Around the third visit, people in restaurants or the local coffee bar or sitting on a bench in the warm sunlight of the town square would nod in recognition. The lady who served espresso during my last visit remembers me as the fellow who marveled, a year earlier, over her lemon granita. She nodded in warm recognition as I entered this friendliest of places saying, *"Ah! Hai tornata. Bene, bene."* (Ah, you have returned. Good, good.)

Early March, in Sicily's south, is on the cusp of cold days trying to turn warmer. Many of the fruit trees, by midmonth, are showing blossoms. I arrived in Racalmuto during my first trip to temperatures much chillier than expected; 2008–2009 had been a colder-than-usual winter here. There was snow in various high places around the island that had not seen it for years. Driving in the direction of Palermo early one morning on the A-19 autostrada where it turns north beyond the exit to Caltanissetta, I saw a huge mountain smothered in white, looming off to the east, a frosty presence almost all the way to the A-19's junction with the Palermo-Messina autostrada.

It was Pizzo Carbonara, or Carbonara Peak. In addition to being the name of a wonderful pasta dish, carbonara also refers to charcoal, which likely was a product produced by people living on the mountain. The peak, part of the Madonie mountain range, is second highest in Sicily at nearly 6,500 feet. (The highest is Etna.) The range extends eastward, joining the Nebrodi and Peloritani mountains that dive into the Strait of Messina. In times when Sicily was connected to Italy, these mountains would have extended into Calabria, hooking up with the Aspromonte range. To take them southwest, in the other direction, this chain, with all its differently named segments, would have plunged into Tunisia.

But here, around the flanks of Pizzo Carbonara, are tiny villages still surrounded by white in early March. I knew Etna could have snow on the summit year-round, but discovering it elsewhere in Sicily was a shock.

Back in Racalmuto, about an hour's drive away and closer to sea level, branches on the fruit trees that surround my bed-and-breakfast were just coming alive. Bare branches, punctuated here and there with puffs of white, on the third morning of my visit, erupted into a sea of blossoms, interspersed with the light green of leaves. All the trees, except for a few tardy walnuts, began to explode with life.

Wildflowers, especially the yellow ones, like the tall margaritas and the shorter coreopsis, were everywhere, and the fields grew greener with the passing of the days, each one slightly warmer than its predecessor. In the midst of this birth of spring,

San Giuseppe's, or Saint Joseph's, feast day arrived in Racalmuto as it always has, on March 19.

This is a festival practiced in many villages, and some, such
as Salemi in western Sicily, make a huge celebration out of it,
drawing tourists from all over. Because this festival also serves
as an altar-bread feast, bakers create intricate examples of their
bread-making art. One sees huge creations in all kinds of
shapes and complicated designs—from large bread crosses
with representations of Christ hanging from them, or the Madonna with child shaped from bread dough and baked, crisp
and light. Some loaves form stars, large and small, or suns,
complete with rays. Others are made into miniature castles or
houses.

Far away from Salemi, in an exhibit room in Racalmuto's
restored Chiaramonte castle, is an entire manger scene, complete with animals, the three wise men, and the baby in a
cradle—all made of bread.

Saint Joseph, of course, is the husband of Mary. He is revered because of his acceptance of the Immaculate Conception
and his role in Christ's upbringing. Racalmuto's day honoring
San Giuseppe is unique, and that is what drew me here instead
of to the huge, tourist-packed festival at Salemi with its own
Web site peppered with dozens of photographs. Racalmuto's is
purely a local affair. It seemed I was the only outsider. From all
appearances over the twenty-four-hour period of festivities,
there weren't even any visitors from surrounding towns; they
likely had their own festivals to attend.

Also, I was curious about why Racalmuto's festivities are
kicked off with what appears to be a unique element: It begins
the night before, on March 18, with a huge *falò,* or bonfire.

Traditionally, friends familiar with the event said, the fire consumed old furniture discarded by villagers. But a few villagers I asked about its origins merely shrugged. That's the way it always has been; no one really knows.

The part about burning the furniture may have been true at one time, Racalmuto resident Concetta Barbieri told me one afternoon. But she surmised that the tradition likely began as a rite of honoring the arrival of spring and later evolved into part of the observance of the saint's feast day.

Originally, she said, old wooden wine casks were burned to symbolize the change of seasons and the preparation for the upcoming growing season. Later, folks may have tossed old, broken-down furniture onto the growing pile in anticipation of the *falò*. The earliest practice, of course, could have its long-forgotten roots as a rite of paganism, which was then co-opted by Christians over the centuries as their religion grew.

During my March 2009 visit, the huge pile to be burned consisted mostly of pasteboard boxes and old lumber, although I did see one broken chair and a few battered dresser drawers in the heap, along with the shattered staves of a beat-up, light-weight barrel. There also were some splintered bed slats, stacks and stacks of wooden crates that once held fruit and vegetables, and piles of tree branches.

The mountain of discards today is a repository for anyone wishing to get rid of things flammable. For a few days before the event, I watched it grow dramatically as folks piled on their refuse.

The fire is scheduled to begin after dark, at 6:30 P.M. in the Piazza Barona. It follows vespers, or evening prayer, in the Church of San Giuseppe, where at least two hundred or more of the faithful are packed into the tiny sanctuary. I listen for a while and then trudge downhill to witness the spectacle. At 5:45 P.M., no one is there. I wander around the square, looking over the edge down toward the unique town fountain, where water spurts out of several pipes and is carried into a long, rectangular basin and then into a semicircular basin farther along. This fountain is next to a newly restored building that was once the village slaughterhouse. Animals drank from the rectangular pool; women washed clothes in the semicircular part. The former slaughterhouse now contains offices for people who help deal with immigrants, mostly from North Africa and points farther south on that nearby continent.

Soon, a large concessioner's truck pulls into the square. Then, a few teenagers ride by on motorcycles, stop, and mill about. With fifteen minutes to go before the scheduled blaze, more people—families with children, groups of teenagers— begin straggling into the piazza.

Finally, about 6:45 P.M., with the crowd quickly building to about three hundred, an elderly man strides up to the wooden pile, shoves a bunch of butcher paper into key places, and starts lighting it. I am told that this gentleman has held the honor for many, many years of lighting the fire. A year after my visit, he had died, and a new fire starter was chosen.

The flames flicker, then grow in confidence and begin to spread. Within moments the jumbled heap, now perhaps twenty feet tall, is overwhelmed. Flames shoot as high as fifty feet, and the crowd inches away as the heat intensifies. It's a spectacle that lasts for perhaps forty-five minutes. As the fire begins to die down, folks start to leave, ambling up the narrow, twisting streets toward Via Garibaldi. There, they hang out for a few moments before disappearing up more side streets. Within a few hours, everything is quiet; the fire is but a low, smoky glow; the square is deserted and dark.

The scene is like the opening of the Federico Fellini film *Amarcord,* his coming-of-age comedy about life in his hometown of Rimini, high on Italy's Adriatic coast. The townspeople surround the great fire—it obviously is their version of the *falò* for San Giuseppe. They dance and chortle excitedly as the flames leap higher and higher. In Racalmuto, the large crowd is all smiles and full of applause, but there is no dancing.

The *festa di San Giuseppe* is the next day, the nineteenth of March. It starts in the morning with a procession billed as *"la processione della sacra famiglia vivènte"* (the procession of the living sacred family), and is for children. I arrive in front of the Church of San Giuseppe, its exterior rough, unadorned, built in the 1600s of brown stone from the nearby hills. The place is packed with families, and in an open area next to the church, a young boy leads a donkey draped in a beautiful, richly pattered blanket. In a strap around the donkey's forehead is stuck a card showing a painting of Saint Joseph holding an infant Christ. Soon, two girls aged around eight and wearing robes are placed onto the donkey's back. I guessed that they were Mary and her mother, Saint Anne.

I'm wrong about Saint Anne, Concetta Barbieri told me later. One little girl actually represents Jesus. A slightly older boy, dressed in rich blue with a red cross over his left breast, takes the donkey's halter rope. He is Saint Joseph. As recently as three years before, Concetta says, these roles were given to poor villagers, and people invited to join the procession were "tramps" who loitered about the town. Now, the roles go to kids of devout church members.

"This is a real honor" for the kids, Concetta says, for these people are very fond of their *chiesa,* the Church of San Giuseppe. The youngsters are into nonstop smiling and obviously pleased at being the center of attention. Proud, smiling parents, aunts, uncles, cousins, brothers, and sisters are taking photographs and cheering the trio on.

It is amazing how a procession like this works in a small village with narrow, steep streets crammed with cars and a space wide enough only to allow room for vehicles—and folks walking a few abreast—passing through. Participants simply make do. A handful of men and women wearing smocks imprinted with TRAFFICO POLIZIA, and looking more like volunteers than regular traffic cops, move ahead to stop cars. Occasionally a vehicle slips through, and the procession stops while participants step aside to let it pass. Then, the group forms again and proceeds uphill, then downhill, then uphill again, the tiny donkey trudging along.

The circuit lasts for about forty-five minutes, ending once again at the Church of San Giuseppe after moving along Via Garibaldi, the village's main street that is punctuated here and there with the clusters of older men typically found in Sicilian and Italian villages. They are dressed in comfortable slacks, well-buffed dress shoes, pressed dress shirts usually covered by light sweaters, and sport coats.

Some wear the traditional Sicilian cap, the *coppola.* They spend a significant portion of their days here, strolling along this portion of the street's single block, talking with one another, enjoying the weather and sweet companionship of life-long friends.

Since this day is an altar-bread festival throughout Sicily, Racalmuto has its offering as well, but on a smaller scale than the event at much larger Salemi. Next to the church, on the bed of a large truck, is a plainly adorned table covered with a white cloth. A bowl of fruit sits in the middle with three place settings. *"La tavola di San Giuseppe!"* a bystander whispers proudly in my ear.

Lined up against the truck railing behind the table are four, nearly six-foot-tall pieces of bread. The bread is in the shape of shepherds' staffs, with crooks at the top. They appear to be in one piece, but I can't imagine where an oven big enough would be found in this small town. Molded onto the surfaces are Christian symbols, such as crosses.

People are served pieces of this bread that, when the procession ends, is ceremoniously broken up and placed in baskets.

Youngsters are taught these traditions, and all seem eager to participate. The little actors are genuinely pleased to be selected for their roles, and the two girls, atop the little donkey, are the most charming of all.

This morning's children's procession and the *falò* the night before mark only the beginning of the festivities. At 6:30 P.M., following a brief service before a standing-room-only congregation packed into the tiny church, the *processione del simulacrum di San Giuseppe,* or the "procession of the sacred statue" of the saint, begins.

Here, near the church's front doors, the *simulacrum* stands erect on a platform with long handles protruding from each side of the base. The six-foot-tall saint is holding a small Jesus. The platform is made of well-polished wood. At San Giuseppe's feet are several clusters of lights. As people pass by the statue—and this is difficult given the congestion in the room—each one reaches out to touch San Giuseppe's foot and silently mouth a brief prayer, then make the sign of the cross. Men, women, teenagers, and young children all do this, seemingly spontaneously and with great reverence.

A group of men are struggling with the main front doors, which are badly in need of restoration. The squeaking fifteen-foot-tall doors eventually swing open, punctuated by grunts from the men (*"Uno, due, tre, spinga!"* Push!). The congregation moves out into the chilly night, a slight breeze swirling pieces of discarded paper around the tiny square. Perhaps 150 folks wearing heavy coats and with scarves wrapped snugly around their necks, are preparing to follow the saint in his procession around this small village.

Eight young men, chosen for the task because of their sturdy builds, assume positions at each of the four long handles protruding from the corners of the saint's platform. They squat down, push up against the rails with their shoulders, and lift the heavy contraption. Think of the horror if the saint tumbled from his perch! An older man positions himself at the front between the rails and another at the rear. They place their hands on the ends of the poles to serve as guides, and keep the saint on course during his journey. The one in front has a wooden stick, intricately carved, that he uses to tap signals on the platform. One tap means "lift"; two quick taps mean "walk," and the platform bearers, like soldiers in close-order drill, step off together, left foot first.

A group of older teenagers and perhaps a few twentysome-things, all dressed in dark navy blue uniforms with white and light blue cords intertwined about their right shoulders, fall in behind the saint's platform. This is the Corpo-Musicale "G. Verdi," or Racalmuto's town band. (All the town bands I saw in Sicily seem to include "G. Verdi," referring to opera composer Giuseppe Verdi, in their names.)

Band members gather in loose formation, not like a shoulder-to-shoulder, rank-and-file precision-marching band in the United States. They seem to have no leader, except for one much older gentleman who takes his place in the second-to-last row among the horn players.

With laughs, smiles, and gentle cajoling, he gets the musicians into some semblance of order: two rows of clarinetists in the front, drummers, and then brass players. On some hidden cue, the snare drummer beats out a brief signal and, without a conductor, the band begins, everyone playing at precisely the right instant.

The group plays wonderfully; no squeaky clarinet reeds, not one player out of tune. Clearly, with no plan or intent to be "in step," the group ambles forward as the loud taps of the stick against the saint's platform ring out. The saint, carried high and proud by the eight confident young men, begins his journey.

The two priests chant Hail Marys through a wireless microphone they hand back and forth to each other and, occasionally, to a member of the crowd, their voices spilling out from a loudspeaker concealed somewhere in the platform. A

group of the faithful leads the procession in front of the priests;
a worshipper, as proud about the honor as the three children
the day before, is carrying the congregation's flag.

The procession stops every fifty feet or so, to give the head
priest a chance to deliver a brief sermon or homily to those
watching along the sidelines or, more likely, to give the statue
carriers a brief respite. It is a slow, exhausting journey down
from the tiny square, through Piazza Barona, where the bonfire blazed the night before. From there, it heads up the steep
Via Regina Elena and then turns up a shorter, steeper, narrower
street and onto the main street through the village center, Via
Garibaldi.

It takes two hours, and it represents for these devout Sicilian Catholics a solemn, serious tradition. The more than two
hundred souls who follow this procession—from toddlers carried by parents, to young children and teenagers, to adults of
all ages, including a large contingent of elderly—stay with it
for the entire route, repeating the countless Hail Marys chanted
by the priests.

Passersby watch respectfully, caps off, as the saint passes. A
young woman sitting behind the wheel of her car waiting for an
opening through the people, makes the sign of the cross as the
saint passes by. An elderly woman in black who is bent with age
and leaning on a cane and with a white-lace shawl around her
shoulders watches from a narrow balcony above. She repeatedly
makes the sign of the cross and mouths words only she can hear.
It is indeed a remarkable spectacle, driven by passion and faith.

This show of respect and faith is much different from what
I have witnessed in northern Italian churches or even churches
in Rome, with the exception of the Vatican. I see few people

attending services; congregations are populated by only a handful of mostly older women.

In Sicily, in the half dozen or so churches I entered during services, nearly every seat is taken, and young people appear to be as involved as adults. For example, processions in the city of Enna, as we will see later, draw children as young as five or six as participants. Catholicism remains very strong in Sicily—and throughout southern Italy—in a nation where fewer and fewer people attend church regularly. As in the United States, attendance is higher only during Easter.

A friend raised in this culture confirms that many Sicilians are believers and take the Catholic doctrine seriously. What they don't like is the organization of the church, the hierarchy, and the Vatican telling them what to do and how to act.

Concetta Barbieri, who agreed one afternoon to show her village to me, says that out of the ten thousand residents of Racalmuto, perhaps four thousand are devout in their regular attendance at church services among the four active churches in the village. This is typical for most Sicilian villages, she says. Four priests and a deacon serve these congregations. They team up, moving among the different services.

Parishioners are extremely loyal to their local churches, and something is going on at each nearly every day. One afternoon, for example, while visiting a church at the top of steep steps—the seventeenth-century Church of the Santa Maria del Monte—I listen to a group of older women bundled in coats against the chill of the stucco interior. They stand in a tight circle, holding lighted tapers, chanting prayers.

———

But more than festivals has drawn me to Racalmuto. This was the birthplace of the Sicilian writer Leonardo Sciascia—someone I wanted to learn more about. Second, it is the ancestral village of a close friend who speaks lovingly of it. And I have spent time speaking with a Sicilian-Canadian anthropologist whose forebears came from here. Hundreds of Racalmutese, like other Sicilians seeking better lives, found their way to Hamilton, Canada, the eastern United States, or South America early in the twentieth century.

Racalmuto's development was influenced not by the Greeks, but by the Arabs who first created a town here, and later by the Normans and the French. It is a village like many others, with a rich ancient and medieval history and traditions that have remained a significant part of daily life.

Another appeal is that this is a village not overrun, or even much affected, by tourism. Its shops serve local people. There are no souvenir shops selling T-shirts or cheap imitations of Sicilian ceramics. I had a hard time even finding a postcard. It has only one or two places where visitors can stay but is rich in restaurants that fill up with locals, night after night, starting about nine o'clock. More than two decades before, while visiting Catania, I was hard-pressed to find a restaurant that was open before nine. The farther south you go in Italy, the later people eat. Most of the places in this village are still full of noisy, laughing diners around midnight.

Daily life is real here; everyone knows everyone else. When out of the presence of strangers, they speak in local dialect that even a visiting Italian from the mainland would find hard to follow.

———

Leonardo Sciascia (1921–1989) ranks up there with a group that includes older Sicilian writers Giovanni Verga and Luigi Pirandello. He also was a contemporary with Italian writers Alberto Moravia and Elsa Morante, Sicilian writer Andrea Camilleri, and Roman writer Dacia Maraini, whose mother was Sicilian. The only living survivors of this group are Camilleri, primarily known for his Inspector Montalbano mysteries, and Maraini, a well-known feminist, playwright, novelist, and newspaper columnist.

Incidentally, Racalmuto is the birthplace of opera tenor Salvatore Puma, born in 1920, a year before Sciascia. Puma was a sought-after singer in many Italian opera houses, from La Scala in Milan and La Fenice in Venice to San Carlo in Naples to the Massimo in Palermo. He died in 2007 in Rome at age eighty-seven. He is revered in his hometown; all his costumes are on display, lovingly kept in immaculate condition in Racalmuto's late nineteenth-century theater.

In each of my visits, different townspeople have gone out of their way to mention him to me; two personally guided me to the theater, eager to show me the costumes.

Sciascia is revered in Racalmuto as well. If the church allowed locals to choose their own saints, he likely would be one, despite his skepticism about the religion of his youth. The Fondazione Leonardo Sciascia is housed in a tastefully restored, three-story, late nineteenth-century structure that possesses a spectacular view of the village. Here are housed in sunny, renovated rooms all of his papers, manuscripts, first editions of his books printed in a variety of languages, and a major portion of his personal book collection. There is a large lecture hall for international conferences and well-spaced tables for researchers who come here to unlock the mysteries of this internationally respected writer.

One afternoon during my fourth trip in March 2010, Steve McCurdy, my Italian-speaking photographer friend and fellow traveler, struck up a conversation with a group of elderly men sitting outside in the pre-Easter sunshine in front of their social club. These retirees, like older men in Sicily, are well-dressed during their morning and afternoon sojourns to the club and their walks up and down Racalmuto's main street.

They invite us to have a drink with them, a *limonata,* or lemon squash. I ask if they know the house where Sciascia was born. Of course, they nod. After all, many of these men likely grew up and walked the streets of the village with him in the afternoons when he would take a break from writing to spend time with his friends.

Lillo Nalbone, a burly, heavily mustachioed gentleman in a black jacket, finely pressed blue shirt, and gray pants, says he will show us. We walk across Via Garibaldi and up a side street, turning left after a few dozen feet onto Via Leonardo Sciascia. There we pause before a two-story house, clearly empty of any inhabitants. No plaque is there to note its famous occupant. The stone is crumbling, the façade is badly in need of paint, and weeds grow here and there around the front door. I can just imagine what the interior must look like. I had been told by Sciascia's daughters that the house was in the hands of cousins.

Lillo points down the street to a corner house. "Sciascia's aunt still lives there," he said.

On the house's second level is a small terrace. It no longer appears like it can hold one person's weight. Looking at it, I remembered a few lines from one of Sciascia's books where he describes how his grandfather, the family patriarch, would sit on that terrace, impatiently tapping his cane when he wanted a drink or a coffee. One of his daughters would come out the door, dutifully take his order, and disappear inside.

Lillo relishes his role as tour guide. He leads us down to the restored nineteenth-century theater, shows us the gilded interior, and then takes us upstairs to a room containing dozens of Puma's costumes. I remember an earlier local guide, Concetta Barbieri, lamenting that they should be protected in glass cases, but there is no money for such an extravagance. Lillo introduces us to the folks who run the theater, and we wander back to the social club, shake hands with him and his companions, and take our leave.

Librarian and curator Linda Graci, a young, lively, engaging *Siciliana* who speaks a touch of English to complement my touch of Italian, is showing me the Sciascia collections housed in his foundation building with its sweeping view of the village below. We put what we know of each other's language together and have an easy visit. Most interesting to me, beyond the scholarly files of Sciascia's papers, are the dozens of prints, etchings, and photographs of famous authors, politicians, and others of various nationalities—although most are Italian— who particularly influenced him. They came from his personal collection, and the foundation has had them tastefully framed. After his death in 1989 at age sixty-eight, Sciascia's family donated them.

The collection includes classic images of Pirandello, Moravia, and Frenchmen Paul Verlaine and Voltaire. There is a stunning print of a newly discovered favorite of mine, Guy de Maupassant, who wrote so passionately about Sicily at a time when most Frenchmen were "convinced that Sicily is an uncivilized country, difficult and even dangerous to visit." The island, de Maupassant insisted, is the "pearl of the Mediterranean."

Sciascia, it seems, collected prints only of those he liked and respected. Two Americans, while not represented in the print collection, also ranked high in his estimation, Linda Graci says: John Steinbeck and Mark Twain. As for his other influences, it seems strange to me that Verga is not present in the grouping. And there are only a few women: Madame Adam (Juliette Lamber), Colette, Gyp, and the French writer George Sand, who, born as Amantine or Amandine Lucile Aurore Dupin, took a man's name to advance her professional life in what was then a male-dominated world.

Linda Graci sheds some light about Sciascia's choices.

"Verga was a realist; Sciascia didn't like this literary form. He liked the *illuminati,* and this is why he liked a lot of the French writers," she told me. And, she continues, Italian or Sicilian writers who are women had little impact on Sciascia. For example, while he certainly knew the Italian feminist and writer Dacia Maraini, who spent her formative years in a village near Palermo, her picture does not appear in his collection.

"Italian men, in particular Sicilian men, are much closed"

when it comes to being influenced by women writers or women artists, Linda tells me. "For the girl, the woman, to write is *molto difficile,* even today.

"That is why, for me, Maraini is very important," she said.

It appears that only George Sand and a couple of others, on the strength of their skills and being French, won a place where most women failed in his estimation.

I had a conversation in Rome with Maraini—author of dozens of books, movie scripts, and plays—several months before, and had asked her about Sciascia.

"Oh, we served on some literary panels," she told me over a lunch of pasta, vegetables, and fresh fruit. "But, you know, he was a man of his culture and very much has Arab blood in his veins. We liked each other, I suspect, but we were not close friends."

I want to visit Sciascia's grave. B and B host Giuseppe Andini, partner of Paola Prandi, says the writer is in the Racalmuto *cimitero.* "It is interesting there because, in tradition here, each family tries to outdo the other families by piling on a lot of flowers onto their relations' grave, but Sciascia's grave is very simple, and usually there is only a single flower, perhaps a rose, placed there. It is Racalmuto's way—the simplicity and cleanness of it all—of honoring him above all others; of not making him the same as the others."

After a few aborted tries to get into the frequently locked cemetery, located on the village's lower edge where the open countryside begins, I finally find it open on a cold, windy, and rain-splattered Saturday morning. The place appears deserted.

I wander around the plots of tightly clustered tombs, some gaudy and ornate, others cleanly simple, but nothing indicates Sciascia.

Then I see a young woman, nearly hidden in a cluster of white tombs with tall headstones, sweeping dried leaves and the clutter of a hard winter off one stone-covered grave. I ask her if she knows of Sciascia's grave. She nods and offers to lead me there. We go back toward the entrance, and she points to a space that is enclosed by a fence of tall, rust-streaked tin.

"It is being changed," she said simply, and then turned to head back to her grave-cleaning task. I walk around the enclosure and find an opening in the back. Through it, I see two unadorned, white-stone boxes partially buried but with their tops protruding perhaps two feet aboveground. This is much in the tradition of the ancient Greeks, Romans, or Muslims in North Africa, I think—places where people aren't usually buried six feet beneath the ground but are sealed in stone boxes that show partially above the surface. The earth around the stone tombs was freshly turned over, and construction tools were scattered about.

I headed for the front gate, passing by the custodian's office. He looks up as I tap on his glass door. "When will Sciascia's tomb be finished?" I ask. *"È a tempo indeterminate"* (It is indefinite), he said, shrugging his shoulder in that typical Sicilian way that says these things take time and who knows. "Why is it being done?" I ask. *"Per la moglie"* (for the wife), he says. *"È morta due mesi fa."* (She died two months ago.)

No one had told me about her death during all my discussions here about Sciascia. I later looked it up. Maria Andronico, age eighty-six, died on January 6, 2009—barely two months before my March visit. She was placed in the tomb next to her husband two days later, on what would have been Sciascia's eighty-eighth birthday. Months later, during subsequent visits, the tin sheets enclosing the gravesite were gone. Two un-adorned white-marble stone tombs surrounded by healthy grass and with carved inscriptions identifying their occupants lay side by side.

Four months beyond that day in the cold drizzle in Racal-muto's cemetery, in the brutal month of July when the warm breath of Africa blows across the island, baking crops and creatures large and small, I stood, at the family's invitation, in Sciascia's study at Noce, the family home in the countryside just outside Racalmuto. On the wall, next to the doorway, was a black-and-white photo of the writer on horseback, being led up the stone steps of the Church of the Santa Maria del Monte, high on a small hill near the center of the village.

He was participating in a festival unique to this place; I could not find a reference to anything similar elsewhere on the island. On the final day of this three-day festival, men and older boys would mount richly decorated horses and, one at a time, be led along the main street to the steady beat of tom-tom drums pounded by a rank of four men. The short procession would turn onto the street at the base of the steep, gray stone steps leading up to the church full of worshippers attending high Mass.

In the photo, Sciascia is wearing a vest with intricate designs. He is leaning forward on his horse as the animal struggles to climb the forty-two steps. There are men on both sides of the animal, gripping its harnesses and shouting to encourage it upward.

To the uninitiated standing at the bottom of the *scala*, looking at the door of the church high above, the exercise looks impossible. An observer might wonder how hard it is on the horses. But every July, for centuries, men have been doing this, and in modern times, Racalmuto is jam-packed with several thousand visitors as well as the locals to witness the spectacle.

Despite the crush of out-of-towners, in many ways this giant festival still exudes a sense of being "local." The five-hundred-foot-long stretch of Via Garibaldi is jammed elbow to elbow, from Piazza Francesco Crispi and its fountain at the south end to the front door of the cathedral at the north. It seems like every one of the village's ten thousand residents is there, along with cousins from families that have, in the last century or longer, immigrated to North or South America.

This festival became the tie that binds. Early on, the original immigrants would return to Racalmuto to witness the major festival of their childhoods and visit family members who had stayed put in this land of vineyards and now-abandoned sulfur and salt mines. Then, they came with their American-born children, who later brought their children. And the newer generations keep coming.

For three days, there is almost nonstop band music and processions, often running late into the night. Food and trinket stalls, run most likely by outsiders who go from festival to festival across this island, are stretched up and down side streets.

The running of the horses up the steep steps comes on the last day, Sunday. I saw that photo of Sciascia participating in a festival he had witnessed from infancy; two days later I was a speck among the masses gathered around the stairway, cheering as each horse and rider struggled upward, horseshoe-clad hooves clattering loudly against the centuries-old stone steps.

Participants in the early festivals rode donkeys up these steps; later came mules; today it is only horses brightly outfitted in colorful drapery held together by gold-colored rivets.

Originally, in past centuries, the peasants brought their wheat harvest to be weighed here. The weighing, according to legend, took place *inside* the church.

Why the wheat-loaded donkeys were originally taken up the forty-two steep steps to the doors at the church's side, no one seems to know. There certainly is an easier way—the street along the front of the church, for instance—for them to get there. And it doesn't make sense in another way: A peasant's harvest would be much greater than his donkey could carry in a single trip.

A Sicilian-American friend who has witnessed the tradition speculates that the grain might have been hauled along the easily accessed street and into the church where it was dumped for weighing. Eventually, perhaps after a good crop year, the farmers may have started the tradition, as a form of thanksgiving, of taking a donkey ride up the stone steps and into the church with a symbolic load of grain. The event likely followed each year's harvest and grew over the centuries in its pageantry—its origins and meaning lost to modern participants.

Nobody today cares about the lack of logic to this event. The festival is a riotous, colorful, musically noisy affair that puts smiles on everyone's faces and incredible local foods and pastries into their stomachs.

The capstone, however, is not the running of the horses up to the base of the steps. When man and beast reach the top, they burst into the wide-open doors of the church, which is full of parishioners attending Mass. I watched six riders and their horses over a period of about ninety minutes, with each being paraded through the village to the unrelenting beat of the drums, clamber up those steps. Once inside the church, just beyond the giant doors, the victorious rider and his steed were met by the smiles of an accommodating congregation.

This Sunday morning's event followed still another spectacle from the night before that lasted until the early hours of the new day: The *u ciliu il cero dei borgesi,* or quest by young, unmarried men of a landowner class, the *borgesi,* for a flag fluttering high atop a tall structure pulled through the main street packed with revelers.

That event is truly steeped in antiquity. A Racalmutese who immigrated to Hamilton, Canada, wrote about it in his 1993 memoir of his ancestral village, *Traditions of Our Fathers: The True Sicilians.* Peppi Pillitteri, a close friend and contemporary, albeit ten years younger, of Leonardo Sciascia, describes the *ciliu* as having deep Arabic origins; its Arabic name was *taazia.* He says in the Arab world that *taazias* "were built as a living proof of martyrdom for a cause and also as an expression to show hope for the future."

This event is tied to another procession conducted as part of this multiday festival. It involves a boatlike float containing a representation of the Madonna housed in the church at the top of the stone steps, the Santa Maria del Monte. This brief procession symbolizes, according to Pillitteri, the discovery in the early 1500s of a hidden statue of the Madonna in a North African cave. A Sicilian prince on a hunting trip reportedly found it as he and his party were seeking shelter from a storm.

The prince transported it, first in a ship across the Strait of Sicily, then by oxcart to his home near Racalmuto. When the cart got to the village, the oxen stopped and refused to move. The church dedicated to the Madonna was built in 1503 on the spot where that cart stopped.

Pillitteri acknowledges that this story has "the untenability of some historical facts. But for the sake of simplicity we would like to adhere to the myth and faith as reported to us by our forefathers."

The procession of the Madonna is well attended, but the *ciliu* is what everyone is waiting for. Late on the night of Racalmuto's *ciliu*, the ubiquitous drummers, who precede just about everything public in Sicily, pounded their way through the crowd. The town band and a visiting band from Calabria, across the water in southern Italy, were arrayed around the fountain in Piazza Francesco Crispi, playing marches. The flag-festooned structure would be pulled along the street ever so slowly. High atop was a trophy flag. A gang of young men, usually in their late teens or early twenties, would suddenly, either spontaneously or on some mysterious prearranged signal, burst out of the crowd from all sides and scramble onto the spiral structure. They would push and shove one another trying to be the first to get to the top and grab the flag, fighting off all those trying to take it away.

In times past, blood flowed freely as the young men clawed

their way to the top. But there seemed to be no hard feelings among winners and losers. The idea is for the winner to take the flag, present it to a young woman he wishes to marry, and then be married before the next year's festival rolls around.

I had heard this story and wanted to witness the event. No one could tell me where the scramble would take place. It was spontaneous, they said, and could happen anywhere along the street.

I got there early in the evening, before the crowd had begun to grow, and sat down on the curb. The evening wore on, the crowd ballooned, various drum groups marched down the clogged street, pushing their way through the tightly clustered throng. About midnight, an engine's roar could be heard. Seconds later, from around a corner, a small tractor pulling the flag-bedecked tower came into view.

The tractor moved slowly down the street, gently nudging revelers out of the way. It passed me as I stood up, watching the tower, waiting for the scramble to begin.

The engine roared again and, erupting from out of the crowd, perhaps a dozen young men, pushing and shoving one another as they fought for position, jumped aboard and struggled upward. It was happening directly in front of me. The scramblers instantly became sweat-drenched—this was mid-July in Sicily, remember—and for perhaps ten minutes or so the battle ensued. No punches were thrown, as near as I could tell; it involved just yelling, pushing, shoving, and the grabbing of sweaty shirts. If there was any blood during this frenzied skirmish, I missed it.

The crowd roared. One young man was standing high atop the structure, waving the banner and shouting in glee. The combatants stopped, clinging quietly to the tower's sides. Slowly, the tractor started up, pulling the tower through the crowd slowly with the victor waving the flag the full length of the street. A few younger boys, perhaps fourteen or so and anticipating their battle for the flag in a few years, climbed aboard quietly for the ride.

This has been going on for centuries here. A woman who had been standing behind me during the battle saw me shaking my head in exhausted wonderment.

"*Tradizione*," she said with a broad smile. "*E ci tiene tutti vivi.*" (It keeps us all alive).

Pillitteri put it nicely as well, his words blending together all that I saw over the period of a year—from Saint Rosalia's procession in Palermo to Racalmuto's pagan *falò*, the *ciliu*, the horses scrambling up the stone steps, and later, Easter processions in Enna—all mixed in with massive doses of Christianity. He wrote: "One of the beauties of faith is the ability to believe in religion, myth, and legend. The great gray area of myth and religion allows one to dream and hope, especially when mystery abounds everywhere."

FIVE

Sulfur

We enter the mountains. Before us lies a region of
real desolation, a wretched land, which seems cursed,
condemned by nature.

—Guy de Maupassant,
Sicily (1889)

Rarely do a visitor's thoughts focus, as he sits basking in
sunlight on a stone bench, on Sicily before the first half of the
twentieth century. Most towns today are well-scrubbed, their
residents driving their late-model cars down narrow, twisting
streets lined with buildings that, in village centers, often hear-
ken back to the Middle Ages. These historic structures may
have an old, somewhat crumbling exterior, but inside many
are modern and comfortable. Some villages have old buildings
that have been abandoned for decades, perhaps from a time at
the start of the twentieth century when owners fled the island's
crushing poverty for North and South America.

For example, Leonardo Sciascia's birth home in Racalmuto

is empty, its façade in disrepair and windows broken. It sits, waiting for some restorer to come along and turn it into the shrine it longs to be. Giovanni Verga's place of birth and death is restored and on display in Catania; Luigi Pirandello's family home—in the *contrada,* or rural neighborhood, near Agrigento known as Caos—draws thousands of homage payers yearly.

Sicilian villages generally do not look like they were cast in similar molds like those in, say, Tuscany to the far north, where one quaint hill town after another can start to look the same. In the last half century or more, most Allied-caused war damage in Sicilian villages has been set right—except for spots of bombed-out devastation that still linger in central Palermo near the port—and modern buildings have spread out around village perimeters.

Modernity is not always good. One of the worst examples is on the approach to Noto, a city in southeastern Sicily. It snuggles against rolling hillsides, its baroque character visible for miles, and in the foreground stands a modern hotel several stories high blocking the once picturesque view of a handful of stunning seventeenth- and eighteenth-century buildings. What could modern folks here have been thinking when they allowed such a structure to be built?

Friends in Noto, when I ask this question, shrug and say that it is the way things always happen: Rules are bent; zoning laws, if they exist, are ignored; a favor is exchanged here and there. Nothing is done about it.

These often sluggish and ineffective building codes aside, life in most parts of the island appears reasonably prosperous. Many older Sicilians have pensions, something that was rare just decades ago. Younger people who are unemployed—the South has an unemployment rate well into the high teens—receive some kind of financial support from the state, and many, if unmarried, still live with their parents.

Long gone are the days of the peasant family that sleeps on straw mattresses on the floor—all in one, maybe two, tiny rooms. Also absent, with few exceptions, is a significant homeless population that many large-city Americans see daily in the United States, a land that Sicilian and southern Italian immigrants a century or so ago viewed as the land of milk and honey with streets paved in gold.

Nowadays, except for the tumble of abandoned structures hidden away in places like Palermo, the only remaining vestiges of World War II are the scattered concrete bunkers sprinkled across ridgelines and the tops of wide, sloping fields. The island's extensive highway system is reasonably well maintained except for some dramatic exceptions deep in the countryside. Nearly all tiny roadways between rural villages, once no more than mule paths, are paved, serving the island's transportation needs quite well despite periodic signs warning of large potholes or places where a significant chunk of one lane has slipped down a steep slope.

Twenty-first-century Sicily seems light-years away from the Sicily of the mid-twentieth century. Enzo Sellerio's black-and-white photographs, taken around the island in the 1950s and early 1960s, show few automobiles, a lot of mule- and horse-drawn carts, growers and their families handpicking grapes and hauling huge grape-filled baskets on their backs, elderly women clothed in black, small children in knee-length pants and ragged sweaters. This was a land still recovering from the ravages of war; northern Italy was well on its way to recovery, while Sicily was still digging out of the rubble twenty years after the last bombs were dropped.

But every decade over the last century showed some progress, however slow. Sicily in the mid-twentieth century may have been where America was in the century's beginning, but it was far ahead of its nineteenth-century condition, either before or after Unification in 1861.

For a look at that era, Giovanni Verga's fictional depictions of such late nineteenth and early twentieth-century living conditions for the Sicilian peasant class are hard enough for Americans to comprehend. But when a famed American traveler visiting the island during the autumn of 1910 describes it, the reality sinks in. That visitor was Booker T. Washington, the African-American principal of Alabama's Tuskegee Institute from 1881 until his death in 1915 at age fifty-nine.

Washington visited Europe with an idea of observing how the lives of the lower classes in various countries compared to those of African-Americans. In Sicily, he came to this conclusion: "The Negro is not the man farthest down. The condition of the coloured farmer in the most backward parts of the Southern States in America, even where he has the least education and the least encouragement, is incomparably better than the condition and opportunities of the agricultural population in Sicily."

It is easy, then, for the casual twenty-first-century visitor—the tourist captivated by the charm of cobblestoned streets and quaint shops full of sweets and other good things to eat, high-end designer clothes, and upscale kitchen appliances and bathroom fixtures—never to know what this place was like for the masses, who over the centuries lived well outside of the palaces and country homes of the rich barons.

One needs to see motion pictures such as *Golden Door* or *Aclá's Descent into Floristella* to really grasp why, in an era closer to our own modern times, southern Italians by the tens of thousands left this land for a new world in North and South America and Australia.

Many years ago, riding on a train south of Naples, I sat next to an impeccably dressed older man on his way to visit his mother in Sicily. I casually mentioned that I wondered why southern Italians and Sicilians left their villages that today draw tourists by the thousands. He held me in a long gaze and said, in precise English, "Well, you can't eat quaint." As a middle-class American, he said in a kindly way, I could have no comprehension of what it was like in the South. Now, many years and plenty of visits later, I begin to understand.

It's the kind of pre-twentieth-century picture Verga paints in his numerous short stories about peasants facing failed crops, landowners taking the workers' share of a harvest because drought crippled production, and malaria taking half or more of the children the poor laborers brought into the world.

Perhaps most compelling is the story of south-central Sicily's sulfur miners, laboring by hand and with sheer brute strength in an era before mechanical equipment, when much of the world's sulfur came from this island.

Leonardo Sciascia knew about this miners' hell. His village of Racalmuto rests in the heart of what once was sulfur country, that region generally northeast of Agrigento. Many of the older townspeople still alive after the turn of the twenty-first century worked in the now closed sulfur and salt mines that peppered this once bleak, dead landscape of rolling, blighted hills.

In the early spring of 2009, I walk into a small two-room building hewn from stone and plastered over. It has a logo next to the door that proclaimed the building to be LEGA ZOL-FATAI SALINAI PENSIONATI RACALMUTO, the village Cooperative of Sulfur and Salt Worker Pensioners of Racalmuto. I am escorted by local resident Concetta Barbieri. She knows the elderly men inside, all of who worked in the mines on the village's outskirts.

One of the mine owners, in 1955, donated this retirement center as a place where the men could meet, talk, and reminisce about their days belowground. Concetta tells me that when it opened, there were three hundred retired miners as members; early in 2009, eighty-four are left. There won't be any others. The last mine closed in 1975.

I had first obtained a sense of how this region had been one of the major sulfur-producing areas in the world by reading a Frenchman's account, *Sicily*, of an 1889 journey through here. Guy de Maupassant, on a grand tour of the island by horseback, had just visited Agrigento and the ruins of its Greek temples. Today's beautiful green and rolling hillsides that surround the temple site and lie at the base of the cluttered city of Agrigento are in sharp contrast to de Maupassant's view of temples that

appear standing in the air in the midst of a magnificent and desolate landscape. All is dead, arid and yellow around them, in front of them and behind them. The sun has burned and eaten the earth. . . . For everywhere around Agrigento stretches the strange land of sulfur mines.

Then he looks beyond the temples as he continues north-eastward on his journey into the region that holds Racalmuto and numerous other villages that relied on sulfur and salt mining. This region, he writes, "seems like Satan's true realm, for if—as was formerly believed—the devil inhabits a vast underground country, full of melting sulfur, where he boils the damned, Sicily is surely the place where he has established his mysterious abode." This reflects what one Sicilian historian once said to me: "Sicily! Where hell and paradise meet."

De Maupassant visits a mine and goes into great detail about how sulfur is hacked out of underground caverns and how the sulfur is processed. He reports all this matter-of-factly. Then, on a steep, narrow staircase, its uneven steps hacked out of the walls of the hot, stifling cavern, he encounters

> a troop of children loaded with baskets. They pant and gasp, these wretched urchins, weighed down under their loads. They are ten, twelve years old, and they repeat, fifteen times in a single day, the abominable voyage . . . They are small, thin, yellow, with huge shining eyes . . . This revolting exploitation of children is one of the most painful things that one can see.

In *Sicily,* a line drawing shows these young boys with baskets balanced on their shoulders coming down a stairway chopped out of stone. They are fully clothed, and de Maupassant never described how they were attired. But it is well-known that the boys, known in Sicilian as *carusi,* along with the adult miners, worked in the hot, hellish pits in the nude or perhaps with only an apron covering their fronts.

The practice of sending youngsters into the mines goes back uncounted decades, perhaps centuries, and ended only in the 1920s or 1930s. None of the men now in the cooperative worked as small boys in the mines, a retired miner told me, but it happened during their parents' and grandparents' generations and earlier.

Nearly a year later, a friend handed me an article he had taken off a Web site. It was written by Tom Verso and entitled "Child Slavery in Sicily in 1910." It confirms what de Maupassant wrote, what I saw in the film *Aclá's Descent into Floristella*, and what the retired miner in Racalmuto told me that March afternoon. The article also refers to Booker T. Washington's book.

Verso writes: "Mr. Washington presents an 'oh-so-not' romantic description of the horrific reality of diasporic Italy, including the de facto enslavement of sulfur mining children in Sicily." The educator, born into slavery, not only watched these child laborers toiling naked in caverns far below the surface near Campofranco, a village only a few miles from Racalmuto, but also he saw youngsters as young as seven working in factories in Palermo and Catania.

His description of the boys' lives belowground in 1910 matches the message found in the movie *Aclá*. The boys are essentially "sold" by their families to adult miners who use them to haul to the surface the rock the men bust out of the mine walls with their picks and sledgehammers. These miners had complete control over the boys' lives—from Monday through Saturday; they could beat the youngsters if they didn't work fast enough, work them long hours and, if they wanted, even sexually abuse them.

In *Aclá*, a scene has the village priest going to the mine to sermonize the miners about their habit of engaging in sexual relationships with each other, including the *carusi*, while housed at the mine, and then going home to their wives on the weekend. The men pay scant attention to the priest's entreaties and laugh when he tries to get them to contribute a few coins to the church.

The young boys worked in this environment for the length of the "contract" the miners had with the families, perhaps for as long as eight years. If a boy tried to escape, as Aclá did, his family and the police would track him down—the police because a legal contract has been broken, the family because it would be forced to pay back the money if the youngster was not returned. Few *carusi* survived the ordeal; those who did became miners themselves; they had no other opportunity, and leaving their village was next to impossible.

Washington's description is emotionally difficult to read; the movie *Aclá* is hard to watch. But the two show, as Tom Verso writes, the truth behind immigrants' "nostalgic recall" and "pastoral romanticism about the conditions in Italy at the time of the diaspora." His argument: They need a jolt of what the reality really was.

A quote taken from a book by Sicilian-American Jerre Mangione, whose father and mother immigrated to the United States, is particularly poignant. The section I read appeared at the beginning of an article by Harvard professor William Granara. In his book *Mount Allegro,* Mangione tells how his father described to his son the Sicily he had left. It was beautiful and full of lovely women and had many "golden sunsets on a blue sea." But the father lowered his voice and described some of the hardships, saying, "Your mother may not like to have me tell you" about the bad things that drove them to America. The mother overhears and does not like it at all. She wants to tell only of the "fruits and flowers beyond the imagination of Americans."

Verso says he agrees with a colleague, Anthony Tamburri of the Calandra Institute, who urges Sicilian-Americans and Italian-Americans "to revisit our past, reclaim its pros and cons . . . we need to figure out where we came from." The land may have been deeply rooted in the souls of these hundreds of thousands of immigrants, but long before it became well scrubbed—made "quaint," as my fellow traveler on the train described it, and thus inviting to hordes of tourists—it was in many ways a killer.

Leonardo Sciascia knew this. His grandfather had been a *caruso* who first entered the mines at the age of nine when his father died. The grandfather "continued to work there until the end of his days," Sciascia writes. But he, unlike many of those boys, survived. He would come home at night and attend classes offered by the priest. As an adult, he became a foreman and then a mine administrator.

He died in 1928, when Sciascia was six. His success, rare among former *carusi*, made it financially possible for young Leonardo to escape that fate. That, plus the practice of using young, illiterate boys was dying out. One of the men in Racalmuto's clubhouse for retired miners told me the practice ended in the 1920s. The film *Aclá* was set during that decade with groups of men walking home singing fascist songs.

Sciascia, in his early novel *Salt in the Wound,* remembers how sulfur affected his village of Racalmuto, thinly disguised in his novel by the fictional name Regalpetra. He writes:

[T]he air in Regalpetra became slightly acrid, the silver tarnished in the mansions of the newly rich, and the bitter odor of burnt sulfur penetrated the very clothing on people's backs. The hills overlooking the town on the north and the high plateau that encircles it on the west took on a reddish hue, and wheat sown in the fields near the mines did not mature.

Then he quotes a fellow villager describing conditions in the mines themselves:

Just try, try to go down those steep steps . . . take a look at those immense caverns, those muddy labyrinths suffocating with infernal vapors, barely lit by the sooty flames of the oil lamps; sweltering heat, curses, the reverberating clang of picks; men naked, pouring sweat, gasping for breath; exhausted youths dragging themselves along slippery steps; small boys who ought to be kissed and petted and set playing with toys instead of subjecting their frail bodies to this beastly labor only to increase the ranks of the deformed.

These laborers, writes Sciascia, while walking back to their houses on Saturday night—"houses broiling in the sun or leaking in the rain"—did so "without consciousness of the world."

The half dozen or so elderly men seated in a semicircle in the darkened room watching a soccer match on a flat-screen television hanging high on the rough, stained wall had looked up with welcoming smiles when I walked through the door of the salt and sulfur miners' clubhouse that March with Concetta Barbiere. These men, the youngest well into his eighties, are the *pensionati*, retired miners on pensions. This two-room, single-story building offers a place where they spend their afternoons when they are not walking back and forth along Via Garibaldi or sitting together on stone benches along side streets.

They greet me warmly, shaking my hand and patting my shoulder, and it's obvious they know and like Concetta, who acknowledges each man. She tells them that I am a visitor from *gli Stati Uniti,* the United States. "They like visitors," Concetta tells me. "It adds variety to their day."

One, who seems to be the spokesman for the group, jumps up to show me around, pointing out a series of dusty, cracking, and faded black-and-white photographs that show stooped-over men—these were taken after the era of *carusi*—carrying large chunks of sulfur on their backs, each piece weighing sixty or more pounds. One photo shows a completely naked miner swinging a pick against a mine wall.

While this work was certainly brutal, the men I met had more modern advantages in motor-driven equipment to do much of the hauling. And like miners everywhere, they have a particularly strong bond. They spend their days together and go to each other's funerals when the time comes.

De Maupassant, Washington, and Sciascia were not the only writers distressed by the lives of sulfur miners. Pirandello, who was born in nearby Agrigento and whose father once was a wealthy sulfur merchant, wrote about it in the short story "Ciàula Discovers the Moon." Verga also describes the life of these children in his short story "Rosso malpelo." This one, set in an underground sand mine, details the brutality some miners directed toward weaker workers.

The man who showed me the photographs told of knowing, when he was a small child, old men who had been child laborers, forced to carry the heavy loads on backs made up of still soft and forming bones. They all walked permanently stooped over, he said.

I bid the kindly gentlemen farewell. Again they shake my hand, wish me a bon voyage, unmute the television, and resume watching their soccer match.

SIX

Sciascia and the Inquisition

Who'er doth enter this horrid tomb.
Here sees the realm of cruelty severe;
Wherefore 'tis writ upon the walls of gloom,
Abandon hope all ye who enter here.
Down here we know not if 'tis dark or day.
But tears we know and pain and cruelty;
And here we know not if we ever may
Hear struck the hour of long-craved liberty.

> —A mid-seventeenth-century
> verse, translated from
> Sicilian, believed written by
> Simone Rao, and found on a
> wall of a cell in the
> Inquisitors Prison, Palermo

ONE BRUTALLY hot July afternoon I found myself standing before Palermo's cathedral. It had started life as a temple that served various pagan interlopers, eventually evolved into a Christian church in the fifth century, and then came under control of Constantinople. It became a mosque during the Arab period, then became, once again, a Western Christian center that saw the coronation of Norman and German kings and their successors. But it really sprouted into full bloom under the Spanish.

Emotionally, I have a hard time with what went on here in the name of the church. It was the Spanish who, under the reign of those great patrons of Christopher Columbus, Ferdinand and Isabella, allowed a revival of the comparatively tame Medieval Inquisition. They let it evolve into what became the feared, despotic Spanish Inquisition that covered much of Europe, including this island off the toe of Italy, and some of the Americas.

In both of its forms, it operated for centuries. Sicilian writer Leonardo Sciascia spent much of his adult life studying that impact on his fellow Sicilians and on an early resident of his home village, Racalmuto.

But before we get into that tale, it is helpful to understand the roots of the concept "inquisition," which date back to Roman times. Edward Peters in his simply titled book *Inquisition,* says that for the Romans, *"inquisitor* was often a synonym for *investigato,"* or someone who "searched for proofs." As time went on, Christianity, even in its earliest iterations, used teaching and persuasion, often in the gentlest of forms, to set right its fallen-away members. This was true well into the twelfth century.

But when *persuasio* failed, other disciplinary means were called for, and in the twelfth century, basing its work on earlier literature, [the church] erected an elaborate disciplinary structure. . . . Such disciplinary measures were aimed more often at protecting the faith of the community rather than explicitly punishing the heretic.

Thus were created the medieval inquisitors. The job was given to the Dominicans, formed by Saint Dominic, who were spread around the realm. The idea was to bring in a group of teachers who had no ties to local politics, and who would judge heresy on ecclesiastical terms, staying above the local entanglements that often led to accusations. And the Dominicans were able to take the process out of the hands of "individual fanatic pursuers of heresy."

One element of the Medieval Inquisition that differed from the later, more barbarous Spanish Inquisition was the way witnesses were used against suspected heretics. In the medieval form, witnesses against an accused heretic may have been kept secret from the general population, but they had to testify and be known to the accused. In the fifteenth century, as the subsequent Spanish Inquisition really got rolling, the accused never knew who the accuser was. And if torture was used by medieval inquisitors to extract a confession—and then only when there were shaky witnesses or proof of guilt was not clear-cut—that confession had to be repeated the following day without torture to ensure the accused really meant what he or she said while in excruciating pain the previous day.

Also, church officials under this earlier, comparatively gentler form, could not condemn anyone to death. The unrepentant heretic was turned over to civil authorities who followed secular law and punished the offender, usually by burning.

Another historian of the Inquisition, Toby Green, tells us

that at the time of Ferdinand and Isabella, a "visitor from Sicily . . . Felipe de Barberis was attached to the old medieval Inquisition in Sicily, and he suggested [to the Catholic rulers that they] found one in Spain . . . Ferdinand and Isabella were convinced." And so the more intense, more dreaded Inquisition began—and at the urging of a Sicilian!

It started in Spain as a way to persecute *conversi*, or Jews who had converted to Christianity but were suspected, rightly or wrongly, of secretly practicing Judaism. Spies were dispatched on Friday nights to the Jewish quarters in Spanish-controlled cities, such as Palermo and Catania and elsewhere in the Spanish empire, where they would watch to see if fires were lighted in the homes. This is something Catholics would have no problem doing on a chilly Friday night, but observant Jews would abstain from the labor of fire building—much as they do today by not operating machinery—as they began to observe their Sabbath. The Inquisition gradually, over the decades, expanded its reach throughout Spain's vast empire deep within the ranks of true believers whom it suspected, again rightly or wrongly, of heresy.

The large, open space that fronts the Cathedral of Palermo is a tranquil spot. It is an escape from the jammed, noisy Via Vittorio Emanuele that, arrow straight for a kilometer or more, slices through the heart of the city, from the Norman palace, now known as Palazzo Reale, to the sea. The Piazza Cattedrale has numerous palm trees defining its far corners and anchoring small squares of hedged-in areas surrounding a massive statue of the city's patron saint, Santa Rosalia. Clusters of schoolchildren on outings, mixing in with camera-toting tourists, lounge around the few brief fringes of green.

The judgments of the Spanish Inquisition were not carried out in front of the cathedral, but it is where hundreds of citizens gathered to view the ceremonies that led up to the actual burnings and to partake of a sumptuous feast. The processions that led to the site where the so-called guilty were "relaxed," as inquisitors euphemistically referred to it, began from here.

Off and on for some three hundred years, between 1478 to the mid-eighteenth century, church leaders adorned in gloriously colored robes started their saunters in solemn processions down the route now followed by Via Vittorio Emanuele. As they neared the sea, they turned right, slowly ambling past the Steri Palace, the headquarters of the Inquisition where so-called heretics were tortured and the religious fathers passed judgment. They would proceed for a few hundred meters more to Piazza Sant'Erasmo, now the site of Villa Giulia. There, a huge pile of wood dominated the open space; erupting from its center was a tall, sturdy post.

Condemned by inquisitors—usually for speaking out against church authority—men and women were burned here, where now beautiful gardens and structures abound. Some sources estimated that upward of five thousand people throughout the Spanish world were "relaxed" in this way; the number for those burned in Sicily from 1487 to 1782 might reach around 250.

Whatever the numbers, these burnings, along with hangings, beheadings, and other brutalities, were conducted in magnificently orchestrated performances known as auto-da-fé, literally the "grand trial of faith." It was better known as the "ceremony" for the punishment of heretics.

Historian Green, in his book *Inquisition: The Reign of Fear,* wryly described one such event, conducted in 1647 in Mexico City, as a "brilliant piece of theater." It likely was a model for what took place elsewhere, including Palermo. All this happened during a time of growing Protestantism and the Counter-Reformation, when the leaders of the Catholic Church, as Green tells us, sought to shore

> up authority over these gargantuan empires. Power was at
> the heart of the Inquisition, and thus, inevitably, did reli-
> gion enter the province of politics. . . . There were always,
> it turned out, others to persecute. But these others could
> remain dormant for decades, their heresies unapparent, until
> some political trigger released them for discovery. . . . For
> the Inquisition provided nothing less than the first seeds of
> totalitarian government, of institutionalized racial and sex-
> ual abuse.

It was a strange, dehumanizing exercise. Men and women were stripped naked, their bodies twisted and bent before an impassive panel of priestly men of God and a scribe who wrote down every detail: The specific type of torture applied, each question, each answer, each scream. The archived records of this body of the church make for difficult reading.

In addition to the politics that may have driven some of the condemnations, the practice was usually coupled with the confiscation of a condemned heretic's land. This led to the creation, particularly in Sicily, of massive estates for church leaders and their friends. At the same time, there certainly were some inquisitors who believed that sending a heretic to the fire was the only way to cleanse his or her soul for entry into God's kingdom. For them and, they believed, for the condemned, the auto was a joyful, necessary experience.

One observation Green makes in his book particularly affects me. He described a painting executed around 1495 by Pedro de Berruguete. It hangs in Madrid's Prado museum and shows various church leaders, including Saint Dominic, presiding over the mass burning of heretics—something he may never have done in reality. His actual role in the earlier Medieval Inquisition is in dispute among scholars, some of who maintain he was never personally involved.

Whatever the reality, the saint, says Green, "is portrayed benevolently, but what is most striking is the air of serenity and justice which envelops the dignitaries around him" as "the little men beneath them" are tied to the posts and flames are licking at their feet. Iron rods protrude suggestively from their crotches, placed there to hold their bodies upright as the flames burn into flesh. What particularly strikes the historian about the demeanor of the church officials in the painting "is the calmness, indeed the indifference, of the dignitaries to the fates of the condemned . . . their suffering is not supposed to be a cause for concern." One prelate even dozes in his seat just below the saint's throne.

Such moments as described in that painting and the Mexico City auto did take place in this Sicilian city in the now beautiful garden area full of tourists and young people, and in other

cities in Sicily as well. The Spanish Inquisition functioned effi-
ciently throughout the centuries-long Spanish rule. This does
not mean that all Sicilians embraced the Inquisition. Green
reports that during a five-year period in the early 1500s, more
than seventy people were burned in autos. In one year alone,
1513, thirty-five people were burned. These numbers began to
gnaw away at the Sicilian soul. The Sicilian Parliament lodged
a protest about the scores of people being led to the stake
"shouting out their innocence in vain and that they had only
confessed under torture their guilt."

News of Ferdinand's death in 1516 was met by mobs filling
Palermo's streets. They sacked the viceroy's palace, burned
the Inquisition's archive, and freed prisoners. Of course, things
settled down, inquisitors returned and, eventually, the perse-
cutions resumed, but at a much slower pace than before.

But the practice continued to flay at Sicilian souls. Friction
remained. A powder magazine in the Inquisition headquarters
exploded in 1593. Inquisitors were nearly killed and, in one
case, one actually died at the hands of a prisoner—a situation
described in a Sciascia story.

After centuries of pain and suffering, it did end, in 1783.
"[T]he Sicilian Inquisition was abolished by royal order, its
buildings and finances were confiscated, its records sealed,
and its prisoners released," writes Green. While the records
may have been sealed, many were burned in the courtyard
of the Steri Palace in Palermo's Kalsa quarter.

The Steri prisons had come into being beginning in 1603 in
the form we see them today. The Inquisition in Sicily, after the
turbulent sixteenth century, had moved into the palace in 1601
and endured there for nearly two hundred years more, until

1783. The first cells, on the ground floor, were built by 1605; another six cells on a new floor above were added some years later. Each cell had an indentation in a wall, with a hole in the bottom, that was used as a toilet. The cell entrances were low, perhaps four feet high, forcing a prisoner to stoop. As many as twelve men would be confined to a single cell, and the only light was from a slot high up on the outside wall.

I am drawn to all this because of Leonardo Sciascia's chilling critique of the Spanish practice and the opportunity I had to visit the prison under the guidance of Sciascia's son-in-law, Nino Catalano, an engineer instrumental in the restoration of the prison.

In *The Death of the Inquisitor,* the writer focuses on the story of a monk from his village of Racalmuto. Fra Diego la Matina, age thirty-seven, a member of the Reformed Order of Saint Augustine—"Impertinent, Pertinacious, Incorrigible"— was burned at the stake in 1658. His final crime: murdering an inquisitor while imprisoned for life adjacent to the Steri Palace. His story is complex. Sciascia is uncertain why the friar first ran afoul of the church. He conjectures that Fra Diego's heresies may have been social, not theological. The friar may have been "a thief and not a man of ideas." This may explain why, until the murder, authorities were content only to lock him up.

Despite his religious standing, he seems to have been in and out of trouble with the church most of his adult life. He was brought before the tribunal several times but escaped punishment by abjuring, or renouncing his crimes. On two occasions, he was sent to the royal galleys. During his second time there, in 1649, he "seduced several galley convicts into his errors." This caused him to be condemned for life to the prison behind the Steri. He escaped once. Some sources say he broke through the walls and commandeered the "rope of torture" that was hanging from the hook in the torture room and used it in his escape over the walls.

Somehow, the friar made it back to Racalmuto, hiding in a cave in the countryside. One writer Sciascia quotes says Fra Diego roamed the countryside "clearing his way with the blood of others." Sciascia does not believe the friar murdered anyone, saying the "blood of others" is a metaphor in Sicily meaning the "property of others." Eventually, the damaged friar, once a man of God, was recaptured and carried away, in chains, back to the Steri.

This was his final incarceration. It was reported that, during a visit to the prison by the chief inquisitor, Monsignor Don Juan Lopez de Cisneros, La Matina came out in a rage and beat him severely with his shackles. Sciascia speculates that the friar was likely being tortured when the attack occurred rather than being subjected to a friendly visit and that somehow he slipped his restraints and broke away from his jailers. The inquisitor died sometime later and was lauded as a martyr. This attack was too much for the Holy Fathers to ignore. La Matina was condemned to the stake in Piazza Sant'Erasmo.

Sciascia gives us a vivid description of the preparations for this auto-de-fé that included thirty-two other prisoners described as including nine women: "witches, possessors of the evil eye, invokers of demons."

It promised to be, in the eyes of the faithful, a glorious affair. A stadium that could hold several hundred spectators was built in the open area in front of the cathedral. Chained into a heavy wooden chair built especially to hold him fast, he was brought there to hear his sentence and to be drummed out of his order.

Reportedly, Fra Diego shouted and cursed as he was carried through the vast crowd. His curses became so unsettling that guards had to place a "brake" in his mouth—probably, speculates Sciascia, a sort of horse bit. The friar was ceremoniously stripped of his office, and the crowd was told only that he was "a heretic, an apostate, a blasphemer, and a parricide for having killed Monsignor de Cisneros." It was the Spanish Inquisition's practice to withhold publicly details of the crimes of all those condemned lest they "offend the ears of Catholics."

The thirty-two other prisoners each stepped forward and abjured their crimes and were absolved. All that was left for the now defrocked friar was for him to be carried, still chained in his chair, on an ox-drawn cart to the stake awaiting him in Piazza Sant'Erasmo. "[T]he wood was fired, and the foul body of the evil heretic was quickly smoked, engulfed, burned, and reduced to ashes, and the mad infernal soul passed on to suffer and to blaspheme forever."

In an appendix to his story, written just a few months after *The Death of the Inquisitor* was first published, Sciascia recognizes that there are many unanswered questions about the impact of the Inquisition on Sicilians. While the joyful Palermitani, on June 27, 1783, publicly burned many of the records, another archive survived and was transferred to Madrid. Sciascia writes: "We hope that some historian will decide to study them."

I am back in Palermo a few days after meeting with members
of the writer's family, including son-in-law Nino Catalano, at
Sciascia's country home near Racalmuto. It is a bright July
morning in 2009. The sun climbs higher, as does the mercury
in the thermometer near the entrance to a coffee bar where I
grab my morning espresso. I had originally planned to be at a
pensione on the east slope of Etna, but Nino's invitation, con-
veyed through his son, Vito, changed everything. Nino is an
engineer and director of the technical department of the
University of Palermo.

He has been involved in the restoration of the prison behind what was once the Steri Palace, known in later centuries
as the Palazzo Chiaramonte. Vito asked if I would like to meet
his father there and see the prison, briefly opened to the public
in 2007 and now closed. I needed no further prodding. I called
the B and B on Etna and delayed my stay there by a day.

Vito and his wife, Anna Kowalska, meet me, and we drive
to the Chiaramonte. At the rear stands the three-story former prison, which later served as an archive. The cells had
been converted into record repositories with floor-to-ceiling
bookshelves covering the newly whitewashed walls. When
the archive was moved decades ago, workers began to find,
beneath two or three layers of whitewash, drawings and inscriptions on the cell walls left there by the generations of
men and women imprisoned while undergoing torture by
inquisitors.

I do not know, nor does his family, if Leonardo Sciascia had
ever been inside before he wrote *The Death of the Inquisitor*. But

he certainly knew about it and about drawings and writings on the wall. In fact, he starts the tale with the words

Patience
Bread, and time

that had been scratched onto the wall of a cell and deciphered, in 1906, by Sicilian folklorist Giuseppe Pitrè (1841–1916). Pitrè had peeled away the layers of whitewash of three cells uncovering vast fields of drawings and scribbling, the medium used coming from feces and charred sticks.

Nino Catalano showed me those three cells and several others that had been restored over the intervening years. At the end of a few hours of studying what his father-in-law, Sciascia, described as this "obscure, anonymous, amorphous drama" of drawings depicting saints, prayers written in Latin, "verses in Sicilian dialect expressing suffering and despair," Nino took me to an elevated landing at the south end of the former prison. There, leaning against a wall, was a drawing by the Sicilian painter Renato Guttuso, a friend of Sciascia's. It portrays a wild-eyed and heavily bearded Fra Diego la Matina, fully manacled, beating the inquisitor.

The spot where we are standing, Nino believes, is where the seventeenth-century beating occurred. Then, he tells a remarkable tale of how, in the early 1990s, well after his father-in-law's 1989 death, a document written by an eyewitness to the beating was found in the Madrid archives of the Inquisition.

According to that account, La Matina was not manacled when he was brought before the inquisitor. Some manacles or other devices made from heavy metal were left on a table in the room, noted the report in typical inquisitorial detail, and La Matina grabbed those when he started his assault.

Nino says, "There is speculation, therefore, that someone wanted the inquisitor killed, and they knew that La Matina was capable of doing it. It could have been a setup."

In rereading Sciascia's story, I wish he had lived long enough to know this development concerning his Racalmu-tese friar.

I have returned to the Chiaramonte Palace a few times since that hot July visit and have wandered into the room beyond the entrance of the main palace, the building in front of the former prison. Near the back of that room is that large hook embedded into a high ceiling beam. This was a torture cham-ber, where ropes were tied to hands behind the backs of the accused. The rope was placed through the hook and the man or woman was yanked upward, throwing their bones out of their shoulder joints. Sometimes a heavy beam was tied to their feet to increase the downward pull.

The only answer the inquisitors wanted to hear to their questions was "I am guilty." Nothing else was accepted. Some knew this and said it quickly; others never knew it and were confused about why they were there; still others, on principle, refused to say the words when they were not guilty of any-thing, enduring the sheer, unrelenting pain.

It was the scribe's job to record every intimate detail, taken down in impassive Spanish script. One wonders: When the scribe wrote, in his dispassionate style, the simple word "ah" as coming from the victim's mouth, what sound actually did escape the lips?

[A]nd when she was brought out she was again ordered to confess.

She said: Here I am; I know not what to say.

And it was ordered that she be attached to the rope, and the ministers attached the beams, and crying she said: If I knew I would say it. . . . And when they hoisted her up off the ground, she sweated and said: My Lord, I know nothing, my enemies have accused me wrongly; help me, Christians; ah, my Lord, you're torturing me wrongly.

. . . And she was let drop . . . Again hoisted high up and again exhorted.

She said: I know nothing.

SEVEN

Sicilitudine

The traveler disembarking in Palermo is immediately assaulted by an atmosphere of violence. . . . The violence of the scirocco, the red wind blowing from Africa, which squeezes your head in a fiery vise. . . . "Once there was a special room in old Sicilian houses," Sciascia tells us, "that was called 'the scirocco room.' It had no windows, or any other communication with the outside other than the narrow door . . . and this is where the family would take refuge against the wind." He adds this melancholy note: "The scirocco, too, is a dimension of Sicily."
— Marcelle Padovani,
Sicily as Metaphor

I HAVE allowed myself to swim around in the soup that is Sicily, a type of minestrone, perpetually simmering and made up of whatever history has tossed into it. Sicily may be *part* of Italy, a political subdivision, an autonomous region, but its people are not *of* Italy. Antonio Gramsci wrote in 1916, "Sicily is the region which has most *actively* resisted this tampering with history and freedom." Sicilians might be viewed in America and elsewhere as "Italians," but in their hearts and souls they are Siciliani.

Siciliani are in a world apart, a world that does not have much to do, really, with what comes out of Rome. The ruling coalition there may want, for example, to attach the peninsula physically to this island with a bridge, but everyone here believes that such an act is neither out of benevolence nor out of a desire to bring the islanders closer into the fold; it's because northerners see euros in such a bridge—in construction contracts, in a way to get northern Italian and European products onto the island faster (but not necessarily as a way to get Sicilian products off and into Europe). If it ever is built, it likely would not have much impact on the islanders' daily lives. It may be physically attached, but Sicily likely will remain emotionally detached from its continental sibling for many lifetimes to come.

This sense of Sicilian separateness, this so-called *Sicilitudine* and Leonardo Sciascia's representations of it, were made clearer during a conversation in Rome with Francesca Corrao, a professor of Arabic literature and language. Born and raised on the island, she shares a look into Sicilian feelings about such things as national government control over it despite its status as an autonomous region. Through Corrao's examples, one can begin to understand why such a thing as the bridge to Messina can be built, despite opposition by Sicilians and many southern Italians.

We are drinking tea in her Rome apartment, from where she commutes to Naples during teaching stints at the three-hundred-year-old Università degli Studi di Napoli "L'Orientale." She tells the story of how her father, Ludovico Corrao, when he was mayor of the western Sicilian village of Gibellina, negotiated directly with the Russian government to sell Sicilian oranges and wine. His sin was failing to go through the appropriate ministries in Rome.

"That's why they destroyed him," Francesca said with barely disguised bitterness. "Even though Sicily has regional autonomy, it does not apply." She points to Sigonella, the U.S. Naval Air Station near Catania. "If we want it, we [Sicilians] should have the agreement with U.S., not the national government. It is in my territory. If Rome does it, they do not give a damn about what is going on down here." Another example: "Say the national government makes an agreement with Morocco to sell Italian automobiles there. In return, Italy imports Moroccan oranges. And the Sicilian oranges? They rot, because they cost more than the oranges from Morocco in exchange for cars."

I realize after numerous conversations with Sicilians over a period of months that others share her anger. But, unlike Francesca Corrao, they offer a characteristic shrug, knowing that such things are beyond their control.

When I see this shrug, I think of an expression I've heard from a Sicilian-American friend that is typically used by people from his ancestral village of Racalmuto: *simmo sùrfaru*. I am told it has slightly different spellings and pronunciations in various parts of Sicily. It means, in its most basic sense, "We are just sulfur," or, *Sùrfaru sugnu*, "I am just sulfur." Literally translated, these expressions indicate that people, like chunks of that nonmetallic element being tossed into a cart for transport, have no control over what is happening to them or where they are going.

———

Chiara Mazzucchelli, in her marvelous doctoral dissertation "Heart of My Race," which she adapted for a paper in the *Tamkang Review*, puts this north-south divide this way: "Admittedly, since Unification in 1861, the Italian southern masses as a whole have experienced various degrees of difficulty in accessing the decisional spheres of institutional power." The industrial North, trying to keep pace with its industrialized European neighbors, had little time to spend on the agrarian South—except as, in Antonio Gramsci's words, "exploitable colonies." The Sardinian-born Gramsci, a leftist political theorist of the early twentieth century, meant that southern Italy and Sicily are a source of cheap labor and a market for northern products.

Gramsci, in the midst of a satirical tirade mocking northern prejudices about the South and southerners, notes that through all this, the South has managed to produce "a few great geniuses, like isolated palms in an arid and sterile desert."

One of those geniuses, of which Sicily has produced many, is Leonardo Sciascia (1921–1989), an intellectual and prolific writer of literature that ranges from detective stories and historical novels to political tracts and memoirs. He became the twentieth century's successor to Giovanni Verga (1840–1922) and 1934 Nobel Prize winner Luigi Pirandello (1867–1936), both of who comfortably straddled the two centuries. Sciascia is a guiding light to younger writers still producing remarkable fiction with a uniquely Sicilian voice. Not an Italian voice, but a *Sicilian* voice.

Sciascia understood his fellow Sicilians. He was born deep
in the Arab-rooted culture of the island's sulfur-rich southwestern edge in Racalmuto. Its name, I was told by historian
Leonard Chiarelli, is derived from the name of a tenth-century
Arab landowner, *Hammud*. Put that with *rahl*, which means
village, and you get *Rahl Hammud*. There are variations on spell-
ing and disputes about the origins, but whatever the etymology, Sciascia cherished his own deeply implanted Arab
heritage.

In an interview, he told a journalist that the original spell-
ing of his name, until Unification in 1861, was the purely Arabic "Xaxa." Francesca Corrao, who was a longtime friend of his
and who speaks Arabic fluently, told me that the name means
"a kind of soft material, like netting."

Sciascia said he was told by the Libyan consul in Palermo it
means "head veil." And as further evidence of his ties to that
ancient culture, he pointed out that there are people in the
southern Italian region of Apulia with the name Sciascia. Apulia,
sometimes called Puglia, is the region that encompasses Italy's
heel, and it is where many Sicilian Muslims were deported—
because of their rebelliousness, not their religion—between
1160 and 1246.

Sciascia believed that Sicilians were perpetually insecure,
a condition generated by the island's continuous colonization
by outsiders. Writes Mazzucchelli:

One can safely say that insecurity . . . affects the behavior,
the way of being, the take on life—fear, apprehension, distrust, closed passions, inability to establish relationships

outside of the private sphere, violence, pessimism, fatalism—
of both the collectivity and single individuals.

It is *simmo sùrfaru* incarnate. Forced colonization and the inability of its inhabitants to follow a course of self-determination
metaphorically imprinted insecurity on Sicilian DNA. Over
the space of thirty centuries, Sicilians sought to cover this
helplessness—again in Sciascia's words—with "attitudes of presumptuousness, haughtiness, and arrogance."

Sciascia's fellow writers, contemporaries as well as predecessors, also appear to hold that belief. Academics put him
into the Sicilian school of literature that includes Verga, Pirandello, Lampedusa, Elio Vittorini, and Maria Messina, who
wrote from a rarely told woman's perspective. Academician
Fred Gardaphé, in the introduction to Messina's book *Behind
Closed Doors: Her Father's House and Other Stories of Sicily*,
writes: "She takes us into another side of Sicilian irrationality
that Sciascia described . . . in a land often constricted by the
spirit-killing irrationality of industrial capitalism, which ultimately sent thousands of Sicilians away from the island forever."

Mazzucchelli believes that it is impossible to discuss Sicily
and Sicilians today "without questioning or concurring with
Sciascia's speculations. Sicilian-ness [*Sicilitudine*] became, in
his articulation, a 'way of being,' the inescapable condition of
a population marked by 'a history of defeats.'" And, in a side
note, Mazzucchelli felicitously points out how *Sicilitudine*
rhymes with the Italian word *"solitudine,"* solitude, loneliness,
"which hints to the isolation of the island."

———

Francesca Corrao has deep insight into Sciascia's thinking. She grew up knowing him during the time her family lived next door to the writer's Palermo apartment, where he spent most winters. Her father and Sciascia were close friends; both were leftists and politically in tune with each other.

"The first time I really remember him was around the time I was a teenager," she told me. "Every morning I would wake up, and he was just sitting in the window of his study in the building in front of our house."

He came often for dinner with her family. Early on, "it was more me being a young lady listening to older people, maybe discussing politics or literature. When I was nineteen, twenty, when I was starting working on my studies, he was very curious about them."

Corrao lived for seven years in Cairo, Egypt, studying Arabic and Arab literature. It was there that she realized that a character from Arab folklore—Juha, a medieval Arab trickster—bore strong similarities to a similar character in Sicilian folklore: Giufà.

"We shared this common love for Giufà," she said of her friendship with the Sicilian writer. Arabic tales about this character were apparently introduced into Sicily in the ninth and tenth centuries during Muslim control and were fully assimilated into the Sicilian consciousness.

"I knew about Giufà because my mother told me the stories. When I went to Cairo, I discovered that my mother's stories were the same ones I found there. Sciascia knew it, too. In his introduction to my book he writes that his grandfather told him the stories of Giufà. He had read them in [Italo] Calvino and [Giuseppe] Pitrè; they thought it was of Arab origin, but no one knew they were the same stories until I wrote the book."

Then Sciascia wrote his own story. It is found in his short-story collection *The Wine-Dark Sea,* titled simply "Giufà." The opening lines state matter-of-factly: "Giufà has been living in Sicily since Arabian times . . . A thousand years later, Giufà still shambles along the roads, ageless like all simpletons and up to all kinds of mischief." It is in this thought about "a thousand years later" where I believe Sciascia takes a backhanded swipe at all the elements of Sicilian society that have held his island in limbo through history and continue holding it in check today: politicians, mafiosi, police, the Catholic Church.

Giufà, a human creature, takes everything literally. He is told to take a weapon and kill something red, meaning he should go after some kind of bird with a red head, for these are the tastiest. He takes down from over his bed an ancient harquebus—a heavy, portable matchlock gun from the fifteenth century—and, as instructed, goes hunting. He sees a red head bobbing along on the other side of a hedge, fires, and drops the creature. He carries it home, presents it proudly to his mother, and she shrieks, "You've killed the cardinal!"

Says Corrao, "In this case, Giufà is too literal, but he is also the paradox of human beings. Sciascia is describing humanity."

In my American way of thinking, I interpret this as a symptom of Sciascia's deep and abiding cynicism. I suggest this to

Sciascia's oldest daughter, Laura Sciascia, a medieval historian at the University of Palermo. In my ignorance of the nuances of the Italian language, my observation comes close to offending her. She immediately sets me straight.

"Oh, no, no, no," she says with finality. "He was *skeptical*! Cynical has another meaning in Italian. To say someone is cynical is to say he has no principles!" She offers an example: A cynic is a person who changes as easily as the wind changes direction—one who can support a cause, and when that cause loses cachet such a person can switch sides and change so-called belief systems without feeling any guilt. Americans might describe such a person as a blatant opportunist or hypocrite; Sicilians and Italians say that person is a cynic.

Hearing this, I think of Tancredi, Don Fabrizio's nephew in Lampedusa's *The Leopard*. He shifts with the tide, doing what is necessary to survive the rapid changes then sweeping the island along with Garibaldi's army. He could be the classic cynic in the Italian/Sicilian definition of the word.

In *Sicily as Metaphor*, Sciascia delves a bit into the healthiness of being skeptical. "Skepticism isn't an acceptance of defeat," he says, "but a margin of safety, of elasticity . . . Skepticism is healthy. It's the best antidote to fanaticism." He sees skepticism "as the safety valve of reason. And so is pessimism, with which many people charge me." As I read this, I remembered a newspaper editor I once worked for who gently chastised me for my extreme American-style cynicism. "Reporters should always be skeptical; that's healthy and a requirement for the job," he told me. "You're too cynical, and that's not healthy."

Francesca Corrao shines more light into the Sicilian character. In her quiet, cool Rome apartment in Trastevere, a neighborhood sprinkled with Catholic convents, she lays out, through precise words and examples, the uniqueness of Sicilians and why they are a people apart from mainland Italians.

She opens the subject by offering up a seemingly conflicting comment about "the two faces of Sicily." Sicilians, she says, are very open and, at the same time, are much closed. For centuries, invader after invader swept across the island, first overwhelming and then subsuming cultural identities with their own—a process that stunts any hope of identity building, generation after generation.

"There was not even this feeling we have now of the word 'identity,'" Corrao says. The peculiarity of being an island is that you cannot run away; you are stuck to the site. [Conversely] the invasions make you rich, in a sense, because you can take the best from the outsiders, but it makes you enclose yourself because you have to struggle to preserve your identity. To do that, you have to be very much attached to your core, and your real core is your heart.

"If you are able to touch this humanity, you become a great person. Otherwise you become aggressive and violent."

Through these statements by a woman who knew Sciascia most of her life and who was in close collaboration with him in adulthood, the nature of the writer begins to show through. By delving into the character of his people and understanding their history and its impact on the vanquished, generation after generation, he got very much in touch with his heart.

"Because you are surrounded by the water," Corrao continues, "it deeply and psychologically means that you must talk to your humanity, so no matter who comes and goes, you have nowhere to run away. The moment you are there, you have to look within yourself, and that's why you're closed and you're open. You are closed the moment the invader is coming to deprive, but you are open because when he is here, you have to deal with him, and you do it in order to survive."

This clearly illustrates why Sicily is unique when compared with mainland Italy—or even other island nations. History shows that while Japan, for example, is an island, the Japanese were able to hold on to their core for centuries because they were never successfully invaded—neither by Genghis Kahn, nor the Chinese, nor the Russians, nor anyone else. That is the difference.

The entrapment of Sicilians and the whipsawing of cultures gradually brought generations to an identity born out of the insecurity that Sciascia described in his writings: arrogance, distrust, pessimism. In many ways, this identity becomes a virtue, and, says Corrao, "this virtue becomes pride, and it becomes attached to our way of being."

"The people," she says, "are like the island itself, like our volcano [Etna]. It is so beautiful, the soil is so rich and it produces a wonderful bounty, but it can destroy you in an instant. You always have to find a middle way in these two opposite faces of Sicily. It is so dry and yet it is so full of flowers; so kind and gentle and yet so violent. The greatness of Sciascia is that he says in words what is impossible for me now to explain how these opposites can coexist.

"The violent and sweet; the sweet and sour. You find it all throughout his books."

For his part, Sciascia acknowledges that each of his books is a retelling of the same themes, over and over again. In *Salt in the Wound,* he says that he is "one of those authors who writes one book and then stops . . ." Then he explains. "All my books taken together form one: a Sicilian book which probes the wounds of the past and present and develops as the history of the continuous defeat of reason and of those who have been personally overcome and annihilated in that defeat."

His targets are constant throughout his oeuvre: politicians, the Mafia, the church hierarchy, the police. Sometimes he has respect for a particular policeman—the northern Italian Carabinieri officer Captain Bellodi in *The Day of the Owl* is one—but he showers disdain on most others, along with priests, politicians and, of course, mafiosi.

One excruciatingly hot July afternoon, I met his youngest daughter, Anna Maria Sciascia, at the family home, Noce, outside of Racalmuto. With interpreting help from her daughter-in-law, Anna Maria told me about what she believed was the most personal of his books and stories. It is a novella, his final work, which he wrote while undergoing kidney dialysis in Milan—*A Straightforward Tale.*

Most of the characters in this story—various police officers, a priest, political figures—are up to no good. There is a professor undergoing kidney dialysis who has insights into what was behind a recent murder. And there is a salesman passing through the area who tells authorities something he saw. He is immediately slapped into jail because, in the mentality of the local police, he is now a suspect—or they want to keep him quiet. When he is eventually released, this salesman on his way out of town inadvertently learns information that tells the readers who the murderers are. But because of what happened to him when he told "authorities" what he saw, he says nothing and leaves.

Sciascia's attitude toward these various "authorities" is a reflection of his *Sicilitudine,* as is the salesman's refusal to get involved after, unjustifiably, being "burned." The author, in nearly all of his writing, clearly demonstrates the supreme skepticism about all authority, secular and religious, that he and his fellow Sicilians share.

This expression of *Sicilitudine,* reflected in *A Straightforward Tale* as well as in Sciascia's other works, draws from his life in Racalmuto and his tender descriptions of his fellow villagers. In later life, after a career as a teacher, he typically spent winters in Palermo doing research at his apartment there. Then, in the spring and summer, he would retreat to Noce, where he would launch into serious writing based on his winter's research. After writing in the morning, he would come into the village and spend summer afternoons with his male friends, walking arm in arm in that wonderful Sicilian-Italian way that older men do, their suit or sport jackets flung over their shoulders like capes, their heads tilted toward each other as they quietly speak into each other's ear.

My visit to Noce during July 2009 allowed me to meet Anna Maria Sciascia's family: husband Nino Catalano, their son,

Vito, his wife, Anna Kowalska, and their daughter—Leonardo Sciascia's great-granddaughter—Sofia Catalano.

Noce, the Italian word for walnut or, simply, nut, refers to the *contrada,* or neighborhood, not just the house. It is a few miles north out of the back entrance to Racalmuto, just off the Agrigento-Caltanissetta highway. A small wooden sign is tacked onto a tree with Noce hand painted in black and an arrow pointing the way.

After a short drive along a narrow, unpaved road, a gate appears on the left, and a tiny lane leads up to the main house between olive and walnut trees that, to the right, nearly hide the outline of an older, shuttered house built toward the end of the nineteenth century. This is where the Sciascia family lived before the present house was built in 1974.

The family is warm and welcoming. Anna Kowalska, a delightful, young Polish woman fluent in Italian and who speaks good English, offers to interpret. With Anna Maria Sciascia, we talk about her father, and it is now that the daughter talks about the final story Leonardo wrote. Three months earlier, her older sister, Laura, had told me that she thought the novel *Candido* was the story that is more revealing of Sciascia's life. It tells the story of a young boy, born just as the Americans invaded Sicily in World War II, who is raised by relatives because his parents are not often present. Sciascia, although born in 1921, had been raised by his aunts. His mother was often not available. Laura sees the parallels; so does Anna Maria. But Anna Maria says *A Straightforward Tale* was written specifically as a denouement to her father's life's work—the concluding "chapter." The two sisters' choices each fit to a certain degree.

Grandson Vito leads me on a tour of the house, built fifteen years before Sciascia's untimely 1989 death of kidney failure, and I am most struck by the author's study on the south side with a great window overlooking a giant, ancient pine tree. Vito tells me that his grandfather's only instruction to the architect was to position the house so that his study overlooked that tree. Beyond the tree and far beyond the rolling countryside are Agrigento and the sea.

The room, perhaps eight feet by fourteen, is dominated by a large, wooden table holding a single Victorian-style lamp and Sciascia's manual typewriter. Books are neatly placed on shelves. In a corner is a tall pot full of walking sticks and canes. The walls are covered by etchings, posters, and prints showing various figures, historic and literary. The eighteenth-century republican Count Di Blasi, who figures prominently in Sciascia's great novel *The Council of Egypt,* is one of them. Others are of the nineteenth-century French writer Stendhal and the late nineteenth-century Brazilian novelist, poet, playwright, and short-story writer Joaquim Maria Machado de Assis.

On a wall to the right of the window are portraits of Sciascia's three great predecessors: Verga, Pirandello, and Voltaire. Next to the door is that large color photograph of Leonardo himself, perched on the back of a gaily decorated donkey clambering up the steep stone steps of a church in Racalmuto during the Festa della Madonna del Monte.

Vito says that when I go to Palermo to meet his father and tour the inquisitor's prison, he and Anna will give me a similar tour of Sciascia's home there. Unoccupied since the death of Sciascia's wife, Maria Andronico, in January 2009, it is preserved exactly as when the couple lived there.

We meet a few days later, and before heading to the former prison where Vito's father is waiting to show us around, the couple takes me to the Sciascia home in a residential area on Palermo's outskirts, just off Via della Libertà. The writer's study resembles the one at Noce; dozens of etchings and prints nearly covering the walls, a desk with another manual typewriter identical to the one at Noce, and a small desk calendar, the kind with tiny cubes in a tray showing month, day, year. It is set to Nov. 20, 1989—the day Sciascia died. "Grandmother kept it set on that day; she never changed it or moved it," Vito says.

This apartment is a repository of thousands of books jammed into bulging bookshelves in rooms and hallways and crammed into closets. I mention a title, and Vito, ever the knowledgeable guardian of his grandfather's property, walks over to a crowded shelf, runs his finger across a few titles, and pulls out the one I mention.

Just as in Noce, Vito knows where everything is. The family donated several hundred of Leonardo's books to the Sciascia Foundation in Racalmuto; these remain. Perhaps they, too, will end up at the foundation, which has employed a librarian to care for the collection there. Vito says there is still discussion within the family about how to use this apartment; perhaps it will become a literary center for writers and scholars.

Much of Sciascia's writings used Racalmuto as a backdrop, either under its real name or as the fictional Regalpetra. He seldom, if ever, wrote about modern Palermo. His focus there was on its medieval or eighteenth-century past. He derived most of his subject matter in Racalmuto and in the villages around it in this closed-in world of south-central Sicily. His descriptions of this world and the people I met there kept me coming back: during the warmth of early spring; through the blistering, soul-sucking heat of midsummer; to the subtle chill of late fall; and again, a year later, around Easter.

Many of the people walking the streets of Racalmuto during my visits were the same people Sciascia loved and returned to year after year, decade after decade. Reading his books and spending time there was the best guide I found in my attempt, however fleetingly as an outsider, to better understand Sicilian life and culture.

It is all there, on the narrow cobblestoned streets and in the eyes and bearing of the men and women who live in the restored medieval houses of the village center. But most particularly for those of us who reside in other worlds far, far away, this *Sicilitudine* is found between the covers of Leonardo Sciascia's books.

EIGHT

Never in Control

The island in ancient times was called, after its shape, Trinacria [three capes], then Sicania after the Sicani who made their home there, and finally it has been given the name Sicily after the Siceli who crossed over in a body to it from Italy.

> —Diodorus Siculus,
> Greek-Sicilian historian
> born in Agyrium (Agira),
> Sicily, during Roman
> domination (ca. 80–20 B.C.)

ON A clear day the view from near the top of Mount Etna, up where clouds begin and black hills seem to roll over one another, offers a staggering look across millennia. If you are on this subtly alive mountain that the Greeks called Aetna early enough in the day and look below the climbing sun, you can see, through the haze and across a wedge of light blue sea, the toe of the Italian boot. And if you are there during the Sicilian winter, you can look while being slapped in the face by the *gregale,* a strong, cold wind that travels southward from central or southern Europe toward Libya.

But in the searing heat of late summer, hot and sweaty from a stumbling climb up a slope of crumbling lava, you can comfortably stand at this cooler, higher altitude on Europe's biggest and most active volcano. Look farther east, beyond the close-by headlands of the Aspromonte range of mainland Italy's Calabria region. Beyond human vision is Basilicata and Apulia, and still farther along, the narrow mouth of the Adriatic. There, on the eastern shore of that tubular sea is Greece, from where the recorded history of Sicily began.

It was while standing here, near Etna's summit in July 2009, that I looked eastward and felt for the first time the full sweep of Sicily's history. For it was from various cities on mainland Greece, their populations outstripping arable land seven or eight centuries before the Christian era, that ships sailed, filled with colonists looking for new worlds and new opportunities. They headed west and forever changed the face of the Mediterranean world.

Fernand Braudel, author of *The Mediterranean in the Ancient World,* writes this about these westbound Greeks:

> At the outset, the sea favored their ventures towards Italy and Sicily. There is a coastal current running northward along the Balkan coastline. Leaving this current behind in the region of Corfu, and if one was prepared to make a direct crossing, it was possible to sail in a day to the Italian coast, there to pick up another current flowing southward. A virtual salt-water river, driving along the coast, it carried ships to the Gulf of Taranto and past the shores of Calabria.

From there it was no distance to the Sicilian coast across the [Strait] of Messina, which [was] not an insuperable obstacle.

We know little about these earliest Greek colonists. Franco De Angelis of the University of British Columbia states simply, in the first line of his introduction to *Megara Hyblaia and Selinous: The Development of Two Greek City-States in Archaic Sicily,* "Archaic Sicily has no history."

The only way to learn about this period is through archaeology. It runs from the time the first colonists landed in 735 B.C. and founded Naxos on the east coast, to around 510 B.C. De Angelis writes that this "heart of the archaic period, which contains centuries of development of the island's communities barely known to us, has even less documentation" than the periods following when writers such as Herodotus began their work. "Archaic Sicily, therefore, is really prehistoric, or at best protohistoric."

The lands these Greeks settled collectively became known as Magna Graecia, or Greater Greece—a landmass much larger than Greece itself. It became, in essence, what America, nearly three thousand years later, represented to the European immigrants of the late nineteenth and early twentieth centuries.

Still more expeditions of this great ancient diaspora, or "scattering," also sponsored by the various Greek city-states, looked even farther to the west than Italy's boot and latched upon Sicily's east coast: Following Naxos's founding, Siracusa was established a year later, in 734; Zancle, where modern Messina now sits, was founded within the next decade.

In those early, pre-Roman years, the Greek-Sicilian cities remained closely aligned with their mother cities on mainland Greece, sharing the same conflicts among one another. Eventually they became more Sicilian than Greek, and cities such as Siracusa grew in power greater than that of their mother cities. Many visitors considered it to be the most beautiful city in the Mediterranean.

Greece, in ancient times, was never a nation or an empire. Its cities had in common language and culture. Brutal conflicts between and among them were frequent. For example, during the fifth-century B.C. Peloponnesian War, which pitted Sparta and its allies, including Corinth, against Athens, Athens launched a major, ill-advised assault on Siracusa, which had been founded by loyal Corinthian colonists.

The entire Athenian fleet was wiped out in Siracusa's harbor; the Athenians never recovered and, eventually, lost the war on the Greek mainland. The giant rock quarry at Siracusa, now frequented by tourists and overgrown with lush greenery, held hundreds of Athenian prisoners who wasted away in brutal captivity. It is told that the aristocratic women from Siracusa, hearing that Athenian men were among the most handsome in all of Greece, observed them from the quarry's rim as the prisoners starved.

The Siracusa quarry is one of my favorite spots in the area for finding solitude. No matter how many tourists might congregate, there is room enough to find peace and relaxation.

There are meandering walking trails, benches to rest on, and, around every turn, beautiful views to record in memory or capture in photographs or on a painter's canvas. I had seen Frenchman Jean-Pierre Houël's eighteenth-century paintings and etchings of this place, showing it to be the kind of Garden of Eden that I found more than three hundred years later.

Trails lead up to a massive opening, either natural or carved by humans deep into a limestone wall. It is known, because of its earlike shape and extraordinary acoustics, as the Ear of Dionysius, named after a Siracusan ruler.

Of course, the various groups of Greek colonists did not come to an unpopulated island. It is thought that humans were there perhaps ten thousand years ago. Sicily, once attached to the Italian mainland, provided prehistoric people a land bridge across what today is the Strait of Messina. Cave drawings dated to around 6000 B.C. in part attest to the presence of these earlier prehistoric peoples.

Robert Leighton, in his book *Sicily Before History,* writes:

Despite being surrounded by sea, Sicily has often seemed to archaeologists and historians to be the least island-like of all the Mediterranean islands, being at once too big, too close to the centre of the Mediterranean and to the Italian mainland to have experienced isolation for prolonged periods.

In the same vein, historian David Abulafia, in his introduction to *The Mediterranean in History,* writes: "It may be a cliché to describe islands such as Sicily as 'stepping stones' between the different cultures of the Mediterranean world, but it is nevertheless true."

Of the people for whom we have a recorded history, the

Sicani may have been among the earliest. They likely came to the island from the west coast of Italy, perhaps around 2000 to 1600 B.C., settling in the western and central regions.

A more mysterious people, the Elymians, came a bit later, establishing cities by 1100 B.C. in northwestern Sicily and eventually displacing the Sicani by pushing them more into the island's central region. These Elymians are thought to have come from as far away as Asia Minor, today's Turkey, via North Africa. They are given credit for first settling Erice, a small, exquisite ancient village on a hilltop near Trapani. They also were likely the first to occupy Segesta to the southeast, today the site of a Greek temple mysteriously left unfinished, along with a theater carved out of a hillside.

The last known group to occupy Sicily before the arrival of the Phoenicians and, later, the Greeks, was the Sicels, or Siculi. They showed up, probably from Liguria in western Italy, around 1200 to 1000 B.C. They seem to have been left alone by the Elymians and the Sicani, settling primarily in the eastern portion of the island.

The Phoenicians, from the land known today as Lebanon, predated the Greeks by perhaps a century or so. They arrived in Sicily between the eighth and sixth centuries and created ports along the northwest coast, including Panormos, today's Palermo; Motya, today's Mozia; and Soluntum, nearly eleven miles to the east, near today's Bagheria.

Panormos, while Greek in name, was never a Greek city. The Phoenicians generally kept to themselves on the west coast when the first Greeks arrived in the east. They held on through much of that colonization before giving way to their more aggressive cousins, the Carthaginians from North Africa, who were descendants of early Phoenician traders.

Through all of this Greek colonization and assimilation in the east and south, the Carthaginians began in the sixth century to dominate the Phoenician cities in Sicily from their base in North Africa, near the modern city of Tunis. This was part of their master plan to maintain control of Mediterranean islands, from Cyprus and Sicily to the Balearics, an archipelago to the far west off the east coast of Spain.

Braudel calls it the "Sicily-Balearic bridge." Sicily was important as a source for wheat and its strategic proximity to Carthage.

Eventually, Braudel writes, around 409 B.C., Carthage took advantage of the "weakness of Athens, following the failure of the Athenian expedition against Siracusa. Immediately the Carthaginians "began to wage war ferociously against the Greek Sicilians, attacking their towns, capturing the inhabitants, and thus acquiring a slave-labor force which was to transform the economy of [Carthage] itself."

The Carthaginians swept eastward, laying waste to Selinous—Selinunte in modern Italian—and Himera and then Akragas, today's Agrigento. Pressing on, they attacked Gela and Kamarina, towns along the southeast coast. Dionysius, the tyrant of Siracusa, stepped in and was routed. He sued for peace. Carthage agreed and retained control of this sweep of south-coast cities, including much of the island's western half. This left Siracusa to the Greek-Sicilians. Other cities, including Messina to the far northeast, also retained their independence.

Joseph F. Privitera, in his wonderfully concise outline for travelers, *Sicily: An Illustrated History,* sums it up nicely: "More than half of Sicily was now under Carthaginian domination; several of the island's cities had perished, and a tyrant [Dionysius] was established in the finest of its cities. The fifth century B.C., after its years of freedom and prosperity, ended in darkness."

Dionysius extended his influence onto the toe of the Italian boot and, as an ally of Sparta, all the way into Greece. He and his successors, along with rulers established in other Greek-Sicilian cities, continued to clash with Carthage and with one another. And while all this squabbling was going on, a movement was taking place in the Italian peninsula that one day would have an immense impact on these divisive players in the Sicilian arena.

It came in the aftermath of the death of Alexander the Great in 323 B.C. Braudel tells us that while Alexander's successors were fighting one another in far-flung Mediterranean theaters well to the east, and because the Greeks and Carthaginians "were at each other's throats in Sicily," Rome, now a republic, was able to conquer Italy, almost out of sight of these other peoples who were wrapped up in their local squabbles.

While Romans were living in mud huts on the Palatine Hill when Greece was in its glory, they slowly, progressively grew in might throughout the third and second centuries B.C., moving out from their consolidated city on those seven hills.

As Rome gained power over its part of the Mediterranean world, it eventually began to covet Sicily as a breadbasket for its growing republic and as a key to the rest of the region. It successfully fought Carthage in three Punic wars, effectively removing forever the Carthaginians from the island and eliminating them as any kind of threat in the Mediterranean. The great sea thus became a Roman lake instead of a Carthaginian lake. (I often wonder how Western history would be different if Carthage had prevailed.) The island's Greek-Sicilian cities came under the thumb of the Republic, as did the cities of Magna Graecia in southern Italy.

Rome did little for the island, which became its first province, beyond exploiting its agricultural prowess for wheat. We know something about it during this time by reading Cicero, the statesman who served the Roman government on the island. Some years later, in 70 B.C., he was asked by Sicilians to prosecute the Roman overseer there, Gaius Verres. This overseer, in a period of three years, "laid waste to the province of Sicily," Cicero wrote in his *Verrine Orations*.

He "plundered Sicilian communities, stripped bare Sicilian homes, and pillaged Sicilian temples." Verres, seeing his outcome as dire, absconded, but Cicero's orations are ripe with descriptions of Sicily and her people under the Romans that he gleaned during his time there.

He writes at one point, "They [Sicilians] are an unduly shrewd and suspicious race." Farther along, he writes, "The Sicilians are, all of them, a far from contemptible race, if only our magistrates would leave them alone; they are really quite fine fellows, thoroughly honest and well-behaved."

More interestingly, Cicero lets us know that Sicilians, despite their rule by Phoenicians, Carthaginians, and Romans, remained essentially Greek in outlook. A Sicilian document he cites still used Greek terminology centuries after Rome assumed control.

However, as it did everywhere else, Rome's influence transferred to the east, and the Western Empire crumbled. Vandals for a short period controlled the island from their perch at the ruined North African capital Carthage. They were supplanted by Goths, but by A.D. 551, the Goths in turn were driven out of Italy. The Byzantine government, new rulers of Rome's former empire and ensconced at Ravenna on Italy's east coast, took over for the next three hundred years, setting the stage for the arrival of the Arabs, a conquest to which many Sicilians today trace their heritage and much of their culture.

One of my more enjoyable walks around modern Palermo is through the Kalsa district, which dates back to Arab and Muslim times. Then, it was a walled palace compound called Khālisa, and it adjoined Balarm, the Arabic name for the city itself.

It is hard to imagine, in this bustling, noisy modern city, what it was like more than a thousand years ago. However, we have remarkable descriptions from a tenth-century traveler, Ibn Hawqal, from his book *Kitab Surat al-Ard*, or the *Book of the Face of the World*. He writes that a wall surrounded Khālisa with gates on all sides except for the unbroken wall along the sea. Within this large enclosure was quartered the sultan and his entourage. There, they enjoyed public baths and a small cathedral mosque.

The area occupied by old Khālisa is bounded today by Via Maqueda on the west, Via Lincoln on the south, Via Vittorio Emanuele on the north, and Foro Italico along the seashore. Surrounding it in various quarters were numerous shops, which Ibn Hawqual meticulously detailed—everything from fishmongers and jar merchants to rope makers, butchers, money changers, and olive-oil sellers.

The palace grounds of Khālisa and the adjoining town of Balarm, tightly wound along the cusp of the seaport, must have been bustling places. Ibn Hawqal counted nearly two hundred shops solely for the sale of meat. In all, he recorded more than three hundred mosques in and around the palace, the town and its various quarters. Standing beside one mosque in Balarm, "I could see, at the distance of a bowshot, about ten mosques, all within view, some of them facing one another and separated only by the breadth of the street."

Situated outside of Khālisa's walls, to the northwest, was, Ibn Hawqual noted, "a great cathedral mosque," today's Catholic Cathedral of Palermo, located in the city's Capo quarter. He said seven thousand persons could be accommodated, standing in thirty-six rows "with not more than two hundred men in each row."

Here, he makes a fascinating declaration: "In it there is a great sanctuary, and a certain logician claims that the Greek sage, that is to say, Aristotle, is in a wooden casket hung in the sanctuary . . . he says that the Christians [Byzantines who ruled Sicily before the Arab invasion] used to revere his grave and come to seek healing from it. . . . I myself saw a wooden casket which could well be this grave."

Imagine that. The bones of Aristotle, who reportedly died in 322 B.C. while in exile in Chalcis, Greece, in a wooden box hanging in the Palermo cathedral? Not likely. Who knows what Ibn Hawqual saw or what it truly represented.

For the casual modern visitor, some incongruities seem to

pop up occasionally on this island: a street sign in Palermo in three languages—Arabic, Hebrew, and Italian; obvious Islamic-style domes on a Christian church; the discovery that Arab and Byzantine craftsmen created the magnificent Christian mosaics in the Palatine Chapel in the onetime Norman fortress in Palermo; Ottoman figures adorn the mammoth gate, the Porta Nuova, that is attached to that Christian fortress, variously known today as Palazzo dei Normanni or Palazzo Reale.

I find that most people, other than Sicilians, have no idea that the Arabs ruled this island for 250 years and that their direct influence lasted for a few more centuries when the island was under Norman and Germanic rule. Plus, they are surprised to learn that many Sicilians, particularly those from the island's western half, consider themselves of Arab ancestry.

Eastern Sicilians may differ on that point. Apparently, as historian Leonard Chiarelli writes, the triangular region of the northeastern part of the island "largely remained a hindrance to Muslim settlement." Therefore, the Greeks were able, in their isolated communities in that area, to maintain certain autonomy. Today, many Sicilians from the island's east consider themselves to be of Greek, not Arab, origin. Overall, however, "the peoples who came to Sicily reflected the inhabitants that comprised the Muslim world from Spain to Persia."

A twelfth-century poet and military leader from Noto in southeastern Sicily, Ibn Hamdīs, for example, considered himself a Sicilian and, during the years of his Spanish exile after the Normans took over, he wrote heart-wrenching poetry longing for the land of his birth.

The Arabs may have controlled Sicily and parts of southern Italy for a mere two and a half centuries out of three thousand years of the island's known human history, but the impact of this relatively brief encounter is shown in the formation of the Mediterranean islanders' attitudes. It is reflected in the origins of many city, village, and family names and in the cuisine. Sicilians followed Muslim methods in the ways they cultivate their land and what they grow. And their closer, innate sense of connection, DNA-wise and emotionally, with North Africa rather than with mainland Europe or even mainland Italy, undergirds their sense of self.

A friend, Sicilian-born poet Alissandru (Alex) Caldiero, put it to me simply, passionately, and profoundly one afternoon: "We are not south of Italy; we are north of Africa!"

The Arab tradition lives on in the stories portrayed in puppet shows that are common across the island and the images on the hand-painted carts that now reside mostly in museums. These conquerors dramatically changed the island's economy from one based primarily on wheat and wool under Romans and Byzantines to one with diverse agriculture. The Arabs introduced oranges and lemons, certain varieties of olives, pomegranates, pistachios, peaches, cotton, eggplants, and apricots. They instituted innovations previously unknown in the island, such as terraces for growing crops in hilly terrain. They devised methods of irrigation still used today.

Jews were welcomed into the slowly emerging society, as were Berbers from North Africa. These disparate peoples lived side by side and were fully integrated with the native peoples and the Greek-Sicilians who had been there for centuries. This is why Sicilians have so much Arab blood in their veins; other conquerors—such as the Normans, French, and to a certain degree the Spanish—did not foster mass migrations of their own people into Sicilian life. They were overseers, rulers, or barons who remained somewhat isolated in their own enclaves, marrying among themselves to preserve their vast estates.

Hundreds of towns and villages take their names from Arabic: Gibellina comes from *jabal,* the word for "mountain"; the Alcàntara River derives from *qantara,* or "bridge"; La Kasbah is still a district of Mazàra, the town where the Arabs first landed in A.D. 827 to begin their seventy-five-year conquest of the island. Just northwest of Mazàra is Marsala, which comes from *mars Ali* or "Ali's port." Caltabellotta, *qal'at al ballut,* means "fortress of oak trees."

Strangely, there is little architectural evidence of Muslim influence in buildings still standing: the Favara Palace in the Brancaccio neighborhood of Palermo and, eighteen miles to the southeast, the baths of Cefalà Diana. At Cefalà, Muslims, then under Norman rule, built the roof on top of old Roman walls that enclosed ancient springs.

The location operates today as part of a historic site where one afternoon I sat with a group of schoolchildren listening to a lecture about what took place there. Ironically, and unnoticed by the young audience, the water that flowed into the ancient baths came from garden hoses slipped under the Roman wall and into channels feeding the various stone tubs. When visitors are gone, the water is turned off by the simple twist of a valve.

The former baths are flanked on one side by a two-story stone structure that served as a resting spot, a way station or type of inn, during Norman times. Now it serves as a storage space for the historic site.

Historian Chiarelli, in the introduction to his landmark

book *A History of Muslim Sicily,* writes: ". . . there is [only] a visual hint of their settlement. A glimpse of the arabesque architecture of the palaces and churches built under their successors, the Normans, brings into view the Arab presence. Their legacy largely remains, however, in the consciousness of Sicilians. . . ."

Chiarelli then quotes early twentieth-century Sicilian folklorist Giuseppe Pitrè, who tells us that his people have forgotten the epochs of the Greek, Latin, and Byzantine; "only the Arab remains alive, although their reign was brief and vague. Everything ancient is [Muslim]: monuments, hidden caches, charming treasures, mountains, farm lands, caves, abandoned ruins, and old trees, especially olive trees."

So the Arabic influence today remains intrinsic, emotional, within the people themselves.

How did the Arabs from the Arabian Peninsula, which today includes Saudi Arabia and Yemen, and Muslims from North Africa get here? Some scholars believe the seeds were planted just twenty years after the A.D. 632 death of Muhammad. They made their first raid against the island, controlled then by Byzantine Greeks who had taken over after the fall of the Roman Empire in the West. The date has been challenged, particularly by Chiarelli, but he does agree that in 669, fewer than two decades later, Muslims captured Siracusa, returning "to Alexandria with captives and booty."

While the exact number of Muslim attacks on Sicily cannot be documented, they "increased dramatically after the Arab conquest of Carthage [in modern-day Tunisia] and the establishment of permanent Arab settlements along the North African coast."

Even while the Arab conquest of Spain was under way, their focus on Sicily never wavered. For Sicilians, the story of how the Muslims decided to move against the island in A.D. 827 is the kind of tale that repeats itself a few times over the course of history. In this case, a Byzantine naval commander, who reportedly was going to be punished for marrying a nun against her will, sought to get out of his predicament by taking control of the island from its governor. Some historians disagree with this story, saying the whole attempted takeover was strictly a political affair.

At any rate, the naval commander and his supporters routed the governor's army at Siracusa, but he knew he could not hold on to the island. So, he traveled to the Aghlabid court in Qayrawan (today Kairouan, Tunisia), now considered the fourth most holy city in Islam, and asked for help.

At first, when the Muslims agreed to help, they did not view it as their own conquest, but that quickly changed. They recruited religious zealots and opportunists, and the goal gradually turned to conquest. With both Spain and Sicily, they could control the entire western Mediterranean basin.

M. I. Finley, author of the classic *A History of Sicily to the Arab Conquest,* set the scene:

> [In A.D. 827] an elite army of more than 10,000 men—Arabs and Berbers from Africa, other Moslems from Spain— landed at Mazara, and the conquest of Sicily had begun. All previous assaults were piratical raids; now the Arabs set out to take the island and colonize it.

The Muslim army had trouble taking Siracusa, but they eventually prevailed after being reinforced by an armada carrying Muslim reinforcements from Spain. Gradually, they gained the upper hand—it took seventy-five years to subdue the entire island—despite being racked by squabbles within their ranks.

This series of events shows clearly how twists of fate determine momentous outcomes. If the naval commander had remained loyal to the Byzantine ruler in Constantinople and not sought Sicily for his own, the Arabs may have never considered conquering the island. (He was eventually executed by the Byzantine defenders when the invaders tried to take the city of Enna.)

The twist-of-fate scenario continued: An invited foreign power steps in and, instead of accepting the gratitude of the person requesting the favor, takes over. It happened when the Normans were invited by one Muslim emir to help conquer two competing emirs 250 years later, and it happened again when Sicilian rebels asked for Spain's help in routing the French in the war of the Sicilian Vespers a few hundred years after Muslim rule.

Under the Arabs, the island, Chiarelli tells us, became "politically and culturally part of the territory of what is today Tunisia"—a land just ninety miles from the island's southwest coast across the Strait of Sicily. Throughout their time ruling the island, however, the Muslims, like their successors the Normans, were regularly beset with discord: assassinations, executions of rebel ringleaders, and civil wars between the Sicilian people and the central and provincial governments.

Sicily, beset by competing Muslim dynasties, became a

stew of simmering divisions, but through it all, North Africans moved to the island by the thousands. Chiarelli writes:

> Many of the immigrants settled in the western half of the
> country, but later established themselves throughout Sicily.
> Most of the Muslim elite and ruling class were composed
> of Arabs, but the Berbers formed a substantial part of the
> population. . . . The Berbers consistently challenged Arab
> authority, which often led to strife, such as the civil wars [of
> A.D. 886 and 898] when the Berbers attacked the mostly
> Arab-led [army].

The Berbers at this time were urban dwellers, farmers, and herdsmen indigenous to North Africa. Many converted to Islam when the Arabs from the Middle East arrived on that continent.

Conflicts between Sicilians and the various levels of government that controlled their daily lives now continued, but this time these conflicts were broken up by periods relatively free of strife.

At one point, around 1020, when an independent Arab Sicilian dynasty known as the Kalbites was facing financial difficulties, the Kalbite emir posed a question to a group of Muslim Sicilian leaders: Should he expel one particular group who shared in the country's wealth in order to absorb their funds? The answer was telling. The Muslim Sicilians advised that, through intermarriage, the islanders were one people. At least some of the island's inhabitants saw no difference in the various groups that, long ago, had settled the island. Says Chiarelli:

It is evident that two hundred years of immigrant settlement from the Muslim world caused an evolution in the ethnic composition of the island, causing the development of a new Sicilian identity. Intermarriage with the native [Greco-] Christian population, as well as large-scale conversions to Islam, not only formed a new ethnic group that bound the immigrants to the island, but also the establishment of a new Islamic society, not unlike that of Spain.

This societal cohesiveness, punctuated by occasional episodes of internal strife, held fast until 1052. That's when a Muslim emir sought the aid of a contingent of Norman knights based in southern Italy to help him overthrow two other emirs. Eventually, a significant portion of the island fell to the Normans, who had effectively displaced the emir's troops and dominated the campaign. But it took the Norman leader, Roger I, until January 1072 to take Palermo, effectively ending Muslim rule in Sicily. It took another eighteen years for the Normans to defeat the last holdout, the southeastern city of Noto, which finally fell in 1090.

In summing up the aftermath and Muslim life under accommodating Norman rule, Chiarelli writes: "The loss of a national government in Palermo, however, did not end the Muslim presence in Sicily. With [many] of the inhabitants Islamicized, it would take another two hundred years to bring the population of the whole island within the sphere of Christian Europe."

———

Once they were Vikings, Nortmanni, or northmen. Eventually, in the early 900s, at about the same time the ruling Arab dynasty took command of Sicily from another set of Arab rulers, these northmen settled in France and, with the complicity of the French king, they stayed and flourished, becoming Christians and Frenchmen. At some point, the appellation "Norman" took over.

Fast-forward one hundred years. In 1016, as legend has it, a group of Norman pilgrims traveled to the Italian peninsula to visit a Christian shrine. Much of southern Italy at this time was ruled by the Byzantines, whose church, based in Constantinople, had been at odds with the Roman Church for centuries. Lombards, descendants of the Germanic people who occupied portions of northern Italy, also controlled large areas of the South.

A nobleman from Bari reputedly approached the Norman pilgrims. He asked their help in driving out the Byzantines so southern Italy could be once again united with the church in Rome. The pilgrims agreed and returned with an army the following year, 1017, and joined with a faction of southern Lombardi. Despite some defeats, the Norman presence grew as their knights and foot soldiers began occupying a significant portion of the South.

By 1035, the Norman mercenary army was selling its services to the highest bidder. At one point, it even shifted its allegiance to the Byzantine Greeks, the people they originally were asked to help subdue. Here's where Sicily comes into the picture. Byzantium wanted to retake the island, which it had lost 250 years earlier to the Arabs. The time was ripe. Muslim district rulers there were in disarray, squabbling among one another.

The Normans agreed to help. In 1038, the Byzantines, with an assortment of mercenaries that included a Norman contingent, landed on the island and within two years occupied thirteen towns and cities. But quarrels ensued among the invaders. The Greek leader was recalled to Constantinople and thrown into prison; the Normans were disgruntled about their share of the spoils, and they left the island. In 1040, the Arabs regained control of the lands lost to the Byzantines in that eastern half.

The years passed. Norman-Lombard-Byzantine intrigue in southern Italy played out in various battles, some involving the forces loyal to the pope in Rome. In 1060, the Byzantines set sail for Constantinople, ending Greek rule in Calabria. Through all of this turmoil, Norman leaders Roger Guiscard and his brother, Robert, kept their eyes on Sicily.

Then the emir, Siracusa-based Ibn Thumnah, who shared control of Sicily with two others, showed up on Roger's doorstep in early 1061. He wanted help getting rid of his two colleagues so he could take control of their shares of the island. In exchange, he would give Roger the eastern half and access to the entire coastline facing the Italian peninsula. According to Norman chroniclers, Roger put together an army of several dozen knights and, along with Thumnah's forces, took Messina easily. Within a decade, the Normans had dominated their Arab allies as well as conquering their Arab opponents. Not satisfied with taking just the eastern half, Roger rode into Palermo in early 1072.

By 1094, Roger at age sixty-three and known as Great Count Roger I, had won complete control. He even sent an army to Malta to ensure that the tiny island barely sixty miles south of Sicily would never be used as a base of operations against him.

The Normans kept Sicily's agricultural milieu the same as it was under the Muslims but introduced a new element into island life: feudalism.

Great Count Roger I died in 1101 at age seventy. Romance-language Professor Joseph F. Privitera, who wrote *Sicily: An Illustrated History,* said that Roger had spent

> [f]orty-four of those years . . . in the south, and forty had been largely devoted to the island of Sicily . . . by the time of his death, though still only a count, he was generally reckoned as one of the foremost princes of Europe. He had transformed Sicily. . . . it had become a political entity . . . in which four races and three religions were living side by side in mutual respect and concord.

Roger I's son Simon succeeded him, but died four years later, giving the throne to Simon's younger brother, also a Roger, who at age five became Count of Sicily; his mother, Adelaide del Vasto, served as regent. At age sixteen, he became King Roger II when he combined the Norman presence in southern Italy with Sicily. He pushed aside other family members who had ruled the duchies of Apulia and Calabria in the far south of the Italian peninsula, and the Duchy of Capua, an area north of Naples. Roger II eventually took control of the Duchy of Naples as well.

His father's reign had sustained the great prosperity earlier fostered by the Muslim rulers. There are no known images of Roger I, and only two known contemporary portraits exist of

Roger II—both in Palermo and both likely created by Muslim and Byzantine artists. In the Palatine Chapel, a carving on a large candle holder shows Roger holding up the throne of Christ. A mosaic showing Christ anointing the new, bearded king is on a wall inside the Church of Santa Maria dell'Ammiraglio. This church also is known as San Nicolò dei Greci and is commonly called the Martorana.

Sometimes people born into power become truly great rulers, as King Roger II did. He started out in good stead with the pope (in exchange for annual payments of one hundred sixty ounces of gold to Rome). From his coronation in Palermo's cathedral on Christmas Day 1130 to his death in 1154, Roger II ruled with a fair hand and embraced many different cultures.

He, and two of his successors—son William I and grandson William II—maintained their courts in a multicultural manner. William I, nicknamed "The Bad," had to deal with overarching barons eager to expand their political clout who saw him as weak. (It was the barons, not the Sicilian people, who considered William I "bad.") There were riots in Palermo, and Muslims faced racial intolerance at the barons' hands. He died young, in 1166, and his son, at age thirteen, took over.

Affairs settled down, and historian Privitera writes that throughout his reign

William II [nicknamed "The Good" because he favored the barons' demands] lived like an oriental sovereign. He had Muslim concubines and kept a bodyguard of Negro slaves; he patronized Arab poets. . . . [Muslims] dominated the

finance department, there were still mosques in Palermo . . .
Even the Christian women in Palermo were said to have
assumed the secluded habits and the dress of Arab women,
while the king himself was known to have worn Moorish
costumes.

Essentially, four generations of Normans had ruled Sicily:
Great Count Roger I, sons Simon and Roger II, William I, and
William II. But all this began to shift in 1189 when William II
died at age thirty-six. His aunt, Roger II's daughter Constance,
was in line and ruled for four years. She traveled north and
married German King Henry VI, who was crowned Holy
Roman Emperor by the pope upon the death of his father,
Frederick I Barbarossa (Red Beard). With Constance as his
wife, Henry VI eventually added the island and southern Italy
to his realm.

Before Henry could move south to take the throne, and
because the southerners disliked the idea of a German king,
the crown briefly passed to Tancred, an illegitimate son of
Roger II's eldest son, also Roger, Duke of Apulia. When Henry
reached Naples, he left Constance there and moved to meet
Tancred on the battlefield. But these events, which seem to pile
up quickly on the written page, in fact happened very slowly.
It wasn't until three years later, in 1194, that he resumed the
march south.

Conveniently, Tancred died early that year; his successor
was his infant son, William III. The baby's mother was offered
favorable terms to surrender the crown to Henry. She agreed.
The terms were broken. She and her son went into hiding in
the south Sicily village of Caltabellotta. She was found, how-

ever, and, according to historian Steven Runciman: "She was imprisoned, and many of her supporters were cruelly put to death; and the child-king disappeared into obscurity."

So Sicily and southern Italy were basically handed off to German control. On Christmas Day 1194, the ever-popular day for coronations at Palermo's cathedral, Holy Roman Emperor Henry VI was crowned king. Meanwhile, a very pregnant Constance, Henry's link to the Norman heritage, was traveling from where she had been taken to a place of safety, north of the Alps, down the length of the Italian peninsula to attend the crowning. She was forced to stop and give birth, on December 26, in a tent hastily put up in the square of the small village of Jesi, near Ancona on the Adriatic coast. Born that day was the future ruler, Frederick II.

Newly crowned Henry wasted no time. He emptied the Sicilian treasury and sent it to Germany. The relative calm that had swept the island during the four generations of Norman rule ended. Sicilians revolted against Henry, a rebellion he put down easily and with great brutality. Fortunately for Sicilians and southern Italians, this anxious young German from the House of Hohenstaufen did not last long. He died at age thirty-two after three rough years on the throne. His son, Frederick II—the one born in a tent in Jesi—became king at age three and ended up being one of the greatest sovereigns the island ever had.

Frederick's reign got off to a slow start. When he became the toddler king, his mother, Constance, was regent. A year later, when he was four, she died, and the pope became his protector. In 1212, he went to Germany, returning eight years later at age sixteen as Holy Roman Emperor as well as king of Sicily and assorted other areas of the Mediterranean world.

Sicily, during Frederick's toddlership and later his absence, had become a land of banditry, and ambitious nobles pretty much had their way with things. When he returned from Germany, young Frederick brought the nobles into line by ordering the destruction of many of their castles.

While still a man of his times whose authority was absolute—heads could roll off the shoulders of those who displeased him—Frederick led Sicily and southern Italy into a new era. He created a university in Naples and developed a code of law that treated everyone—Lombards, Greeks, Arabs, and Franks—the same; under the Normans, each of these groups had been governed by their own separate laws and customs.

While he protected law-abiding Muslims, he could not tolerate efforts by members of the surviving Islamic communities to be independent. He deported many, sending them to Apulia on the Adriatic coast at the heel of the Italian boot.

Privitera maintains that Frederick did this "because they were rebels, not because of their religion." Differences in religion certainly didn't seem to concern him. As a Catholic, he battled throughout his reign with different popes and was repeatedly excommunicated for keeping Sicily separate and not a fiefdom of the church. He made ecclesiastics pay taxes like everyone else.

Historian Steven Runciman writes:

But to Sicilians it was not the same as in Norman times. Then Sicily had been the heart of a self-contained kingdom. It was from Palermo that the mainland provinces had been governed; and the Norman kings, for all their ambition, had remained essentially kings of Sicily. Now the king of Sicily was also the emperor of northern Italy. Even in the Sicilian kingdom he did not seem to favour the island more than the mainland.

Runciman also points out the biggest influences on the island, through the century of Norman rule, remained Greek and Muslim. "But in spite of the diversity, a Sicilian national consciousness was arising. . . ." It was this tiny spark of national consciousness that would smolder for a few more decades and erupt into one of the most significant events in Sicilian history: an ill-fated rebellion, perhaps the only time that Sicilians had a real shot at establishing control over their own destinies. This became known as the Sicilian Vespers.

Frederick II died in 1250. Over the next fifteen years, civil discord rocked the island. Most of Frederick's children and grandchildren were killed outright or imprisoned. Sicilian cities, much like the Greek model of ancient times, warred against one another. Messina fought battles with Taormina; Palermo rose up against Cefalù. Bandits plundered the countryside. Briefly, an English king's eight-year-old son, Edmund of Lancaster, who was favored by the pope, ruled as king of Sicily. Then a successor pope, a Frenchman, got the youngster deposed.

Here, the history gets a bit muddled; kings came and went with great frequency. A bastard son of Frederick's, Manfred, was crowned in 1258, but in 1266, the French pope had his way and got a Frenchman crowned, Charles of Anjou, who then proceeded to get rid of Manfred. That happened after a pitched battle on the mainland where Manfred was killed. Next in his line of succession would have been his fourteen-year-old nephew, but Charles had him imprisoned and then beheaded. It was often tough being a child born into royalty in those brutal days.

This, in 1266, put Charles and the House of Anjou, its members known as the Angevins, in control of the island of Sicily and much of southern Italy, especially Calabria, from Naples southward. It would be another two centuries before this combination, under a different ruler, would become officially known as the Kingdom of the Two Sicilies.

Sicilians, by this time, were used to being controlled by foreign kings who maintained their courts on the island. They were dismayed that their new French king preferred Naples to Palermo. In fact, Charles visited the island briefly only once. It was this apparent lack of interest in the island, Charles's oppressive rule, and his heavy taxation to fund an expedition he was planning to launch against the Byzantines in Constantinople that frustrated Sicilians.

Add to this a growing sense of nationalism among Greek and Muslim Sicilians that led, sixteen short years after his takeover, to an outpouring of rage against the occupying Angevin French. Historian Jean Dunbabin also points out that by 1282, "Angevin rule was not as well established in Sicily as in southern Italy."

Charles had used brutal methods, twelve years earlier, to put down a rebellion in Augusta, a city between Catania and Siracusa on Sicily's southeast coast. "[L]ittle had occurred to erase the images of ferocity and brutality created in those years," says Dunbabin. And, finally, "Palermo and Messina, the great towns of the past, watched the rise of Naples with jealousy." Naples represented foreign rule to Sicilians who could not identify with either that city or Italy in general.

More than anything, though, Dunbabin pegs what happened on Easter Monday in 1282 on the crushing tax burden Charles imposed for another foreign war.

The Church of the Holy Spirit, or Santo Spirito, stands in all its iconic Norman glory in the midst of Palermo's massive cemetery, Sant'Orsola. Made of volcanic stone, it is not overwrought in its construction as so many churches can be on this island of devoted churchgoers. The ceiling inside is painted wood. The church is not large and, except for morning and noon Mass and funerals, the wooden front doors are generally shuttered; the tiny piazza before those doors is usually empty. The only vehicles allowed are hearses; sometimes several funerals a day are scheduled.

The piazza in front is surrounded by magnificent crypts, some two stories high and topped with Islamic-style domes. There is a memorial in the square, honoring soldiers killed during the northern Italian fight for Unification. Heavy vegetation surrounds the square and infuses the cemetery with an almost woodslike quality. Along one edge is a rank of oleander trees preparing in late March to erupt in white, pink, red, and yellow blossoms.

The air in this third month—this time of year in the southern Mediterranean marks early spring—is comfortably warm, the evenings in Palermo are mild and, away from the heart of the city in this vast cemetery, quietness pervades. As evening approaches, swallows swoop through the darkening air, feasting on insects; the hum from the main road just outside the faraway gate, near where the flower sellers and stone masons operate, is nearly gone.

During a visit, with my son Brad and friend Conchita Vecchio in November 2009, the church was shuttered tightly and we wandered among the gravesites too long. The main gate was locked for the day. The maintenance people don't seem to mind that we were there; they wait patiently to show us the way out through a tiny gate farther along, obligingly kept open for folks who miss closing time.

I returned in mid-March 2010 with my friend Steve McCurdy, arriving more than seven centuries after an event, on Easter Monday, March 30, 1282, when Sicily's history took another sharp turn. Then, a crowd had gathered for early-evening vespers at the church that was barely a century old. The piazza so long ago was likely rough and unpaved, but it was large enough to hold those from the neighborhood and visitors from Palermo less than a mile away. These vespers were part of a traditional festival associated with Easter Week.

Historian Runciman reports that a handful of French soldiers also was there, observing the people who were "gossiping and singing" while waiting for vespers to begin. A soldier made what we moderns might call a "pass" at a young, married Sicilian woman. Her husband pulled his knife and stabbed the soldier. The crowd suddenly erupted in support for the act. Angry Sicilians "armed with daggers and swords" and with their burning resentment boiling over against the foreigners who presume to rule over and tax them for foreign wars, grabbed the other soldiers, murdering them on the spot.

At that moment, Santo Spirito's bells, marking the start

of vespers, started ringing. At the sound, "messengers ran through the city calling on the men of Palermo to rise against the oppressor . . . Every Frenchman that they met was struck down . . . Sicilian girls who had married Frenchmen perished with their husbands." None was spared, including the children of the French occupiers. By morning, the rebels controlled the city, and two thousand Frenchmen and their women were dead.

All of this raises the question: Was the incident at Santo Spirito spontaneous? It certainly happened after a Frenchman threatened the honor of a Sicilian woman, something the crowd could not have anticipated. Or was it already in the planning stages and waiting only for a match to ignite the fire that first swept the city and then the entire island?

The answer is uncertain. What is known is that within a week or so, rebel troops had swept across Sicily, toward Trapani on the west coast, Caltanissetta to the south, and Messina on the east.

The earthshaking event that took the rebellion beyond Sicily and turned it into a major European event was that the emergency halted in their tracks the plans of Angevin King Charles I to attack Constantinople. This, of course, was much to the relief of the Byzantine emperor. Some reports indicate he hurriedly provided gold to support the rebellious Sicilians. Meanwhile, French soldiers were dispatched from the Italian ports where they had been gathering for the assault on Constantinople and sent to the Strait of Messina.

Battles, particularly over the city of Messina, took up much of that summer. Eventually, the Sicilians, despite their early successes in routing the French, came to realize they could not go it alone against the much larger and better equipped army.

Here is where a Spanish king, Peter of Aragon, enters the picture. Aragon, a self-proclaimed kingdom in northeastern Spain, was ruled by Peter and Queen Constance. She happened to be from the House of Hohenstaufen, the dynasty that once ruled Sicily through Henry VI and his son, Frederick II. This tie was enough for the Sicilians to seek the couple's help.

"The Sicilians had been unwilling at first to substitute the rule of one foreign potentate for that of another," Runciman tells us. "But they could not stand alone." A group of Sicilians met with Peter and agreed that his queen, Constance, "was their lawful queen to whom the crown should be given, and after her to her sons, the Infants of Aragon." Eventually, Peter agreed to "place his wife upon the throne of her ancestors" and become, as her husband, king of Sicily.

He organized his army and sailed to the west-coast city of Trapani, landing there on August 30, 1282, just five months after the incident at Santo Spirito. Peter began his march across the island, first toward Palermo, where on September 4 he was declared king of Sicily. Then he led the army on a slog through the center of the island to Randazzo and across the north slope of Etna toward Messina to confront the bulk of the French army. He was victorious in keeping the French off the island.

The act of Peter being named king of Sicily demolished what Roger II had accomplished more than 150 years earlier: the unifying of southern Italy and Sicily. All that was left to the French were the Kingdom of Naples and portions of the peninsula's southern end.

Runciman gives the Sicilians credit for fighting unaided for so long. The arrival of the Aragonese allowed them to take the island under their control. It wasn't until the 1440s, when Sicily and Naples were reunited under Spanish rule, that this part of the Mediterranean world became known as the Kingdom of the Two Sicilies.

But first, a comedy had to play itself out. The two kings, Peter and Charles, in 1283, challenged each other to a duel. A site in Bordeaux in France was chosen. The date was set, but not the hour of the day. Peter showed up with his retinue early in the morning; no one was there. He left, saying he won by default since his opponent was a coward and hadn't showed up. Charles arrived sometime later, found the field empty, and made the same declaration. Each man claimed victory.

Charles I of Anjou, onetime king of Sicily and Naples, "died a failure," writes Runciman. In Foggia, on Italy's Adriatic coast, he died in 1285 and his body was carried to Naples for burial. His successors, including his son Charles II, were not up to the challenge, even with the support of the king of France and the pope, and Charles I's great ambition to dominate the Mediterranean world came to an end.

The result of all this is that for the next four centuries, Sicily was under the thumb of Spain. Messina had been the favored city on the island under the French; now Palermo once again, and for the last time, became the capital.

The new king, Peter, may have treated Sicily as a kingdom separate from Aragon, but the Spanish aristocracy started to acquire estates on the island in exchange for military service. When Peter died in 1285, just ten months after his mortal enemy, Charles I of Anjou, Peter's son Alphonso took over the crown of Aragon and second oldest James was given Sicily.

Alphonso died, James succeeded him and named third oldest brother Frederick as governor in Sicily.

Then James, beleaguered by a spate of internal problems and outside threats, gave Sicily to the church, which was going to turn it back over to the French Angevins. The Sicilian Parliament could not stomach being returned to the French they had chased out in 1282 and so found a friend in Frederick, who challenged his brother's supremacy on the island. With Parliament's blessing, he was elevated in 1296 to the crown of Sicily as King Frederick III.

He continued to battle the Naples-based French Angevins as the war of the Sicilian Vespers was still being fought. The French often landed on the island, burning crops, uprooting orchards, destroying forests, and disrupting commerce. Because of these incursions, the island's Muslim-built irrigation system was destroyed, famine killed peasants by the thousands, and "Sicily had fallen prey to greed and ambition, and had become an island of hollow, frightened, and starving people," according to historian Runciman.

Finally, in 1302, Naples, tiring of these decades-old battles, demanded that for Sicilians to remain independent, Frederick III must pay an annual tribute to the pope and call himself king of Trinacria, after the island's ancient name, instead of king of Sicily. He was to marry a daughter of the French royalty in Naples and, at his death, the island would revert back to the French. This became the Treaty of Caltabellotta, signed in that south Sicily village in August 1302.

Frederick died in 1337. His son Peter II took over, but he died in 1342, and the treaty's requirement that Sicily revert back to the Angevins was ignored. The Kingdom of Sicily was reunited eventually with the Spanish Kingdom of Aragon. For the following four centuries the rulers of Sicily never lived on the island. Instead, viceroys managed baron-controlled commerce, and peasants, as usual, suffered the most on the famine-wracked island.

Between the viceroys and the barons, corruption reigned and Spanish rule nearly destroyed Sicily's economy. The island had to contribute to all of Spain's wars, providing taxes and men for the army. Eventually, revolts broke out in Sicily's largest cities.

By the beginning of the eighteenth century, Spain's time in Sicily was nearing a shift in power. King Charles II, who ruled from 1677 to 1700, had no son. When his will was read, "Spain and Sicily found themselves bequeathed to Phillip V, the Bourbon grandson of [French] King Louis XIV." But before Phillip could take over, the island was bequeathed, by members of an international congress, to Vittorio Amadeo di Savoia, in Piedmonte, northern Italy.

Sicily was ruled by Vittorio for five years, by the Austrians for fourteen years, and then, beginning in 1719, by the Spanish Bourbon ruler in Naples.

Identifying the Bourbons can be a complex matter. The current king of Spain, Juan Carlos I, descends from the Bourbon line, an ancient dynasty that had its beginnings in the early thirteenth century where its lord was a vassal of the king of France. Its members, over the centuries, spread across western Europe, often through intermarriages with other lines. Eventually some of the Bourbons became rulers of significant portions of the Western world, primarily in France and Spain, some specializing in the possessions, like the Kingdom of the Two Sicilies, of those countries.

Again, these rulers were interested only in getting as much money out of Sicily as possible. And again, the kings did not live there. The Spanish tried, periodically, to regain control, but failed after the Austrians, who held on to the island until 1734, took control.

Eventually, the Spanish Bourbons reentered the fray. Phillip V of Spain sent his son, Charles of Bourbon, to retake Naples and Sicily, and in 1734, Charles became Charles III, king of the reunited Two Sicilies. As the Bourbons held sway, Sicily's fortunes ebbed and flowed. A plot to replace the viceroy with a republican government was uncovered in 1797, and its leader was beheaded. Sicilian writer Leonardo Sciascia wrote a novel about this period, *The Council of Egypt*.

One of the successor kings held two titles. In Naples, he was known as King Ferdinand IV. In Sicily, he was King Ferdinand III. When he brought the two kingdoms under one command—once again to be called the Kingdom of the Two Sicilies—he renumbered his name to become Ferdinand I.

His rule, including that of his progeny, kicked off four revolts between 1820 and 1860. The first two, if they had succeeded, might have created an independent Sicilian nation. The last two called for unification with Italy. Ferdinand died in 1825 in the midst of all the nationalistic turmoil. He was followed by son Francesco I, then by Ferdinand II, who died in 1859, on the eve of the Giuseppe Garibaldi–led northern Italian invasion of Sicily and southern Italy.

Early in 1860, revolts broke out in Palermo, Trapani, Marsala, Messina, Corleone, Cefalù, Misilmeri, Caltanissetta, and Agrigento. News of these events had convinced Garibaldi that the time was ripe for the invasion by his Red Shirts of northern volunteers called the One Thousand (the actual number was 1,070). The reign of Ferdinand I's successor, Francesco II, while housed in Naples, says historian Privitera, "barely got under way before he had to flee the Garibaldi forces."

Italy today, with Sicily, Sardinia, and southern Italy under its control, is a relatively new nation at a mere 150 years old. Garibaldi landed at Marsala on May 11, 1860. A day later, at the inland town of Salemi, he proclaimed himself dictator and began the process of routing Bourbon troops throughout western Sicily. He took Palermo on May 25. By July 20, the island was his, and the Sicilian people loved him for his efforts. He crossed the Strait of Messina and, on October 1, it was all over in the South. Garibaldi had routed the Bourbons, driving them out of Naples, where he issued a decree "ordering the incorporation of the Bourbon Kingdom of the Two Sicilies into the Italian realm" under the rule of King Vittorio Emanuele II of Piedmonte.

Also that month, a vote was taken in Sicily on whether to go with the new nation with the promise of Sicilian autonomy. It passed, of course—the rigged "unanimous" vote is clearly shown in Giuseppe di Lampedusa's *The Leopard* and Visconti's film of that magnificent novel—but many Sicilians had wanted Garibaldi as their leader. Now they were under the thumb of one more monarchy, this one made up of northern Italians. To get their vote of support, they had been promised self-government, but their new northern leaders, who declared creation of the Kingdom of Italy early the next year, 1861, reneged.

It was a tough situation. As Privitera tells it, "[King Vittorio Emanuele] and his fellow Piedmontese saw themselves as coming to deliver Sicily from bondage whereas Sicilian opinion was that . . . they themselves had launched the liberation of Italy."

These northern overseers found a culture in Sicily and the South that was foreign to their own. They found Sicilians, not Italians. The people spoke a different language and resisted the requirement that they learn Italian. The island, as was true so many times in the past three thousand years, was once again drained by taxation; its young men were drafted into the Italian army, and over the next several decades were used as cannon fodder in a number of senseless wars. Small landowners went broke; food and political riots were common.

Things got so bad that in 1866, says Privitara, "a major revolt in Palermo was put down by the shelling of the city by the Italian navy and by the arrival of forty thousand troops. But unlike 1860, no Garibaldi arrived to support the revolt." The northern Italians declared martial law that lasted for several years. Many Sicilian insurgents were summarily executed.

Again, as happened so many times in Sicilian history under brutal invaders, these were incredibly tough times. Only now it was driven by northerners, Piedmontese, attempting to paint Sicilians as "Italians."

Martial law was again declared in 1894. Privitera continues: "By the end of the century, Sicily was no better off than it had been under the Bourbons. The island was under-educated, overtaxed, neglected, and impoverished." It was in this era of post-Unification that the Mafia got its pincers sunk deep into the soul of the island.

What all this did was start one of the greatest movements of people from one nation to another. The great diaspora of the late nineteenth and early twentieth centuries took millions of disenchanted, hungry Sicilians and southern Italians to North and South America.

Eventually, after World War II, Sicily, along with Sardinia and a few other regions in northern Italy, was given regional autonomy. But in Sicily's case, it was only done to stop that growing separatist movement that hadn't gone away after the North reneged on that 1861 promise of self-government. This political solution succeeded, keeping the island under the Italian flag.

Today, Sicilians remain Sicilians in their hearts, souls, and culture. The talk of secession is debated, quietly and in confidence, sub rosa, among friends.

NINE

A Mother's Rage

I had imagined myself standing on Demeter's Rock
and looking down onto the shores of the lake, watching
Persephone, sharing Demeter's moment of distraction
and the horrible clutching of her bowels as she turns
her gaze back and Persephone is no longer there.
—Mary Taylor Simeti,
On Persephone's Island (1986)

IT'S A Sunday in March. The days are warm, and the almond
petals, five to each pink bud that just a month earlier ignited
the trees in the countryside around nearby Agrigento, are fluttering in the breezes of early spring. Racalmuto is quiet following the feast day of San Giuseppe a few days earlier. The brass
band that followed the processions is silenced. Pounding drums
that announce everything traditional in this tiny village of
nearly ten thousand souls are put away until the next festival.

The bronze statue of Leonardo Sciascia, frozen in mid-
stride, stands alone on the sidewalk, his cigarette dangling as

it did in life, between the first and middle fingers of his right hand. No one is here to affectionately touch that hand as they pass. The massive gray iron doors to the cathedral just ahead are closed. The last real sound I hear is from the bells ringing out the noon hour.

I came into town for a midday espresso. But the door to the bar just across the street from the smiling Sciascia is shuttered behind the long strings of beads that usually serve as a doorway. Nothing to do here, I think to myself. I bid farewell to my friend Leonardo, affectionately rub the patina a tiny bit brighter on his right hand, and head for the car. Pergusa, about an hour away and just down the slope from the imposing city of Enna in Sicily's center, is in need of a visit.

That small town is intriguing simply because it sits near the shore of a tiny lake that figures heavily in the pantheon of Greek mythology. Before I knew much about Sicily, or even knew that its recorded history began with the arrival of Greek colonists nearly three thousand years ago, I assumed the Greek myths I had read all took place in Greece.

The same was true of the Greek plays I read in college and saw performed on the university campus in my home city. Weren't they all written in Greece? Some were, of course; others were conceived and created by Greek playwrights in Sicily. Some of those writers were born here, some were merely passing through, and others were born elsewhere and died in Sicily after becoming Greek-Sicilian.

Many of the better known plays were performed at the giant stone theater in Siracusa. *The Persians* by Aeschylus was performed there; born in Greece, he died around 455 B.C. in

Gela, on Sicily's south coast. Sophocles and Euripides had plays presented here, as did the Greek-Sicilian comedy writer Epicharmus.

That Greek myths didn't all occur in Greece began to sink in during readings of *The Odyssey* and a literary guidebook I used to make sense of early Mediterranean geography. Both made allusions to the episode of Odysseus's battle with the cyclops taking place along Sicily's east coast.

Over the years, other travel narratives described a Sicily shrouded in Greek myths. The one about Persephone and her kidnapping and descent into the underworld caught my attention. This reputedly took place in central Sicily, around a small spring-fed lake just off the south slope of the Enna plateau. The idea that it all occurred near modern-day Pergusa seems older than time itself. People on this island have always been aware of the myth and nod knowingly when it is mentioned.

In Pergusa, in a small park with a clear view of the lake—now shrinking in size, I am told, as the springs that feed it are commandeered for drinking water—sits a modern statue that looks like a representation of Persephone being gathered up and kidnapped by her uncle, the nether god Hades, in preparation for his golden-chariot ride into the underworld.

The lake, surrounded by a track where locals race cars, is difficult to get to. There are conflicting campaigns: one to remove the track and create a wildflower-filled park along the shoreline; the other to turn it into a Formula One venue. The track, for the time being at least, seems to be winning.

The next best thing is to find a bar where I can get an espresso, a sandwich, and blood-orange juice. I return to the park with my lunch, sit on a bench, and consider the statue, the lake, and the impact the story of Persephone had on this once magical island.

The origins of the myth are unclear. Marguerite Rigoglioso suggests that there are indigenous Sicilian versions of the story "that far predated the arrival of Greeks in Sicily. . . . The idea that the myth of the grain mother and her maiden daughter originated in Sicily is rendered not so farfetched. Perhaps it is only later, with the arrival of the Greeks, that they came to be known as Demeter and Persephone."

By the way, it is important to note that these gods and demigods have many names. Persephone is the Greek name that the Romans changed to Proserpina; Hades, Zeus's brother, becomes Pluto under the Romans; and Demeter, Persephone's mother and Zeus's sister, becomes Cerere or Ceres. Zeus, the maiden's father and king of the gods on Mount Olympus, becomes the Romans' Jupiter. Yes, all are of the same family. Zeus and his sister Demeter conceive Persephone, and Zeus conspires to have his daughter become the bride of his brother, her uncle. Incest happened among the gods and the ancient Greeks. To understand why the gods acted as they did, one need only look at the culture of the ancient Greeks—daughters often were married off to uncles to preserve a family's fortune, for example—who endowed their myths with their own standards of behavior.

Gods and goddesses were not bound by the conventions of humans, with whom they interacted and even shared offspring. But they were still gods, ruled by Zeus, and they could leap from land to land with ease and cause great calamities or events of great fortune, depending upon their moods at any given time. The goddess of the grain, Demeter, who taught humans the secret of agriculture, wanted to protect Persephone from lesser gods who were pursuing the beautiful girl.

Then, one beautiful, sunny day on this most fertile of Mediterranean islands, Persephone sat picking wildflowers along the shore of this lake.

Hades—did his brother Zeus direct him to Persephone's location?—was clambering about aboveground. He saw her and, charmed by her beauty, gathered her up, placed her in his golden chariot pulled by a brace of black horses, and rode off toward Siracusa to the southeast. There, he and she disappeared into the bowels of the earth. A nymph, Cyane, tried to stop him, but Hades turned the nymph into a spring that feeds the short, beautiful river—the Ciane—that to this day runs into the harbor at Siracusa.

Demeter heard only that her daughter was missing. She did not know her brother Hades was behind the disappearance or where the maiden had been taken. She raced to the lake's shore but found she was too late. In her anguish, she wandered all of Sicily for nine days and nine nights looking for Persephone, swinging her scythe to cut pathways through the lush green of the island. During the night, she carried torches lighted by the fires of Mount Etna. Her grief-fed anger was so intense that everything on the island began to die; the soil became infertile, starvation began to take hold, and the human race was in danger of extinction. Demeter lost her scythe along the way; some say the scythe-shaped promontory of the western Sicilian city of Trapani is where it landed.

Zeus, as was usual in these kinds of stories, eventually heard the pleas of the starving populace. He intervened and sent a messenger to the underworld to confront Hades and urge him to release Persephone. But the young woman had grown attached to her captor. Secretly, Hades had fed her a couple of seeds of the pomegranate, a fruit that inspires love. And once you eat in the underworld you can never return to the surface.

However, Hades yielded to Zeus and agreed to let her come to the surface part of the year; for the remaining months, she was to return to join him in the underworld, where she sat on the throne as his queen.

Rigoglioso points out that in Sicily, there are really only "three main seasons, not four—autumn/winter, spring, and summer." Grain is planted in the late fall and harvested in late June, so "[s]ummer is the time when the land lies barren and fallow under the fierce sun. . . ."

Thus, according to Rigoglioso, Persephone returns to the underworld at the beginning of summer, "the time in Sicily associated with barrenness and death." Ancient festivals honoring Persephone were held not in the springtime, but just before the goddess was to retreat belowground to sit on her throne as queen of the underworld.

In ancient times, Greek-Sicilians held a flower festival known as *anthesphoria* during the advent of spring. Celebrants would gather flowers and twine them into garlands, which is what Persephone was supposed to have been doing when Hades kidnapped her. Women wore these flowery crowns in their hair during the festival; the Romans called it *floralia*. Variants of this practice often can be seen in a variety of cultures across Europe. Some believe it does not have anything to do with honoring Persephone, but it marked a time when ears of corn were carried to the temple.

Sicilian-American folklorist and storyteller Gioia Timpanelli uses the Roman names of the gods and goddesses when she refers to this myth in her novella "Knot of Tears," which is contained in her scintillating book *Sometimes the Soul*. Her character Costanza, a young woman living at the turn of the twentieth century who isolates herself in a large house in Palermo—"the dark, cool house, the quiet study where sometimes she worked until dawn"—would imagine ancient times and places.

> . . . [S]he might see a large migration of eagles flying overhead or travel to the luxuriant meadows of wildflowers outside of Enna, the fields of her ancestors where it was said that Ceres' daughter had been stolen: *Proserpina fell from the fields of Enna / Fields where purple convolvulus grow / Down to the folds of the dark / Underworld.*

Gioia, in a telephone conversation after my March 2009 visit to Lago di Pergusa, told me that she first heard the Demeter and Persephone story from her grandmother when she was only five years old.

"I remember she had tears in her eyes as she told me that story," Gioia said. The fact remains that this great Greek myth fosters great intensity among Sicilians. They all, from small children to the aged, know it. Hotel and B and B rooms across the island have the names of these gods on the doors as names for the rooms. As I write this, I am sitting in a room in an Enna B and B with KORE on the door. *Kore* is still another name for Persephone meaning "young maiden."

Just a kilometer or so up the street is the Rocca di Cerere, site of a former temple dedicated to Demeter. She is powerful on this island; there are numerous such sites around Sicily where ancient Greek-Sicilians practiced animal sacrifices. Today, visitors stand on the rock to savor magnificent views of the countryside of central Sicily and of snowcapped Mount Etna to the east. A prominent church here is built on the foundation of a temple to Persephone.

I sense from all this that myths developed, in the eighth century B.C. and earlier, as a way for early people with no knowledge of astronomy or physics or chemistry to explain the mysteries of nature: Helios drove a golden chariot to push the sun across the sky before the blazing globe eventually disappears into the west. It then returns to the east after twilight by sailing across the ocean. And it was the ancient Greeks who imagined how a god's sword can cleave a human in two, flinging the feminine half in one direction and the masculine in another, each side doomed to wander the earth looking for its perfect other half.

But there is one thing about these ancient gods that we must never forget: The gods—Zeus, Hera, Demeter, Hades, all of them—did not care much for humans. They wanted humans around only to offer sacrifices. So when Demeter, in her anguish over her lost daughter, caused the great famine and humans were in danger of extinction, Zeus was forced to relent and demand that Hades return his bride to the surface of the world. To let humans die out would mean the end of sacrifices to the gods.

And humans, in order to understand their world, relied on the gods to explain why good things as well as bad things happen. As Homer tells us in *The Iliad,* "All men have need of the gods." And the gods need us to offer sacrifices to them.

Most of us lost those particular gods long ago during the

rise of the world's great religions. But maybe, deep down inside, we haven't. That bonfire, the *falò,* I attended in Racalmuto likely originated as a pagan rite of nature, as did the decorated pine tree early peoples worshipped near the winter solstice of late December. The understanding of the origins of these rites may have been lost generations ago, but they are still part of the very soul of this island.

For the return to Racalmuto at the end of this pleasant day communing with Demeter and Persephone, I choose to stay off the autostrada and instead follow the tiny lines on my map that represent narrow two-lane roads. This allows me to pass through, at a leisurely pace, one small village after another: Masseria Scioltabino, Pietraperzia, Borgo Braemi, Sommatino, Canicattì, Castrofilippo.

There are many ways to get from one place to another in Sicily. The narrow roads, like spiderwebs, plow across land that is waking up in March; wildflowers in fallow fields are blooming, heat is building under acres and acres of white plastic sheeting that covers factory-operated fields, and the green of the rolling hills of south-central Sicily—still light-years away, one hopes, from being overwhelmed by American-style subdivisions—rise in clear, tangy air through which an observant traveler can easily imagine the past, feel the present, and wonder about the future.

TEN

Aci Trezza and the Cyclops

A grim loner, dead set in his own lawless ways.
Here was a piece of work, by god, a monster
built like no mortal who ever supped on bread,
no, like a shaggy peak, I'd say—a man-mountain
rearing head and shoulders over the world.
—Homer, The Odyssey

I HEARD a story about the folks who climbed Etna each day and carried the large blocks of ice wrapped in protective green ferns down its steep, rich slopes so they could preserve the early morning catch of fish. The ice, made from snow packed by peasants and preserved for summer use deep in lava tunnels on Etna's slope, was stored some distance from the coastal fishing villages that stretch out north and south from cluttered, overcrowded Catania.

I thought about this daily ordeal one bright July Sunday when I dropped down along the narrow, confusing mountain roads from Trecastagni to a little village on the Ionian Sea, Aci

Trezza. This is the village made famous by a Giovanni Verga novel, *I Malavoglia,* the name of the family in the story. The English translation carries the additional title *The House by the Medlar Tree.* It tells the tragic story of a fishing family that lived out their lives in that tiny village in the late 1800s.

The good folks in Aci Trezza depend on tourism these days as well as fishing, and they capitalize on the fame of this book and the 1948 Luchino Visconti film, *La terra trema,* based on the story, which Visconti set not in the late eighteen hundreds, but in the mid-1940s. Visconti used only local people, nonactors, who spoke only their local dialect. The result was a tribute to his abilities as a director.

I learned that only two of the townspeople appearing in the film were still alive. I met one during my usual stroll around the town's main square overlooking the port. He is a retired fisherman, Salvatore Vicari, now seventy-two. At around age ten, he was "Alfio the boat boy," the brother of the film's hapless hero, 'Ntoni.

Salvatore revels as the town star; he loves meeting people who have seen the film and who remember the Visconti character despairing as he watched his family disintegrate within the grinding poverty of the fisherman's life. The final scenes are particularly touching as he goes, hand in hand, with his brother to find work on a fleet of new boats, enduring the brutal badgering of the bosses as they ridicule the fishermen who tried to defy them.

Today, Salvatore, looking like he could be in his midfifties or early sixties, his face, nut-brown from a life at sea, has a winning smile and an easy manner as he greets visitors eager to shake his hand. Men of his generation never went to school. The host of my bed-and-breakfast tells me, "Most of the older men can't read. A man from the north reads news and documents to them."

Looking at the young people of Aci Trezza today and their easy interactions, they seem no different than American teenagers. This easy socialization was much different in the 1940s when *La terra trema* was filmed. No unmarried young girl among the townsfolk could be found who was willing to be kissed onscreen. It would have been disgraceful; the shame would have been too much to bear. No man would have married her if she had done that.

So Visconti, for the kissing scene down on the windblown beach on a pile of rocks battered by crashing waves, found a minor professional actress in Catania. That clip was memorialized in the 1988 film *Cinema Paradiso* as one of the scenes the censoring priest ordered removed, ringing his little bell as a signal to the projectionist.

For book and film lovers, Aci Trezza offers a stone house by a medlar tree, a shrublike plant that produces a fruit similar to crab apple. The house is in the heart of the village that is set in a small, natural bay immediately north of Catania's sprawl and near the community's church. The house features three rooms that in the 1800s would have served three separate families.

One room, full of black-and-white movie stills and an original poster, is dedicated to the making of the film. Another, just across a tiny courtyard, is simply outfitted with a single bed and assortment of fishing nets, net-making gear, and domestic implements. The bed, I was told, was the very one used in the movie where a dying grandfather lay before he was carried off to an old-folks home in Catania.

All the room's furnishings occupied the same spots as they did in the film.

"Everyone else would sleep on the floor," the museum guide said, pointing to the small area around the bed.

But one domestic implement that caught my attention was a solid-metal cylinder, roughly the size of a bar canister for mixing drinks. This was used, our guide told us, "to pack in a bit of the ice from Etna" to make what is still known today as granita, that supremely refreshing repast for hot July and August days. Today, this refreshing dessert is available in all kinds of flavors: melon and rose, black currant, watermelon—the list goes on.

But back then, it involved filling the container with shaved ice, popping in a bit of sugar, and mixing in the juice of Etna's lemons: a thrilling but certainly infrequent treat for incredibly poor fishing families of the late nineteenth century.

Ice and lemons from Etna—the story of how difficult it was then to make and haul ice great distances in a premechanical era, while a small story, underscores the rigors of life in this land even just a century or so ago.

Tales of these rigors—the extremely brutal life of families drawn so closely together for survival, whose livelihoods depended on the vagaries of the dangerous sea before them, the tremors of the massive volcano above them, and, elsewhere in Sicily, the fickleness of the seasons that either produced an abundance of crops or burned them up for lack of moisture— are what make the works of Verga and Pirandello so unrelentingly powerful. The rich landowners stayed rich, the peasants suffered continually, and the only people they could really trust were members of their own families.

Neighbors could turn on them in an instant over a per-ceived slight or a baseless rumor; fish buyers could cheat them, as in *I Malavoglia;* landowners and banks could take the hovels in which they lived if money was gone. If they didn't pray hard enough to the Madonna, the crops could fail, the fish would disappear, and they wouldn't have anything with which to survive the winter.

The new conquerors, northern Italians who followed in the footsteps of the Spanish, French, Normans, Arabs, and others, could conscript their sons into armies and then turn a blind eye to the suffering of the South while enriching the North.

Fascism, in the early twentieth century, offered hope briefly, and many of the peasants and middle-class Sicilians flocked to its cause. But Mussolini failed them as well. So all these people, the peasants and the fishermen, had to count on was family. This is why the power of family is so deeply ingrained in Sicilians.

The appeal of this place for tourists goes beyond its connec-tion to Visconti's film. People here also capitalize on a Greek myth that led to the naming of these places with the appella-tion "Aci." There is Acireale, the largest of the three coastal fishing communities, and, a bit inland, Aci Santa Lucia and Aci Catena. In all, I counted nine villages in the area with names preceded by Aci.

What they have in common is the tiny Acis River, laden with rusty-colored, mineral-infused water that trickles down

Etna to the sea at Capo Mulini, between Aci Trezza and Aci-reale. The river is usually dry during the summer months, as are many of Sicily's rivers. This name is tied to Greek mythology of a time when only gods and half-humans/half-gods roamed the fruitful land.

The story is a charming one, and it is worth mentioning because one of the characters in this drama is the one-eyed cyclops, Polyphemus, who figures in *The Odyssey,* Homer's tale of Odysseus's ten-year journey home following the Trojan War.

But before Odysseus and his fellow warriors showed up, the giant Polyphemus, who tended his sheep and worked in Hephaestus's forge in the volcano Etna, was in love with the nymph Galatea, who cavorted with her fellow nymphs on the beaches that ring the harbor of today's Aci Trezza/Aci Castello. Unfortunately, Galatea had fallen in love with the shepherd Acis, son of the Greek god Pan. This enraged Polyphemus, who crushed Acis with a large boulder. Galatea was distraught, and Zeus, the most important god in the Greek pantheon, took pity on her grief. Using her tears, he transformed Acis into that river that flowed through Galatea's realm to the sea. Eventually she recovered from her grief, married Polyphemus, and bore him three sons. Ah, the fickleness of it all.

Odysseus and his men, during their long journey home, land near the mouth of the Acis River, where they encounter Polyphemus. A monster with cannibalistic tendencies, he captures and imprisons them in his cave on the slopes of Etna, where he keeps his flock of sheep. There he begins eating the hapless crew two at a time, day by day, promising Odysseus that he will eat him last.

Of course, wise Odysseus conjures up a plan of escape. The

warrior takes the cyclops's olivewood club, sharpens an end, and makes the point hard by charring it in the giant's fire.

Waiting until Polyphemus falls asleep, Odysseus and four of his men pick up the huge club and jam the point into the monster's single eye and "bored it home/as a shipwright bores his beam with a shipwright's drill . . . till blood came boiling up around that smoking shaft . . . and the broiling eyeball burst." The men hid from the now blind, enraged cyclops who was suffering excruciating pain. Later, the men escaped from the cave by grabbing hold of the undersides of the sheep as the monster let the animals out of the cave to graze. As they escaped to their ship and set sail, Odysseus badgered the giant, and the enraged Polyphemus ripped off "the peak of a towering crag [and] heaved it so hard the boulder landed just in front of our dark prow. . . ." The monster threw other massive rocks as the warriors rowed out to sea, rocks that still rear up out of the dark water just off the harbor of Aci Trezza. Tourists now swim and scuba dive among these massive boulders, some more than a hundred feet high.

Of course it's all myth, conjured up by deep-thinking Greeks trying to explain the mysteries of the world. My Sicilian-American friend Alissandru (Alex) Caldiero has a different take on the story. Over coffee one morning in a shop near his Utah home, he told me that he believes the tale of Polyphemus the cyclops is an "allegory for the Greek takeover of the island. It is my observation, my reading of Mediterranean culture, that this is true.

"In one dialect, the word *ciclopu* means 'man of the woods,'" he told me. "And cyclops means 'round eye,' not 'one eye' but 'round eye.'" Alex is convinced that the "cyclops" represented the indigenous peoples of Sicily—the people who were on the island when the Greeks arrived in the seventh and sixth centuries B.C. They had built their own villages, which the Greeks overtook and destroyed en route to building their own magnificent cities.

"The Greeks crushed these earliest peoples, these *cyclopi*, and erased them, hence the story of Odysseus outsmarting the giant."

This is a lot to think about and impossible to prove. Many theories abound of the origins and meanings of myths. But it makes good fodder for the imagination as I sit on a bright, hot Sunday morning on the terrace of an Aci Trezza *pasticceria* sipping lemon granita, looking out over the harbor and its dozens of small fishing boats tied up or hauled onto dry land. Bikini-clad women and Speedo-adorned men carrying coolers and towels, and some with scuba gear, are lining up on a long, narrow stone pier jutting into the harbor. Dozens of small boats oared by local men picking up a few euros are hauling these sun-worshipping tourists to the rocky outcrops cast there millennia ago by an enraged, newly blinded giant. I am distracted by thoughts of myths and of poverty-struck families of late nineteenth-century fishermen struggling to survive in a land once populated by gods, demigods, and nymphs.

I was brought back to reality when I found a parking ticket on my rental car's windshield. It took standing in line for nearly two hours the next morning at the Trecastagni post office to pay a €38 fine, plus €1 postal tax, to bring me back into the modern world.

ELEVEN

The Language

Un populu
diventa poviru e servu
quannu ci arrubbanu a lingua
addutata di patri:
è persu pi sempri.
(A people
becomes poor and servile
when the language
inherited from their forefathers
is stolen from them:
they are lost forever.)

—Ignazio Buttitta (1899–1997),
Sicilian dialectal poet
translation by Alissandru
(Alex) Caldiero

T HE HERD of cows, showing patches of white, brown, and
black, their udders nearly touching the asphalt of the narrow
Sicilian road, moseyed into view over the crest of the hill just
ahead. I stopped as this swarm of bovines, perhaps twenty or

so, broke around the car. On this trip, with photographer Steve McCurdy, the encounter was our second with herds or flocks deep in the remote western Sicilian countryside. Earlier that March day, around Piana degli Albanesi, a flock of scrawny sheep, bells tinkling and on legs that seemed too fragile for walking, likewise had surrounded us. A clutch of sheepdogs, moving constantly, had kept the woolly creatures in a tight pack as two herders, one in front and the other behind, controlled the dogs with shouts and whistles.

Now, a few hours later and on the outskirts of the tiny village of Montelepre—I wanted to see the birthplace of the infamous twentieth-century bandit Salvatore Giuliano—it was the cows' turn to envelop us and to remind us that we were traveling far from any urban influence or main highways.

A young man, perhaps in his early twenties, followed behind the herd, giving our vehicle only a brief glance. Steve grabbed his camera and jumped out of the car to follow the herd for a few hundred feet. He speaks near-fluent Italian, and I saw him engage in conversation briefly with the young herder.

"I couldn't understand a word he said," Steve said, climbing back into the passenger seat. "And he didn't seem to understand a word I said. Italian is certainly not his language."

It's likely the young man was speaking a local dialect of Sicilian, a language separate from Italian and one that some authorities believe was the first Romance language. And the reason that the herder didn't acknowledge any understanding of Steve's Italian.

If he had spoken Italian, it likely wouldn't have been the formal language Steve speaks, but a broken Italian-Sicilian combination you often hear older Sicilians speak in villages far away from the larger urban areas of Palermo, Catania, or Messina.

This is the view of folklorist, poet, and university professor Alissandru (Alex) Caldiero, a Sicilian by birth, a U.S. citizen since age eight. Alex is fluent in both Italian and Sicilian and has spent most of his adult life studying the vernacular of his Mediterranean birthplace. He has translated documents and compiled his own *Grammar of the Sicilian Language;* a language that he believes is dying.

When this happens to a language, he says, "The first thing you lose is how to write it. Then, you lose how to read it. Third, you lose how to speak it, and, fourth, you lose how to understand it. Perhaps twenty-five years from now, hardly anyone will understand Sicilian. The young man you described likely understands Sicilian but probably doesn't write it or read it."

The area where we encountered the young herdsman was deep on the south flank of the mountains that surround Palermo. The capital may have been less than an hour's drive once the main highway was reached, but this particular area is deep in those mountains and considered remote. Such areas, Alex said, are among the Sicilian language's last bastions.

The film *La terra trema,* Visconti's 1948 movie of life in the eastern Sicilian fishing village of Aci Trezza, is one of the last records of the original language.

"The only time you hear even a bit of Italian in that film is near the end when the boss man comes around," Alex says.

When I visited Aci Trezza some sixty-two years after the movie was released and met retired fisherman Salvatore Vicari, a child actor in the film, many of its older residents certainly could carry on conversations in Italian, but during the evening *passeggiata,* when I would sit on a bench in the town square and overhear the spirited banter of the older, retired fishermen sitting or strolling arm-in-arm nearby, their words were unrecognizable. Among one another, they were speaking the language they grew up with—a Catanesi dialect of Sicilian and a subdialect spoken only in the village. I remembered that the first, unrestored version of the film I had watched had subtitles—in both English *and* Italian!

Nowadays, educated Sicilians in the more urban areas primarily speak the language imposed on them in the late 1800s by their new national government. They speak a form of mainland Italian, particularly to visitors and, perhaps, in their business dealings. Among themselves, Alex says, they might speak a vernacular that is dialectic, with localized combinations of Sicilian and Italian words—a sort of new form of "proto-Sicilian" that has developed since the early 1900s.

He notes that Sicilians who fully embrace Italian—he referred specifically to his cousins who live in Rome—will occasionally slip into Sicilian phrases when they want to make an intimate statement or a particularly strong point about something that affects them deeply.

"You defer to Sicilian in moments of anger or of real tenderness. For those moments, there is an appropriate Sicilian phrase that is ingrained in us, that we heard since childhood, and that we fall back on at the appropriate moment."

One of Italy's most prominent authors—and one of the world's bestselling who is still writing in the twenty-first century—is the Sicilian Andrea Camilleri. Raised in the area around Agrigento on Sicily's south coast, Camilleri, now in his eighties, lives in Rome. Incredibly prolific, he has written, along with a few dozen other tracts, nearly twenty mysteries rife with subtle humor and featuring the laconic, skeptical, nearly burned-out detective Inspector Salvo Montalbano, whose only joys in life are found in the food he eats, his friendship with a few close comrades, and his often fractious relationship with his longtime, long-distance girlfriend, Livia.

Identified nearly everywhere as an "Italian" writer, Camilleri remains truly Sicilian; his books reflect the culture of his island of birth, the speech patterns of its residents, and their jaundiced view toward authority, lending authenticity to his characters.

Stephen Sartarelli, Camilleri's English translator, points out the translation challenges in Camilleri's writing. The Montalbano novels "are written in a language that is not 'just' Sicilian dialect, but a curious pastiche of the particular Sicilian of his native region (Agrigento province) combined with 'normal' Italian, contemporary slang, comic-stage dialogue, lofty literary flourishes, and the sort of manglings of proper Italian made by provincials who have never learned it correctly."

This kind of speech is retained in the popular Italian television series based on Camilleri's books. Actors deliver it rapid-fire; it is almost as if the person writing the subtitles for an English-speaking audience has trouble keeping up. Despite my barely basic knowledge of Italian, I have trouble recognizing most of the words the characters deliver.

One trait that I caught was the Sicilian way of putting the verb after the noun phrase. For example, whenever Montalbano knocks on a door and announces himself, he will say *"Montalbano sono!"* (Literally, "Montalbano I am!") Sartarelli chose "Montalbano here" for his English translations. A Sicilian-American friend, historian Leonard Chiarelli, overheard, while stopped along a Sicilian highway under repair, a classic example of this. Workers had just painted a white stripe along the road and had put up orange cones to keep motorists off the fresh paint. A woman ignored the cones and drove over the line, spreading paint across the asphalt. A worker turned to his colleague, shrugged his shoulders matter-of-factly, and stated, *"Fimmina era"* (A woman it was)—a typical male Sicilian remark with a typically Sicilian noun-verb construction.

Camilleri's style offers a challenge for all his translators: His work is translated into at least nine languages, including Greek and Japanese. Each translator must make different choices about how to render Sicilian speech patterns into the appropriate language so that readers in all of these disparate countries can understand what is going on.

Emanuela Gutkowski has written a study of the obstacles translators of Camilleri's novels face. She chose Camilleri's Montalbano novel *L'odore della notte* (*The Smell of the Night*) for her essay *Does the Night Smell the Same in Italy and in English Speaking Countries?* The reading of this interesting work shows the complexities of translating a Sicilian or a Sicilian-like Italian phrase into English. A classic example from *L'odore della notte*: *"Ho avuto una botta di culo incredibile"* becomes, when translated literally into English, "I had a terrible ass-hit," which means nothing to the English reader. So, in *The Smell of the Night*, the phrase becomes "I hit the goddamn jackpot," which is closer to the essential meaning of the Sicilian phrase.

Laura Sciascia, daughter of Leonardo Sciascia; Palermo. *(John Keahey)*

Anna Maria Sciascia, Leonardo Sciascia's youngest daughter, and her son, Vito Catalano; Noce, Racalmuto. *(John Keahey)*

Francesca Corrao, Leonardo Sciascia; Gibellina, ca. 1988. *(Courtesy of Francesca Corrao)*

Sciascia statue; Racalmuto. *(Steven R. McCurdy)*

Festival for the Madonna del Monte, Racalmuto. *(John Keahey)*

Racalmuto. *(John Keahey)*

Santo Spirito, site of the start of the War of
the Sicilian Vespers; Palermo. *(John Keahey)*

Inside Palazzo Lampedusa; Palermo. *(Courtesy of architects Gabriele Graziano and Alice Franzitta)*

Prisoner painting on cell wall in the Inquisitors Prison; Palermo. *(Steven R. McCurdy)*

Franco Bertolino, cart painter; Palermo. *(Steven R. McCurdy)*

Men playing *scopa*, Vucciria; Palermo. *(Steven R. McCurdy)*

Salvatore Tranchina; Scopello. *(Steven R. McCurdy)*

Pirandello home; Kaos. *(Steven R. McCurdy)*

Judge Giovanni Falcone with bodyguards; Marseilles, France, 1986, six years before his Mafia hit. *(Gerard Fouet-AFP-Getty Images)*

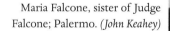

Maria Falcone, sister of Judge Falcone; Palermo. *(John Keahey)*

Salvatore Vicari, who played Alfio the boatboy in *La terra trema*; Aci Trezza *(Steven R. McCurdy)*

Good Friday; Enna. *(Steven R. McCurdy)*

Camilleri's work represents not only escapist mystery-novel fare—the novels follow a predictable formula and can be read quickly—but they are enlightening for the insight they show into the Sicilian mind-set: Often people don't report a crime because they feel it is none of their business or they don't trust the police not to consider them suspects. Public officials are often involved in dirty work. Sometimes the guilty are never caught, even though the police know who is responsible, because they are ordered by higher-ups to back off. Police are held in low esteem by the general populace, who call policemen *sbirro*, which, Gutkowski tells us, is an "untranslatable term . . . used as an insult in a place where the state is perceived as an enemy, often missing if help is required, yet always present if it has to arrest the underdog." That may be true for Sicilians' use of the word; in Italian, it simply translates as "cop."

Fortunately, Montalbano is a "good" cop who stands up to authority, usually catches murderers and terrorists through Sherlock Holmes–like deduction, and is generally faithful to his girlfriend, Livia, despite a lot of temptations. He also has the respect of his colleagues and many of the citizens of his town, Vigàta, a fictional Sicilian city modeled after Camilleri's birthplace, the Agrigento suburb Porto Empedocle.

In one telling passage in *The Snack Thief,* one of the more emotional reads in the Montalbano series, Camilleri captures a moment that offers a major clue as to how Sicilians view relationships. His trusted associate Fazio, knowing his boss better than anyone else on the small Vigàta police force, takes the initiative to do a task without being told, saying, "So I figured out what you wanted me to do, and I did it."

The inspector "felt moved. This was real friendship, Sicilian friendship, the kind based on intuition, on what was left unsaid. With a true friend, one never needs to ask, because the other understands on his own and acts accordingly."

City officials in Porto Empedocle, eager to capture the tourist trade of Montalbano fans, commissioned a life-size statue of the fictional detective that, in reality, looks nothing like the actor who plays the television series Montalbano. The statue is similar in style to the statue of Sicilian writer Leonardo Sciascia in nearby Racalmuto; both were done by the same sculptor, Giuseppe Agnello. It stands on a sidewalk, posed like a plainclothes cop leaning against a light post. Ironically, Montalbano's gaze is directed across and down the street toward a bigger-than-life statue of Luigi Pirandello, also a son of Porto Empedocle and winner of the 1934 Nobel Prize for literature.

In correspondence with Camilleri, I asked why Montalbano holds allure for so many readers from so many different cultures. His answer, which he likely has given many times, was simple and illuminating: "I think he owns many characteristics of good relationships. He is the friend I would love to have."

Most linguists agree that the Romance languages began to evolve in the various provinces of the dying Roman Empire sometime around the fifth century A.D. Joseph F. Privitera, in his slim volume *Sicilian: The Oldest Romance Language,* writes that "with the disappearance of the Roman administration, the speakers of Romance vernacular from different parts of the former Empire became increasingly unable to understand each other."

The Latin of the Romans was being displaced, and "the new Latin-derived languages known as Gallo Romance, Italo-Romance, Hispano-Romance, Rheto-Romance, and Balkan Romance" began to emerge, and peoples who spoke one of these forms could not understand those who spoke another form. Eventually, these languages developed into what we know as Spanish, French, Tuscan, Calabrian, and so forth.

Here, historian Privitera tosses a bomb into the discussion. He asserts that Sicilian did not come out of this period. It was already there and had been for more than a thousand years.

"It is clear," writes Privitera, that by the year 200 B.C., "Proto Sicilian had already emerged and had been cemented as the new Sicilian language." This position, of course, is not held by some linguists who believe the language came after the Normans took control of the island in the eleventh and twelfth centuries. This was the time when the new rulers supplemented the once Arab-speaking population with immigrants from mainland Italy—from Tuscany to Calabria.

Privitera defends his thesis by pointing to the large number of words—about one-seventh of the five thousand offered in a Sicilian dictionary—that come from Greek. So at the third century B.C. in ancient Sicily, during the time of Roman domination, there were four major influences among island speakers: administrative Roman Latin, the people's Latin found among the general populace, plus Greek, and probably Carthaginian from the pre-Roman, North African colonists.

Following the Romans were the Byzantines from the east, the Arabs, the Normans and, briefly, the Germans and the French before the longer-lasting Spanish arrived.

Alex Caldiero says that in the separate Italian language,

any words that show Greek, Spanish, or Arabic influence came from Sicilian. As a side note, he points out that while many Sicilians today consider themselves to have evolved from some of the various conquering people—western Sicilians often claim Arabic patrimony, for example—many on the island's eastern flank consider themselves more Greek than anything else. He mentions his ancestral village of Licodia Eubéa, in the province of Catania, built by Greek colonists on an earlier Sicel site and inhabited prior to 600 B.C.

"We've seen them all," he says of the original native peoples and the various conquerors who swept across the island over the last three thousand years. And he recalls hearing, during visits as a young man to the place of his birth as recently as the early 1960s, different pronunciations of Sicilian words and phrases from one end of the small village to the other. That's how intensely local—even neighborhood by neighborhood—dialects could be at that time. Those differences are now disappearing as older generations pass on.

For a quick understanding of how Sicilian differs from Italian, I turned to an article written by Leonardo Vigo sometime in the early 1870s. The piece, which appeared in *Raccolta amplissima di canti populari Siciliani*, which literally means "very large collection of popular Sicilian songs," was translated by Caldiero and included in the appendix of his unpublished *Grammar*. It gives a quick summary of the differences between the two languages, showing how, as certain Sicilian words were incorporated into the Italian language over the centuries, Italian speakers and writers modified them.

The biggest influence in the language's development beyond 200 B.C. was Arabic.

María Rosa Menocal, in *The Arab Role in Medieval Literary History,* points to evidence of the influence Arabic had on Sicilian writing and even administration. "Arabic was the language of learning as well as the native tongue of Frederick II [the Holy Roman Emperor and king of Sicily based in Palermo] some two hundred years after the Arabs had lost all political power in Sicily and at a time when Frederick was actually carrying out certain repressive measures against Muslims there."

Most intriguing is the fact that there is no future tense in Sicilian. This could also come from the Arabic language that, even today, has no future tense. Twentieth-century Sicilians have adopted the Italian, which has a definite future tense as, of course, does the English that immigrant Sicilians embraced in the great diaspora of that century's earliest years. As Alex points out, those immigrants were suddenly immersed in a culture that believes you can be anything you want, that you have the power to shape your future.

"This is where grammar reflects the inner life of the people and the way they construct their reality.

"Remember," he says, "Sicilians have always been dominated by other cultures; they never had self-determination as a people. Their blood constantly told them that they have no control over their lives, that everything was controlled by the will of God."

This attitude is reflected in numerous short stories by Giovanni Verga. His peasants, facing one failed crop after another because of drought or pestilence, of invaders laying waste to the land, bemoan the fact that they must not have prayed hard enough to the Madonna, or that God, not nature, is punishing them; or that when malaria had killed the father, the breadwinner, or the mother, or most of the children, especially the boys who could have helped in the fields, that it is "God's will."

In the story "Malaria," contained in Verga's *Little Novels of Sicily,* neighbor Carmine who lived by a lake where mosquitoes flourished

> had lost all his five children, one after the other . . . three boys and two girls. But the boys died just when they were getting old enough to earn their bread. So now he was used to it; and as the fever got the last boy under, after having harassed him for two or three years, he didn't spend another farthing, neither for sulfate or decoctions, but drew off some good wine and set himself to make all the good fish stews he could think of, to provoke the appetite of the sick youth.

It was all to no avail, of course. The last boy died, and the survivors "bent like a hook with brokenheartedness," went on, the story continues. A neighbor, Nanni the carter, summed it up simply: "The lake gives and the lake takes away. . . . What's the good, brother?"

Thus, the future is not something you can *will.* Pre-twentieth-century Sicilians deal in the future as an obligation, Alex says. "Instead of saying 'I will do it,' they say, *'l'aiâ farsi.'* [I have to do it.] It's all in that one grammatical difference." Instead of saying "I will sing," it's "I have to sing." Instead of "I will bring it," it's "I am about to bring it."

One of the more surprising discoveries about the Sicilian language is the influence it had in the development of Italian as a national language. We know that the Tuscan language in which Dante wrote *The Divine Comedy* in the early fourteenth century eventually became the national language of Italy. Less known is the role that spoken, sung, and written Sicilian played in the development of that language.

Around the mid-thirteenth century, wandering troubadours from France made their way into Italy and Sicily. This was the time of that relatively enlightened Holy Roman Emperor, Frederick II—a man responsive to artistic tastes in his court in Palermo, from where he ruled Italy, Germany, and Burgundy.

The troubadours wrote and sang poetry, and their arrival had a tremendous influence on Sicilian poets who found the form of troubadour-style verse compatible with Sicilian lyric poetry—poetry of the heart, or courtly love.

Sicilian poet Giacomo da Lentini, a notary in Frederick's court, and others entered the scene and took this poetic form to a new level, creating the sonnet, which later spread to Europe and England, where Shakespeare used it with great success.

At some point, the works of the so-called Sicilian School of poets came to the attention of such notables as Dante and Petrarch. In the early fourteenth century, some believe, they incorporated into their works the style and a significant portion of the Sicilian language that had been adopted into Tuscan, including Dante's *The Divine Comedy*.

Thanks in part to many of the Arab-influenced works that Frederick II made available in 1227 to the university in Bologna, then Italy's intellectual capital, "Dante may indeed have been strongly affected [by] . . . the whole Arabic cultural and ideological entity . . . ," Menocal writes. After all, Arabs had written about Muhammad's trip to the otherworld. Why shouldn't Dante Christianize such a story?

The editor of the anthology *The Poetry of the Sicilian School*, Frede Jensen, in his introduction, underscores this connection in a more general way: "The decisive role of the Sicilians in the development of a refined poetry in an Italian vernacular can hardly be over-emphasized. The Sicilian School is the fountainhead from which a splendid tradition has never ceased to flow."

Menocal puts an end to the debate, at least as far as she is concerned, over who influenced whom: "Under his [Frederick's] patronage was born and thrived . . . the first lyric poetry in an Italian vernacular." She then translates a poem that may have been heard "in the hallways and *salotti* [salons] of Frederick's courts at Palermo and elsewhere":

> *I have been killed by the looks of*
> *women like statues, between the*
> *whiteness of teeth and lips of dark*
> *purple;*
> *After having said that my youthful folly*
> *was now over, here it is once again*
> *making me insane with love and passion;*
> *In her face I have seen the moon,*
> *smiling with her radiant look. Did she*

appear to me, I ask my eyes, while I was
awake or in a dream?
That look is a true mystery! It makes my
body sick, but it also cures it.

(The Italian translation from the Arabic is from Rizzitano, 1958; English translation from the Italian is Menocal's.)

I read this and imagine a couple of older men, perhaps in their sixties or seventies, sitting in a café drinking coffee and admiring the young waitresses who serve them week after week. These men realize their youth is gone, and they do not delude themselves, knowing the young women have no interest in them beyond getting the job done in a friendly manner. But the pair can admire from the distance of multiple decades and, for a moment, relive their own pasts. It's a universal theme, as true today as then, that probably goes well beyond even the time of the early Arab-Sicilian poets.

This example is but a single fragment of Arabic poetry, Menocal informs us, from a "reputed twenty thousand verses written by a hundred and seventy poets . . . [that were] "written in Sicily, from the tenth through the thirteenth centuries." The tenth was the last full century of Arab domination of the island, and Sicilian Arab poets were writing there and in southern Italy for another three hundred years. Most of this poetry has been lost.

Menocal finally emphasizes: "This lapse in our knowledge of the period, of the flavor of court life, of this other world that existed within the same walls as the one we think we know so well, is a serious one."

TWELVE

The Mafia

It was invented by man, and as all human creations, it
has a beginning. And it will have an end.
— Giovanni Falcone, anti-
Mafia judge, murdered
May 23, 1992

Giovanni Falcone, the judge who was blown up, along with
his wife and three bodyguards, while driving at high speed
along a stretch of highway southwest of Palermo, never
wanted to predict *when* the Mafia would fade away—only that
he believed it would. He knew that it is like a festering cold
sore that periodically and painfully erupts and then subsides,
waiting just under the skin for the next eruption. "The octopus is inside all of us," he once said.

Their deaths, along with the violent deaths of a handful of
other judges and police officials, launched a movement that
drove the once rural family bands back beneath the surface of
Sicilian society. As each mafioso is captured, the state confiscates

their property and, in many cases, it is turned over to the public for its use.

In mid-August 2010, for example, Sicilian police announced the arrest of a former Mafia chieftain's associate and the confiscation of more than $1,000,000,000 worth of assets that will be given to anti-Mafia and other community groups. A hideout of one boss is now a bed-and-breakfast. Another is a retreat for journalists. Insurance offices once owned as a Mafia money-laundering front now house, in Palermo, the Fondazione Giovanni e Francesca Falcone. In late December 2010, the anti-Mafia group Addiopizzo moved its offices into a large Palermo apartment a crime boss had once owned.

Falcone was part of a generation of new judges who rejected the social relations between Mafia and magistrates "that were commonplace in their fathers' day," and this would allow them "to distance themselves from those they would prosecute," say American academics Jane C. Schneider and Peter T. Schneider in their essay "Giovanni Falcone, Paolo Borsellino and the procura of Palermo."

The new breed of prosecutors formed themselves into a pool that tried new ways of building cases against mafiosi, abandoning methods that had long failed. The Schneiders, who also wrote the book *Reversible Destiny: Mafia, Antimafia, and the Struggle for Palermo,* tell us that the jurists cultivated Mafia turncoats, or *pentiti,* willing to testify in open court. Falcone, drawing on his early experience as a bankruptcy court judge, developed methods of scouring financial records that laid out the Mafia's money trails.

The result of all this work, periodically punctuated by

Mafia hits on some of his colleagues, was the so-called 1986–87 Maxi Trial in Palermo involving 475 defendants. Some 344 mafiosi were found guilty, others were tried in absentia, and more than 2,500 years of prison sentences were handed out. Other trials were held in various Sicilian cities with similar results. The Mafia was cornered. The bosses went underground, some hiding out for years in the Sicilian countryside.

The toll on the personal lives of the judges was phenomenal. Some of the men and their families, for their safety, had to withdraw from the world. In an interview with Falcone shortly before his death, Deborah Puccio-Den reports that the jurist acknowledged that "the thought of death is always my companion." In preparation for the Maxi Trial, the Schneiders tell us that Falcone and his then-fiancée, magistrate Francesca Morvillo, whom he later married, and her mother, together with another judge and life-long friend, Paolo Borsellino and his family, were housed on the island of Asinara, off the northwest corner of Sardinia.

The irony here is overwhelming: To jail mafiosi, prosecutors were forced to set up house in a maximum-security prison, under guard around the clock.

That same summer prior to the trial, a handful of police officers were murdered. The Schneiders write that "the more the police went after the fugitives, the more the Mafia would attempt to destroy the police."

As if the pressures against the prosecutors were not enough, in the midst of the Maxi Trial another shot was fired, this one a literary blast from none other than revered Sicilian author

Leonardo Sciascia. He wrote, in the Milan daily *Corriere della Sera,* that he saw the prosecutors as politically ambitious men, calling them *professionisti dell'antimafia,* or anti-Mafia professionals. He particularly went after Paolo Borsellino, who in earlier days had neo-fascist leanings and thereby offended the strongly antifascist Sciascia, a well-known and much beloved leftist. His pen was powerful; a champion of the people, Sicilians listened to him.

Borsellino had been promoted, over the heads of more senior magistrates, to a position as prosecutor in Marsala on Sicily's southwest coast. This proved, in Sciascia's mind, that the judge was in the anti-Mafia game only for the advancement. The writer's treatise "created a storm of shocked protest," the Schneiders wrote. Then, just four days later, Sciascia retracted his allegations and, according to Alexander Stille in his book *Excellent Cadavers,* apologized to Borsellino.

I ask the murdered judge's sister, Maria Falcone, sitting in her office at the Falcone Foundation, about Sciascia's attack. "I'm glad you asked me that," she says firmly. "I appreciated Sciascia as a writer. He opened for us a road against the Mafia. [But] he really didn't understand what the Mafia was—as Giovanni understood it during his investigations."

Her face clouds over during this part of the conversation. She obviously is bothered by the impact Sciascia's remarks had on her brother and on Borsellino.

"When he [Sciascia] dubbed them 'the professionals of the anti-Mafia,' Giovanni was very pained by that appellative. And what Sciascia didn't know [about Borsellino] was that he left Palermo for Marsala because he had three children; he needed a bit more tranquillity because of his family." In other words, the pressure of the Mafia prosecutions—the time spent in isolation under twenty-four-hour guard—was getting to the judge and those closest to him.

Unlike Borsellino, Falcone and his wife had no children; their lives, Maria Falcone told me, were devoted to the anti-Mafia crusade. "Out of the presumptuousness of the writer, Sciascia never understood the work of the magistrates."

The author died in 1989, three years before the bomb that killed Maria Falcone's brother, her sister-in-law, and the three policemen. How Sciascia would have reacted to that tragedy remains buried with him in the *cimitero di Racalmuto*.

Despite the apology, the damage was done. Sciascia's attack helped to fuel other criticisms of the judges and investigators who some people thought were violating civil rights of many Sicilians in their quest for bosses and their henchmen. At this point, Mafia bosses could have retreated from public view and let public opinion come to their rescue, but they did not. Killings increased in intensity.

Despite the great success of the Maxi Trial, Falcone came under attack; his group was shut down as part of criminal-justice reforms. He continued to work, but funds were short; support for his efforts remained unenthusiastic.

Then, in March 1992, all should have been well: The verdicts in the Maxi Trial were upheld by Italy's highest court. That decision was "a dose of poison for the mafiosi, who felt like wounded animals," write the Schneiders, quoting a *pentito*. "That's why they carried out the massacres."

Two months after the high court ruling, the Falcone party was riding in a high-speed caravan between Palermo and the airport that today bears his and Borsellino's names. Near the exit to the town of Capaci, a Palermo suburb, "their armored cars passed over a culvert where mafiosi had hidden five hundred kilograms [more than half a ton] of explosives, packed into plastic drums and covered by a mattress." The explosion was set off by a remote-controlled signal triggered by a man sitting on a nearby hillside.

In the immediate aftermath of those five deaths, a sense of hopelessness seemed to pervade Palermo and the rest of Sicily. During mass anti-Mafia demonstrations in Palermo in days that followed, Rosaria Schifani, the wife of one of the murdered bodyguards, spoke to the crowd, saying the Mafia had turned Palermo into "a city of blood. There is no love here; there is no love here; there is no love here!" Video of her tortured remarks and the sound of agony in her voice are difficult to see or hear, as are the words of Falcone's fellow anti-Mafia judge Paolo Borsellino.

During a tribute to his colleague, best friend, and childhood playmate, Borsellino said Falcone's work was "shattering the accepting attitude of living side by side with the Mafia, which is the real strength of the Mafia."

Fewer than two months later, on a hot July Sunday afternoon, Borsellino, with five bodyguards, climbed out of his armored car that had just pulled up in front of his mother's Palermo house. A massive explosion from a bomb planted in a nearby parked car laid waste to the street. All six men were killed.

Borsellino's words—along with the cumulative effect on Sicilians of the Mafia hits on the judges, combined with years of almost weekly hits on competing mafiosi, judges, Carabinieri, police officers and, in some cases, shop owners who refused to pay protection money—finally lifted ordinary Sicilians out of their denial. Posters appeared that laid out such statements as YOU DID NOT KILL THEM. THEIR IDEAS WILL KEEP WALKING ON OUR LEGS. Or, YOU CAN KILL OUR BODIES BUT NOT OUR SOULS. The relentless violence, capped by the deaths of Falcone and Borsellino, became too much to bear. *La cosa nostra* had gone too far. And it kept going.

Other magistrates and policemen were killed. The following year, bombs hit targets in Rome and elsewhere, including a bomb at Florence's Uffizi Galleries. Authorities increased pressure on Mafia leaders but also started directing their efforts toward prosecuting compliant political leaders and some prominent businesspeople. This sweep was known as Operation Clean Hands. Several thousand Italian business executives and politicians were investigated. A score or more of Italy's leading businesses were probed. More than a thousand individuals had corruption charges brought against them, many of those charges to be summarily dismissed months, even years later. A dozen committed suicide.

The backlash to this process led prosecutors to be put on short leashes once again: Such prominent citizens, except for the most egregious offenders, are almost forbidden fruit for law enforcers in Italy. But the Mafia, if not compliant politicians, remains under siege. Now, nearly twenty years after Falcone's death, most Mafia bosses have been arrested, along with their accountants and fellow "men of honor."

"Almost on a daily basis there have been arrests," the martyred judge's sister says. "All the biggest heads of the Mafia are in prison now. The last one who is still a fugitive is Matteo Messina Denaro . . . who at this moment is considered to be the *capo* [boss]. They are burning the ground around him because they recently arrested people who are very close to him; they are getting to him."

Palermo's chief prosecutor Francesco Messineo, speaking to a reporter for the Italian news service ANSA in March 2010, said that the "aim of their strategy against Messina Denaro was to 'dry up the water he swims in.'"

The history of the Mafia dates back to the mid-eighteenth century, with roots that go back even further. But it began to take form as we know it following Unification in 1861, after the northern Italian military leader Giuseppe Garibaldi and his one-thousand-strong Red Shirts drove the Bourbons out of Sicily. As Garibaldi diverted his attention to the Bourbon rulers still ensconced in Naples, banditry filled the ruling vacuum and claimed the Sicilian countryside. Brigands attacked police, kidnapped rich landowners, stole livestock, and often brutally executed their opponents.

The term "Mafia" was not in much use in those days. But some of the individuals in the 1860s who evolved into that loosely constructed confederation were known then, as they are now, as "men of honor." Even Lampedusa, in *The Leopard*, uses the euphemistic phrase. Near the end of the book, in scenes not used in the film, Father Pirrone is visiting family members and dealing with his sister Sarina's emotions over her teenage daughter's unwed pregnancy. If the girl's father, Vicenzino, knew she was pregnant, he would kill her.

"He'll kill me, too, he will, because I didn't tell him; he's what they call 'a man of honor'!" the sister laments. Lampedusa makes note of Vicenzino's "perpetual swelling of the right trouser pocket where he kept a knife" and how this made it "obvious at once that Vicenzino was 'a man of honor,' one of those violent cretins capable of any havoc."

A Pirandello one-act play "The Other Son," which became an episode in the Taviani brothers' film *Kaos,* graphically illustrates the horror of the banditry that swept rural Sicily during the post-Unification years. In the late nineteenth century, groups that later evolved into the Mafia worked with the police to help rid the countryside of the bandits, whose presence likely threatened growing Mafia control. This further endeared the "men of honor" to the peasantry.

As for the police, Alexander Stille writes: "In exchange, the government allowed the Mafia to continue its more subtle form of economic crime." This set a stage for cooperation among police, politicians, and the Mafia that lasted well into the twentieth century.

Eventually the state, in the 1870s, cracked down. Bandits were captured but, the Schneiders tell us, "crimes against property continued; indeed, animal rustling flourished with the growth of urban markets." The reaction by landowners and civic authorities to this continued economic mayhem, then, led to the unholy alliance with the early Mafia families, whose members were made up of "an incipient entrepreneurial class of carters, muleteers, itinerant merchants, bandits, and herders . . . Forming themselves into *fratellanze,* or 'brotherhoods,' . . . they offered protection for a price."

From the mid-1860s on, the word "Mafia" began to enter the Italian vocabulary. There is a lot of confusion over the word's origins. According to the Web site sicilianculture.com, some believe it derives from the Arabic *mahias,* meaning a bold man or a braggart, or from *Ma 'afir,* the name of the Saracen tribe that ruled Palermo. A third theory of Arab origin relates mafia to *maha,* a quarry or a cave in a rock. The *mafie,* the [tuffa] caves in the Marsala region, served the persecuted Saracens as hiding places and later provided hide-outs for other fugitives . . . rebellious Sicilians had hidden out in the *mafie* near Marsala and had therefore subsequently . . . been called mafiosi, the people from the mafia.

Other sources believe differently. Historian Peppi Pillitteri believes it comes from the Arabic-based words *ma 'fiu,* which originally meant "I can do it." He continues, "Like a weed, secret organizations found fertile land in the despair and suffering of Sicily, always trying to better one's lot in life by rebelling or taking the law into one's own hands."

Whatever the origins, these men were hired by beleaguered landowners to provide security in the fields against rustling or the stealing of crops. Banditry, under pressure from these new, increasingly powerful protectors, eventually diminished. It is from this period that the image of the field guard, which gained prominence in the first *Godfather* film, was of a man wearing the black pants, white shirt, black vest, and Sicilian cap and carrying a sawed-off shotgun, known as a *lupara.*

Surprisingly, one of the best, most concise explanations of these early beginnings of the Mafia comes from Booker T. Washington, the American educator who visited Italy and Sicily in 1910, and who published two years later a classic book, *The Man Farthest Down.* Washington compared the Mafia to "the White Caps, the Night Riders, and the lynchers in our own country, as a means of private vengeance."

He, of course, was looking at the Sicilian phenomenon in the context of his own experience by referring to the Ku Klux Klan. In reality, the Klan had nothing much in common with the Mafia other than the brutality with which it conducted its business. Washington sums up the Mafia's origins simply.

> In the course of time, these field guards became associated in a sort of clan or guild . . . No property owner dared install a guard without consent of the chief . . . the mere knowledge that a certain plantation was under the protection of the Mafia was in itself almost sufficient to insure it from attack.

Rural Sicilians therefore came to rely on the Mafia, rather than the police, "to ferret out and punish the criminals." If they needed someone to settle a dispute with a neighbor or to find out who may have rustled their cattle or sheep, they went to the head of their local family, not the authorities, and this *capo* decided what to do. The winning party then owed the boss a favor, to be collected at some unknown time in the future. The loser accepted the decision and kept quiet. To protest meant problems, perhaps even his death, for him and his family.

The close relationships among public officials, police, politicians, and mafiosi grew. "By controlling substantial blocks of votes, Mafia groups helped elect politicians who, in turn, helped them," Stille writes. It solidified the Mafia's unfettered control of the island and kept generations of politicians and public officials in its hip pocket.

An autobiographical, mid-twentieth-century tale of how the Mafia worked can be found in "The Mafia at My Back," published in an anthology, *Mafia and Outlaw Stories: From Italian Life and Literature*. Sicilian writer Livia De Stefani (1913–1991) describes how the *capo* of the local Mafia clan, midway through the twentieth century, gained control over her family estate, Virzì, near Camporeale in western Sicily.

At one point, when she refused to replace her own trusted field guard with a person of the *capo's* choosing, she arrived home to find her threshing floor and her entire harvest of straw bales and wheat in flames. De Stefani had been warned, in a letter, that such an event would happen unless she acquiesced. She had ignored it. When the fire erupted, she knew it was a direct message from the local Mafia chieftain, Vincenzo Rimi.

The investigating Carabinieri officer, a northern Italian who had been posted to the far south and who never had been able to make a single inroad against the local Mafia, begged her to tell him that the fire was intentionally set. Both knew it was. She refused, saying only, "Spontaneous combustion, sir. Precisely that."

She writes, "He spread his arms open, let them drop to his sides like logs, and turned his back on me. Only as he got on the seat of his motorcycle did he make a sign of goodbye, stiffly giving me a military salute."

De Stefani later had a meeting with the Mafia boss and agreed that he would appoint her field guard. The one concession she got was that the *capo* would allow her to keep her long-time field guard through the fall harvest, several months away. Then, the crime boss's man would take over. When that time came, her faithful guard knew exactly what would happen. He emptied the shells from his *lupara*, stomped them into the ground with his hobnail boots, turned the weapon over to the police authorities, and went back to being a sharecropper.

What was her reaction to answering the Carabinieri officer about the fire's origins the way she did? "I did it, though I felt sorrow . . . which gave me a sense of malaise that still comes over me to this day." The night after the fire, she was hit by an inescapable realization.

> I was not the owner of Virzì. I was simply the one who paid the taxes, who vainly pronounced that this must be done, not that. In short, I was a pathetic puppet. Someone else was wielding the command on my land; the reins of power in the entire province—and maybe beyond—were in the hands of someone who remained unnamed.

It is precisely this kind of acquiescence, this kind of acceptance, of the Mafia's influence over the decades that troubles Sicilian journalist Angelo Vecchio, who has been writing about the Mafia for forty years. I met Angelo one warm afternoon at an outdoor café in Palermo. We were joined by interpreter Conchita Vecchio. They are not related, Brooklyn-born Conchita told me, although they have roots in the same town, Licata, on Sicily's south coast. Angelo worked in Catania for the now defunct newspaper *Giornale del Sud* and, at the time of our meeting, in Palermo for *Giornale de Sicilia*.

I tell him about a Sicilian businessman I met who claims he does not pay protection money, known in Sicily as *pizzo*, or euphemistically, "a beak full." The businessman had told me he somehow befriended the neighborhood boss. They occasionally talk when they meet, say, in the local barbershop. And as a result of this, the businessman is exempted, and his business is never bothered. I did not ask this businessman if he was ever expected to return the favor.

Angelo takes no prisoners in his view of such a "friendship."

"Everyone pays," he said bluntly. "If you don't pay [under an unspoken agreement with a *capo*], you are a friend of mobsters—you are one of them."

He recognizes that there is a movement in Palermo among business organizations, Addiopizzo, whose adherents refuse to pay. He said that businesspeople can seek police protection when they take a stand against the Mob. Journalists also can be given police protection, something authorities have offered to do for Angelo when he has written particularly hard-hitting news articles.

He said he always refuses the offer. This despite an attack many years ago in Catania, where a man walked up to his car while Angelo was stopped at an intersection and attempted to slash him with a knife, only landing a bad cut on his arm before Angelo was able to drive off. He had published, the day before, an article about Mafia involvement in international car smuggling.

Messages not to publish come in different ways, Angelo said.

"Someone will make a phone call to the newspaper, quietly

suggesting that the article not run. I get these every now and then. I don't pay much attention to these things. One night, when opening the door of my house, a man I had never seen before greeted me warmly, as if he knew me. He asked me if I was 'still writing about old things. Why do you do that?' he said to me. That's the way they warned me—a friendly threat.

"If the Mafia wants to hurt you, they will simply kill you. But now there is not much killing going on; the Mafia is laying low. I just don't worry about it."

With certainty, someone will step into the shoes of the current boss of bosses, Matteo Messina Denaro, if and when he is found and arrested. Perhaps the Sicilian Mafia will splinter and become like the Neapolitan *camorra*—a disjointed collection of families operating independently from one another. In other words, the *camorra* has no *capo* for authorities to focus on; it is like an octopus—when one tentacle is cut off, another grows in its place.

This, according to Maria Falcone, is what makes that criminal organization—now far more violent than the Sicilian Mafia—a harder nut to crack. The *camorra* is thought to have its origins in the sixteenth or seventeenth centuries, when southern Italy and Sicily were under Spanish rule.

Then there is the Calabria-based organization known as the 'Ndrangheta, from a Greek word *andragathía,* meaning "heroism" or "honor" or "virtue"—still more ironic euphemisms. Maria Falcone describes this group as the most violent of the southern crime organizations. Its strength is its worldwide drug operations, which have billions of dollars at stake.

And to the east in Italy's boot, in the region of Puglia, still another criminal organization exists, the Sacra Corona Unità, which means the "sacred united crown." All these loosely confederated organizations continue to grow and become far more violent than the twenty-first-century Sicilian version of La Cosa Nostra ("our thing"), which grew out of the rural Sicilian landscape of the mid-nineteenth century.

The fact that it has taken more than a century for police authorities to make headway into Sicilian crime families undoubtedly stems from the refusal, for many generations, of ordinary citizens to acknowledge the Mafia's existence. A Sicilian-American friend, born and raised in the United States and who visited extended family on the island in the 1960s as a teenager, tells how he asked about the Mafia. "There is no such thing!" scoffed his Sicilian aunts and uncles, who then hastened to change the subject. Such denial mirrors a typical Sicilian response: "I know nothing, I have said nothing, and if what I said is said, I didn't say it!"

Maria Falcone hopes that the spate of arrests of leading Mafia chieftains in recent years will work to change that attitude, but she recognizes that the fear of Mafia power is deeply entrenched among ordinary Sicilians.

"For you Americans who take into high regard the state and the nation, it is difficult to understand the normal Sicilian," she told me, her piercing southern eyes—her strongest resemblance to her martyred brother—pinning me to the chair. "Sicilians do not have the sense of the state within them. For centuries, Sicily has always been dominated by foreigners, even [northern Italians]. Giovanni [Falcone] was called the 'Sicilian Anomaly' because he had this great sense of the state within him, which his fellow Sicilians didn't have."

She says part of her work, and the work of the Falcone Foundation, which she started just months after his death, is to instill in Sicilian and Italian schoolchildren, through educational programs, "the values Giovanni believed in, especially democracy. Children and young people still haven't understood that. We don't have this."

Some Sicilians believe progress is being made, especially with schoolchildren. Each year around the May 23 anniversary of Falcone's death, thousands of youngsters and teens from throughout Italy arrive on ships docking at Palermo's waterfront. They arrive to pay homage to the anti-Mafia judge and to attend Falcone Foundation–sponsored conferences stressing the importance of the fight against the Mafia.

In late March 2010, during Easter Week, a time when most children are out of school, I witnessed a succession of groups of local young people visiting the so-called L'Albero Falcone, or "Falcone tree" growing in front of the apartment once occupied by Falcone and his wife, Francesca Morvillo, forty-seven. It is a large magnolia tree that has become so big it almost blocks the front stoop at Via Notarbartolo, 23A. Its trunk was covered with hand-lettered posters and short missives penned by schoolchildren and others.

Three weeks after my March 2010 visit, the tree was vandalized overnight. All of the messages and posters disappeared. Then, three months later, on July 18, the eighteenth anniversary of Borsellino's death, vandals smashed life-size plaster of Paris statues of Falcone and Borsellino that had been set up the day before along one of Palermo's main boulevards, Via della Libertà. The statues were models that were eventually to be cast in bronze. The midday attack was witnessed by several people; no one would come forward with what they saw. Vandals elsewhere in the city ripped down posters announcing a march in memory of the two judges.

Deborah Puccio-Den, writing a chapter in the book *Shrines and Pilgrimage in the Modern World: New Itineraries into the Sacred*, talks about how Giovanni Falcone, since his death, has become "the object of a civic cult." She says people post crudely lettered signs on the tree saying, "You are my saint; pray for us." The May 23 ceremonies are commonly referred to as pilgrimages.

Puccio-Den makes a case that the martyred judges are being held, in the Sicilian psyche, to the same level as Palermo's patron saint, Santa Rosalia, that twelfth-century Norman aristocrat who left the material world and lived on a mountaintop outside of Palermo. She became Palermo's savior, with the faithful believing she ended the plague. Now she shares that role with Falcone and Borsellino, says Puccio-Den, who urges her readers to look at the judges' isolation on the Sardinian prison island during preparations for the Maxi Trial and compare that with Rosalia's self-imposed isolation on a mountaintop.

A small suite of offices, set anonymously in an outer neighborhood on Palermo's western fringe, announces in tiny script on a lone doorway that it is the home of Addiopizzo, Goodbye Protection Money. The offices, which nine months after my March 2010 visit were moved to the former Mafia boss's apartment, also housed Libero Futuro, Free Future. Both are made up of groups of Palermo merchants who have banded together and refuse to pay protection money. Similar in some respects to chambers of commerce in the United States, they also give merchants solidarity against yielding to the long-held tradition of paying "a beak full." Their slogan: *Pago chi non pago* (I pay those who do not pay), meaning I give my money to businesses that refuse to submit to Mafia intimidation.

I met with Enrico Colajanni, one of the *anti-pizzo* organizers. He tells me the groups have 450 members; their goal is one thousand. They hold street fairs featuring the products and goods of its members as a way of recruiting new ones. Eventually they want to take the message to villages, towns, and cities beyond Palermo.

Colajanni said that for fifteen years after Falcone's and Borsellino's deaths "nothing happened" against the Mafia. Then, in 2004, seven people anonymously came up with the Addiopizzo concept. "They decided this situation of protection payments is impossible. We have to do something.

"The first message was that people who pay have no dignity. It was posted on stickers placed anonymously across the city." He said the first year, one hundred merchants signed up. Then, in 2007, Libero Futuro was organized to bring together buyers and sellers.

But it wasn't easy. When the participating merchants denounced paying *pizzo*, "banks closed the door to them getting loans, saying their risk is going up." The group's goal: "We have to open this door," Colajanni said.

While banks may not be cooperating, authorities are. Police continue to give twenty-four-hour security once a business denounces *pizzo*. Business owners can call the police to come to drive them to work. Ironically, a major hindrance is that "there are a lot of people here who are more afraid of the police than the Mafia."

"There has been no violence so far, and our membership has leveled off," said Colajanni.

Can such a campaign be effective against such an entrenched, albeit under-siege criminal organization? Colajanni understands the question and acknowledges the reality.

"*Pizzo* is a small part of the Mafia's income. Compared to drugs and other rackets, it doesn't amount to much. But they enforce it to keep power over everyone; it's a way to keep control over the people. It's like a state within a state."

Then, he adds a chilling thought. "Right now, the Mafia strategy is to lay low. It has suspended committing the violent murders of the past. But, given a change of strategy, it could begin again, targeting us, the merchants, the police, and the prosecutors. We all know this and live with this. But if we are many, we are surer of success."

THIRTEEN

The Forge of Hephaestus

> *. . . And Sicily's land by Aetna's craigs*
> *Was filled with streams of fire which no man could*
> *Approach, and groaned throughout its length . . .*
> —Carcinus, tragic Greek poet,
> quoted by
> Diodorus Siculus,
> Greek-Sicilian historian

Europe's biggest and most active volcano is somewhere ahead. Adrift on the A-19, moving southeast and then eastward at a too-high rate of speed, I am contemplating the foolishness of preconceived notions about how Sicily's interior would look in July. I expected countryside burned over by the intense Mediterranean sun; instead, I see rolling hills of green and golden fields where wheat has recently been harvested, stretching to the horizon. And as I enter the northern edge of the Plain of Catania, there is a subtle shift in the landscape, a sense that I am gradually moving down, toward the Ionian Sea, still out of sight to the east. The hills ahead start to roll lower; plateaus, like the one cradling Enna, are behind me. The sky just above the hills ahead takes on a slightly different hue; strangely, I can't tell if it is darker or lighter. It is just different from that shocking blue, cloudless sky that had been above me as I left Palermo.

Where, I wonder, is Etna? I am close enough, and I certainly know it dominates the island's eastern landscape. It takes a few moments, then to my left, toward the northeast, I sense a massive outline towering above a series of foothills. I had mistaken this outline for sky; the colors of both, slight variations of hazy blue-gray, are nearly identical. This mountain, my unseen companion for perhaps thirty minutes, grows sharper the closer I get to Catania and the sea.

I prepare to turn northward onto the north-south A-18 toward my exit at Acireale. The darker sky color morphs into views of green mountain flanks punctuated by narrow black fields of lava formations. This mountain, called Mungibeddu in Sicilian, stays with me for five days as I lounge on its slopes in a tiny bed-and-breakfast in the mountainside town of Trecastagni. I see its southeast cone, wisps of smoke floating skyward, through my bedroom window as I awake each morning, and it is never far from my view as I walk around Trecastagni or drive from village to village in search of something new: a nice restaurant far from tourists, a bench in a quiet park, a friendly bar and a cup of bitingly strong espresso.

Villagers here seem always aware, consciously or subconsciously, of its presence—not just because it can erupt suddenly and bury them in cinders and lava, but because the mountain gives them life.

"Where are these lemons from?" I ask the lady at the fruit and vegetable store a few blocks from my B-and-B. "Etna," is her reply, delivered with a warm smile as she shrugs her shoulder in the direction of the mountain just outside her front door. A bottle of wine is sitting on a table display in another shop. "Etna," the man says, referring to the vast vineyards that blanket the slopes. I look closer. The label reads: "Etna DOC."

DOC stands for Denominazione di Origine Controllata, or Controlled Denomination of Origin. A DOC, then, is a zone, one of many throughout Sicily and Italy, where wine production is tightly controlled to maintain quality.

"It is very robust wine, from the lava," the man tells me, meaning the soil created by the black, sometimes reddish, molten rock bursting from the mountain's deep interior—the mythical home of Hephaestus, blacksmith to the gods. (He is Vulcan in Roman mythology.) The wine seller offers a sip from a tiny plastic cup. For reasons of health, I politely decline. *"Sono astemio"* (I am a teetotaler), I say with honest regret.

I imagined that I would journey to the top. I had read that there is a cable car at some place on the volcano's south flank that roughly follows the path of French writer Guy de Maupassant, who went up the mountain in 1885.

I expect to drive to Nicolosi, just a few kilometers from Trecastagni, to begin my ascent, following maps and well-trod routes. De Maupassant started his climb in Nicolosi, today a village full of hotels and B-and-Bs catering to Etna-bound tourists. He had gotten there via a train that carried him "through fields and gardens full of trees growing in the pulverized lava" and was met by guides and pack mules for a trip that took two days. They left at four o'clock in the afternoon, he writes in his travel classic *Sicily,* traveling upward through a maze of steam and lava vents that he describes as "the sons of Etna, grown up around the monster, which thus wears a necklace of volcanoes." They traveled well into the night through a growing storm and eventually stopped at a woodcutters' cabin, where they spent a few hours before daylight on flea-infested mats.

Later the following day, they left the mules and climbed a "frightful wall of hardened cinders." It was well into nighttime, and the travelers awaited the sunrise. The sun started its climb, and they could see all of Sicily from the crater's rim. Off to the east and across the Strait of Messina were the hills of Calabria near the toe of the Italian boot. They headed back down, and eventually found "under our feet, the indented and green island, with its gulfs, its capes, its towns and the great sea, so very blue, that encloses it."

My plan was to start early in the morning and, thanks to modern roads, cable cars, and being able to forgo mules, be back in time for a wonderful plate of pasta and a freshly opened bottle of water—"Etna water," boasted my Trecastagni host, Beppe Stiolmi, as he proudly handed me a bottle upon my arrival the day before.

But when I told him of my plan to do Etna solo, he shook

his head. "No, you must do it with a guide, a man of nature who can explain to you how the mountain works, the differences in the lava, the fauna. It is not enough to go up, look around, and say, 'How beautiful. Look, I can see the Ionian Sea, and beyond, why, it is Calabria!' That does not let you *know* the volcano," Beppe said with finality.

I believed him. And, of course, he knew just the guide. But, he said, it would be too expensive to hire a private guide. I must go with a small group. Sixty euros (about $80 at the time). "I can arrange," he said. Later that evening, he called to tell me that the guide would pick me up at nine fifteen the next morning, just after breakfast. There would be seven other people, a French family of four and a Scottish family of three. "The guide speaks excellent English," Beppe said. "And he speaks French. No problem."

It isn't a problem. Mario Giaquinta is on time. We bounce along in his nine-person van, taking the confusing, narrow, twisting roads to Nicolosi to pick up the other seven. It will be a long day, Mario tells me. We will go to the northeast side of the volcano to make our way up—"the south side too hot, too hot today"—and then, after several hours high on the mountain, we will cool off in a shady gorge, the Gole dell'Alcàntara, that was carved out by the Alcàntara River through a deep, narrow flow of lava laid down millennia ago.

"We will return around seven thirty. OK?" Sure, it is OK. It will be a ten-hour excursion. I am going to get my €60 worth.

We pass tiny villages, always going up, up. Occasionally, the volcano's southeast crater—the one I see every morning when I get up—pops through a picture-perfect setting, with green trees and vineyards in the foreground, contrasting against darker soil from centuries-old flows or rigid piles of sharp, deeply pocked rock from more recent eruptions.

Mario is full of information, speaking nonstop, first in French to the couple in the front seat and their two teenage daughters next to me in the middle seat, and then in English to the Scots and me. Then he moves on to a new subject and once again the French-English rotation.

For example, we pass through a small village that is only a few streets deep but stretches out like a belt holding in the mountain's girth: Zafferana Etnea. "This is a place famous for the honey," Mario says. "There are five varieties: lemon, orange, *mandarino,* chestnut, and wildflower. There are seven thousand inhabitants, and seven hundred produce honey."

He points out that lemons are grown in the lower part of the mountain, at about seven hundred meters (nearly 2,300 feet) above sea level. "The landscape changes quickly," he declares, pointing to acres and acres of vineyards above the citrus groves. "We grow what we call 'black' wine. It is very strong red wine, because of the soil from the lava."

When we stop several hours later for a picnic lunch of soft bread along with various assortments of salami and cheese, Mario produces from his rucksack a bottle of this so-called black wine, and the other members of my party attest to its roughness. "It is very aggressive," the Frenchman allows as he eagerly seeks a second glass.

Now, we are passing through Milo, "the last village," Mario announces. "From here we have only nature, and we are going into the terraces, the old way of growing wine," he says, pointing out the centuries-old lava-rock walls similar to the ones I had seen several years ago in northern Italy's Cinque

Terre, south of Genoa. "Only older people remain here to practice agriculture."

We are climbing higher, and Mario gets serious about his
volcanology. Etna is a young volcano, only about fifteen thousand years old, and much more active than its more famous,
smaller cousin to the north, Vesuvius. Etna grew in the place
of various prehistoric predecessors as far back as 140,000 years
ago or more. According to the 2001 book *Volcanoes of Europe* by
Alwyn Scarth and Jean-Claude Tanguy, Etna's direct ancestor
is known as the Ellittico volcano, a much bigger giant that
helped, along with its predecessors, to create much of Sicily.
Scientists also call it Ancient Mongibello, a bilingual term for
mountain: *"Mon"* is Latin for mountain and it is joined to another word for mountain, *"gebello,"* a corruption of the Arabic
gibel. Sicilians, in their language, call it Mungibeddu (beautiful mountain). Whatever the appellation, the mountain we
know today as Etna had a catastrophic eruption perhaps fifteen thousand years ago and began to build to the shape we
now recognize.

Just a scant century ago, in 1909, Etna had only one crater at
the summit. This was the crater climbed in 1885 by the Frenchman de Maupassant; now it has four active ones. The southeast crater that greets me daily from my window in Trecastagni
appeared during a 1971 eruption.

Other facts shared by Mario: After a lava flow, it takes four
to five centuries for trees and bushes to grow in the soil that
forms as the lava rock breaks down; it takes six to seven centuries before agriculture can take place on that flow. We drove
through the 1971 flow on the volcano's northeast edge; it was
a moonscape. No tiny plants peeking through. Seven hundred

years from now, there would be dense woods here and, if some-one is still around to farm it, beautiful rolling vineyards.

This breakdown of rock to soil occurs because specialized lichen begins to grow on the stone surfaces, tearing it down through a natural chemical process. This is further facilitated by development of plants such as the deep-rooted *Genista aet-nensis,* or Mount Etna broom, a beautiful, ubiquitous bush with tiny yellow flowers. Toss in a lot of wind, snow, and rain erosion, and you eventually have the kind of deep, rich soil that drew the Greeks, Carthaginians, Romans, and a whole host of other invaders here nearly three thousand years ago.

En route to our hike, we stop and Mario opens the back of the van and hands out yellow hard hats. He pulls out a rope and a large flashlight to show us caves made by flowing lava. Deep in a birch forest, we come across a group of local women scal-ing the bark from long poles that will be used to replace old, rotting pole fences encircling small openings in the ground. These are entrances to the caves below.

Mario tells us the remarkable story about how early resi-dents of the mountain would come here in winter and shovel huge amounts of snow down into these holes, filling the caves. There, it would turn to ice. In summer, men and women would return each night, around one o'clock in the morning. The men would enter the caves, chop the ice into large blocks, and haul them out and then lash them onto the backs of mules.

The women would cover the ice with layers of green ferns collected from the surrounding woods, and the ice would be hauled down the mountain to ports around Catania. There it would be used to preserve the fish caught early each morning. Day after day these workers did this. It was many miles to the various port villages—a remarkable daily undertaking.

I later read that in medieval times, blocks of Etna ice would be hauled to Messina and put on ships bound for Malta. After all, the volcano was the only regular source of snow-to-ice in the southern Mediterranean.

Mario told us that the prolific French painter Jean-Pierre Houël captured, in the mid-1770s, a scene of men, each hauling a large ice block on his back out of the cave's mouth, the slight hole in the ground near where we were standing. He said that painting is in the Hermitage Museum in Saint Petersburg, Russia. I could find no representation of it there, but the *Encyclopedia of Kitchen History,* referring to a book by Houël, not a painting, says

> In Sicily, the Bishop of Catania claimed a considerable revenue from snow and ice harvested from Mount Etna's slopes. . . . To keep ice throughout the hot Mediterranean summer, according to the painter-engraver Jean Houël's *Voyage Pittoresque en Sicilie* (Picturesque Journey in Sicily, 1784), the Order of Malta established a lava-roofed grotto on Mount Etna consisting of double carved wells into which workers compressed snow. They loaded the frozen chunks onto mules for delivery to boats carrying them to kitchens on the shore.

Later, as our group of nine sat in the dark in that "lava-roofed grotto," perhaps twenty feet below the surface, with droplets of groundwater sprinkling us from the bumpy lava ceiling that scraped our hard hats as we shifted about, we could only imagine what it must have been like.

"Remember, for us Etna is a paradise, not a hell." Mario admonishes us later up the road as we leave the van behind and hike up to the top of a massive crater two-thirds of the way to the top. Thinking about how de Maupassant described his slippery ascent more than 120 years earlier, I fear for the worst on my hike. But the trail is well defined through the packed lava cinders, and it gradually, gently, skirts the hills. But this lower crater is as close as we will get to the three-thousand-meter (9,842 feet) summit.

We stopped at a point where we had a perfect view of craters of various ages laid out in successive waves before us. On the summit is one of the four active cones; today, only a gentle hint of smoke floats above it. Just below that cone is *monte frumento delle concazze,* an inactive crater formed five thousand years ago. Below that is a cone formed from an 1865 eruption that wiped out hundreds of acres of birch trees. One hundred and forty-four years later, a scattering of low-lying vegetation is barely poking through the now crumbling lava from this flow. This patch of lava is just beginning to show plants with names like Etna tansy, achillea, and Etna milk wetch. A few centuries from now, the yellow-flowered *Genista aetnensis* will show up, followed by birch and pine forests.

The mountain is a regional park; much smaller Vesuvius, near Naples, is a national park. This is a point of contention for Sicilians who believe Etna should get the national designation. Etna has 270 craters, Mario says, every one of them representing an eruption. Some eruptions cause little damage, but some have been murderous.

De Maupassant obviously did his research. He detailed several, including the ancient Greek lyric poet Pindar's report of one in 474 B.C. There also was an eruption in 1669 that destroyed much of Catania, including its port. The duomo there used to be next to the water; today, it is several blocks away; the land in between rests on top of the lava flow.

Some of Etna's eruptions, of course, occur out of the four summit cones, like the last big ones in 2001 and 2002 that wiped out tourist stations, ski lifts, hotels, restaurants, bars. The 2002 eruption lasted twenty days and was "very violent. It sent up a cloud shaped like a cypress tree. The Catania airport was closed for three months because of the ash" potentially fouling airplane engines. Other eruptions shoot out of vents lower down on Etna's flanks, like the one that caused the 1669 Catania disaster.

The "cypress tree" image formed by smoke during an eruption must be a common phenomenon. A nineteenth-century American writer, Bayard Taylor, witnessed an eruption in 1852 as he rode in a carriage along the sea while traveling from Catania to Messina. His carriage stopped just before Taormina, and he saw, pouring out of the summit, "a mass of smoke four or five miles high, and shaped precisely like the Italian pine tree. . . . It was like the tree celebrated in Scandinavian sagas . . . that tree whose roots pierced through the earth, whose trunk was the color of blood, and whose branches filled the uttermost corners of the heavens."

Just a few hours earlier, while he stood on the streets of the coastal city Acireale to wait out tremors and listen to a thunderous noise from the summit, a local resident standing next to him commented, "'Ah, the mountain knows how to make himself respected. When he talks, everybody listens.'"

Mario, our guide, looks at me. "American people often see it as a 'gentle giant.' It is a giant, but not gentle. We respect it and take from it when it lets us."

In January 2011, just eighteen months after my visit, the volcano came alive once more. No new cones were formed, but existing ones spewed lava and ash, forcing authorities to close Catania's Fontanarossa airport for a few days. This time, no villages were affected; property damage was minimal.

After going a bit higher and taking in the hazy view across the Strait of Messina toward Calabria, we hike back down. There is one more destination, this one primarily for the two French teens and the Scottish teenager who have been delightful, involved companions on this journey. It is Gole dell'Alcàntara, the gorge carved out by the river through lava. The teens want to wade in the cold, cold water of the river after the long hot day in the van with a broken air conditioner.

It's an hour's drive. We clomp down more than two hundred stone steps into a magnificent gorge with incredible lava formations revealed over the eons by the rushing river, now at a low level after the flood-level spring.

Mario confides to me quietly, as the two families frolic in the water amid several dozen other waders, that this is his least favorite part of the trip. "I love the geology," he says, pointing to the rolled-oats shape of the stone and the tall, narrow walls shooting up to a tiny patch of blue sky. "But the people"—he gestures at the loud, raucous Sicilians surrounding us—"don't respect this place for what it is. Look at the trash," he says, pointing to plastic water bottles and candy wrappers, some floating in the river. "People say to me, 'You live in a paradise! Why does everyone here treat it so badly?' To me, it is a mystery."

FOURTEEN

Food

Eat to live, or live to eat are not axioms [Sicilians] adhere to: they eat, of course, to satisfy nutritional needs related to the body, but they live also because through eating they want to satisfy needs of a spiritual nature. This is so even if they are about to eat *pasta con le fave* [pasta with beans].

—Giuseppe Coria,
(1930–2003) *Sicily: Culinary Crossroads*, translated by Gaetano Cipolla

Uɴɪᴠᴇʀsɪᴛʏ ᴘʀᴏꜰᴇssᴏʀ Francesca Corrao grew up in the Sicilian interior and Palermo. In the midst of my visit to her Rome apartment, where we spend four hours talking about a range of subjects dealing with the place of her childhood, she excuses herself to make lunch. After a few moments in the kitchen of her comfortable home, located a few streets up the side of a hill opposite the Trastevere train station, she set a table on a sun-dappled terrace overlooking a Catholic convent for Eastern European nuns.

Sicilians and Italians love to eat out-of-doors, even in chilly weather. But this is July, and Rome in July is sweltering. At one point she grabs a short hose and waters down the light tan deck tiles baking in the Roman sun.

"I am doing something very Arabic," she shouts from the terrace over the gurgle of running water. "They would pour water over tiles in their North African or Sicilian houses to cool them down and make it pleasant to sit. Please"—she motions—"come. Sit."

A finely decorated table, starched-cloth napkins, heavy knives and forks, all in place, greet me. She sets down a large bowl of pasta coated in what appears to be a light tomato-based sauce sprinkled throughout with herbs, spices, and bits of vegetables. Then she sets down a covered skillet. "Chicken," she says. "I hope you like chicken. It will be our *secondo*."

She has prepared three courses in fewer than fifteen minutes. A green, leafy salad also was presented in typical Italian fashion: at the end of our meal. "Amazing," I say. "I have Italian friends who can throw together a meal this wonderful almost as quickly. When I cook, it takes hours. How do you do it?"

Francesca shrugs. "I don't know," she says. "But when you learn to cook at age eight standing at the elbow of your grandmother, it becomes fast and easy." No recipes, she says; they are all in her head.

It seems that cooking comes naturally to Sicilian women and some men. Food is the center of family life, and children are usually surrounded by two or more generations of aunts, grandmothers, and sometimes uncles and grandfathers, who are more than willing to teach. It becomes, as Francesca Corrao indicated, second nature. She doesn't really remember learning; she just did. It was like, decades ago, when a journalist I knew asked ski professional Stein Ericksen at what age he learned to ski. Ericksen was puzzled by the question. "I don't know," he replied after a few moments' reflection. "Do you remember learning to walk?"

There are at least dozens, if not hundreds, of cookbooks boasting the finest recipes in Sicilian cuisine. Some appear to be thrown together with little explanation about how they represent Sicilian versus Italian cooking. Others might call for substitutions of products easily found in the United States that no self-respecting Sicilian would ever use. Still others are full of history, the literary equivalent of, say, Burt Wolf's television series *Travels & Traditions*, in which he places the food he talks about in fascinating and detailed historical perspective.

Among the best cookbooks—and there are others as well—are *Sicily: Culinary Crossroads* by the late Giuseppe Coria, and Clifford A. Wright's *A Mediterranean Feast*, in which he examines the culture of food and its culinary origins in several Mediterranean areas.

Coria's book is wonderfully translated and in a new edition by Oronzo Editions. It breaks down, in its introduction, the contributions of the eleven periods of foreign domination by various nations or groups of colonists and warriors that have occupied Sicily for good or for ill over the centuries. Since it's impossible for historians to discern the diets of the indigenous peoples on the island who greeted the first settlers, the Greeks, Coria starts with what the Greeks brought: great cooks and writers of some of the earliest cookbooks. He says that "[F]rom the fifth century B.C., Siracusa, Agrigento, and Gela were the birthplaces of the finest cooks."

Even the Greek luminary Plato was impressed with the colonizers' culinary traditions. He wrote of the people of Agrigento, the south-central Sicily city that has a collection of the most durable Greek temples in the world: "They always build as if they expect to live for eternity; they always eat as if they expect to die the next day."

Mary Taylor Simeti, writer of several books and articles about Sicily, tells us, in an article in *Gastronomica: The Journal of Food and Culture,* that "the first cookbook in the Western world (unfortunately lost to us) had been written by Mithaecus of [Siracusa]," where a professional cooking school had been established. And she writes that Greek-Sicilian chefs trained there went on to serve aristocratic Roman families.

Another thing she points out is that the first *"pasta asciuta,* dried and then cooked in boiling water," was "documented in Italy in twelfth-century Sicily." Prior to this moment, an Arab geographer mentions that a substance known as *itrya* was produced—a type of vermicelli.

Meanwhile, Coria informs us that Greek-Sicilian writers described soups full of crustaceans, and they wrote about how Odysseus was drawn to the Sirens not only by their sexual power, but also by their "grilled anchovies, roast suckling pig, young squid accompanied by a superb wine for lunch, and then with fat mullet, bowfin fillets, and scorpion fish for dinner."

A third-century B.C. culinary writer offered descriptions of all kinds of fish, "and for each the best method of preparation." Coria described a variety of breads, and what each type should be eaten with (olive oil, wine, vinegar, cheese). Others wrote about how to prepare tuna roe, where to find the best honey (the Iblei Mountains near Ragusa), and ways to cook various birds, including a type of quail known as skylark, which Coria said is still consumed in Sicily. I didn't see that particular dish on any menus, but I am sure skylarks are still consumed in some homes.

These early Greek colonists, then, began mingling with the indigenous peoples on the island, particularly in the east. Within a short period of a century or two, as we have seen, the Greeks evolved from colonists to Sicilians. Then, by the first century B.C., the Romans came onto the scene and took over for four centuries. Sicily was the Roman Republic's first province, and by this time, Greek influence had been spreading across the island for as many as six centuries. Rome left around A.D. 307 as the empire neared its end.

During Roman rule, the island was controlled by various functionaries, some of who robbed the islanders, enriching themselves and their republic-turned-empire.

It is well-known that Sicily was Rome's breadbasket, primarily growing the wheat that fed much of that particular empire. So bread was never lacking among the general populace, Coria tells us. But foodwise, writes Coria, "the Romans left few traces." There was something called *cudduruni,* a type of flatbread that could be referred to as the first "pizza," although that honor rightly goes to the Neapolitans many centuries later.

Different kinds of small breads, *focaccia*, were developed, including some with various ingredients cooked into the bread itself. Sicilians call these *'mpanate*. The Roman writer Cato handed down actual recipes for some of these bread dishes, including one called *placenta*, "made with flour, cheese, and honey from the Iblei Mountains" north of Noto and west of Siracusa ". . . and the recipe for *mustaceos*, which would become the pasta *mostaccioli*," a smooth or ribbed tubular pasta cut at the ends on a diagonal and about two inches long. It is a bit longer than the more common penne.

Coria credits the Romans for developing Sicilian appreciation for asparagus and for teaching them "to eat only fresh meat and cook it well, never to age it; to store snow in caves for use in summer." And the Romans taught Sicilians to "cook liver in nets." The "net" in this case refers to the fibrous membrane taken from a pig's abdomen and boiled in water for a few moments. A pig's liver is cut into chunks; the now pliable, stretched-out membrane also is cut up to wrap around those individual chunks. Properly seasoned, these pieces can be pushed onto skewers and roasted over a fire, or they can be fried in a skillet with finely chopped onion and bay leaves.

Coria's book has the precise recipe for *ficatu nno 'ntrigghiu*. The dish is well-known, I am told, in Siracusa. I never came across it during four or five visits to that city. I am still debating whether to make the dish; I may have to taste it alone.

Beyond a handful of such unique dishes, the Romans also get credit for bringing many species of fruit trees to the island before they were supplanted by the next wave of invaders: the Franks, Goths, and, for another long stretch, the Constantinople-based Byzantine Empire.

There is a recipe from Messina that Coria included in his book. It is simply "Oven-baked Pasta," or in Sicilian, *Pasta 'ncasciata*. He describes the name as "Pasta in a Chest" and writes: "It was originally cooked inside a pan that was covered with embers placed on top of the cover, so that the pasta was cooked with heat from above and below." It is a process similar to Dutch-oven cooking. This recipe, published with permission of Oronzo Editions, makes its preparation a bit easier.

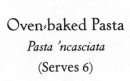

Oven-baked Pasta
Pasta 'ncasciata
(Serves 6)

Ingredients

Extra-virgin olive oil

1 onion, finely chopped, divided

10 ounces (1¼ cups) diced pork

¼ cup pork rind, roughly chopped

10 ounces (1¼ cups) firm, dried sausage, crumbled

2 cloves garlic, finely chopped

1 tablespoon *strattu* (thick Sicilian tomato paste) diluted
    with a little water

3 tablespoons chopped fresh or canned tomato

sea salt
2 pounds cauliflower florets
1 pound rigatoni
caciocavallo cheese, sliced finely
grated pecorino

For the sauce, heat a little olive oil in a skillet over medium heat, and gently fry half the chopped onion until golden. Add the diced pork, pork rind, sausage, garlic, and tomato extract. Fry, for a few minutes, mixing well, then add the chopped tomato and enough water to cover. Cook until the sauce has thickened. Season with salt to taste.

Bring a large pot of salted water to a boil and blanch the cauliflower until just tender, about 5 minutes. Strain, reserving the water for the pasta, and set aside. Coat the bottom of a skillet with olive oil and gently fry the cauliflower florets and the remaining onion. Bring the pot of water from the cauliflower to a boil and cook the rigatoni until al dente, 8 to 10 minutes. Drain.

Heat the oven to 350°.

Once drained, mix half the pasta with one-third of the cauliflower, one-third of the sauce, and a few slices of *caciocavallo*. After blending, pour this mixture into an ovenproof casserole (the "chest") and layer on some of the sauce, cauliflower, and cheese. Put the second half of the pasta over these layers and then add the remaining cauliflower, sauce, and *caciocavallo* slices. Top with an abundant amount of grated pecorino. Bake covered until the cheese has melted and the flavors are combined.

VARIATION

Some people add fried eggplant and slices of hard-boiled eggs between the layers.

Still another of Coria's recipes is worth mentioning here: Ragusan Meatballs, or *Purpetti di maiali*. He writes that "Sicilians love meatballs so much there is no food they have not shaped into balls." He especially finds that meatballs made from wild hare and wild rabbit are exceptional, and that ball-shaped sardines are classics. Cooks can also make balls out of vegetables, such as eggplant, potatoes, mushrooms, and artichokes—and even certain sweets.

An interesting note here: Coria informs us that "meatballs are prepared at home, not in restaurants, where they are never made: Sicilians are suspicious by nature."

Ragusan Meatballs
Purpetti di maiali
(Serves 4)

Ingredients

Olive oil for frying

1 onion, finely chopped

½ bunch fresh flat-leaf parsley, chopped

2 or 3 cloves garlic, finely chopped

1 pound ground pork
2 eggs
1 tablespoon red wine
sea salt
pepper
caciocavallo cheese

In a large skillet over medium-high heat, warm the olive oil.

In a medium bowl, combine the onion, parsley, and garlic with the ground pork. Incorporate the eggs, red wine, sea salt, and pepper to taste, and add the shredded *caciocavallo*. Take small amounts and form them into the shape of meatballs (walnut-size, oval-shaped balls, not too thick, but do not flatten them). Fry the meatballs, turning occasionally, until browned, about 7 minutes. Drain the meatballs on paper towels and serve right away or they lose their aroma and crispness.

VARIATIONS
The initial mixture for the meatballs can be made thicker with the addition of bread crumbs, or softer with the addition of a little milk.

⌣·⌐

The dew lay heavy on the field of wildflowers carpeting the ground where olive trees spilled down a hillside. This crowded grove is sliced in two by the road to Caltabellotta, a small village with a commanding view of the Mediterranean. On a clear day, I suspect, one could see North Africa from here. Heading north past the town on narrow roads is Corleone, deep in the hilly interior. And north from there is Palermo. But that was not my plan.

These trees are massive, twisted, gnarly, and whorled at their base, indicating their advanced age. They grow shorter in Sicily than they do elsewhere, and therefore the olives are easier to harvest, usually in October, than they are in Greece or mainland Italy. Planted hundreds of years ago on the flanks of this mountain below Caltabellotta and northeast of the south-coast city of Sciacca, they were young at a time when much of Sicilian history passed by.

They looked like trees I had seen many years ago in a remote, lightly traveled section of Calabria. There I had encountered an old man with a freshly sawn olive-wood log perched on his shoulder. He told me that many of his trees were planted at the time of Christ. And this Sicilian grove also resembled trees surrounding a pensione in Sardinia. Those trees, the property owner had assured me, were a mere six hundred years old.

This Sicilian hillside appeared to have been in a fire long ago. But the black tree trunks were producing fresh, young olive branches festooned with long, thin, silvery-green leaves. One trunk was split down the middle, as if hit by a lightning bolt. It, too, was showing healthy, thick new growth on both sides.

I had once been intrigued enough to look into olive-tree lore. Some authors, particularly American writer Mort Rosenblum, report the existence today of groves in France and Italy that indeed could have been planted by imperial Romans as many as two thousand years ago. But while trees growing today are not likely that old, their deep, sturdy root systems could be.

Those ancient clumps of roots are capable of surviving fire, extended drought, earthquakes, and rampaging armies. When the aboveground tree dies of old age—the upper torsos do not usually survive beyond seven hundred years—new sprouts will emerge from the original root system, a cycle repeating itself endlessly until the roots are dug up to make room for a road, a house, a parking lot.

In modern times throughout the Mediterranean, such removal does not necessarily mean the death of a tree. There are tree farms that sell, for thousands of euros, large reclaimed olive trees set into sturdy wooden containers.

It was the Greeks who introduced to Sicily, perhaps by the sixth or fifth centuries B.C., olive trees and grapes for wine. Today, the island, with its volcanic soil, delightful climate, and rolling hills with a slightly cooler elevation, produces perhaps ten percent of Italy's crop.

The Web site OliveNation (olivenation.com) describes Sicily's oil as "sweet and delicate. Others can be as strong and peppery as their Tuscan cousins to the north. All are fragrant and appetizing . . . so much so that it has been said that the ancient Athenians preferred Sicilian olive oil to their own, even though some of the varieties grown in Sicily and Greece were the same!"

My tongue is not nuanced enough to discern significant differences in oil grown in different places, but I can tell the difference between light and heavy. This difference is particularly found in the oil from olive trees grown near Trapani, on the west coast, around the tiny village of Scopello. It is light and not meant for heat in a skillet. This light, slightly nuanced oil is best used for dipping bread, or sprinkling on salads or mounds of steaming, fresh pasta.

In rural Sicily, pointing your car in just about any direction and going for it reaps wondrous rewards. You can find small villages that suddenly appear on hillsides or hilltops and possess perhaps a handful of streets and one, maybe two, local restaurants that almost never see a tourist. There might not even be a menu; guests are served whatever is being prepared that day.

Such experiences have always turned out well; experiences in heavy-duty tourist-oriented restaurants have not. You know the places. They are the ones with large asphalt parking lots with long painted stripes that indicate parking for tour buses. Many times I have wandered into a tiny room with a handful of tables where the father is clearing off one to make room for a new customer; the son or daughter is collecting orders; and the mother, cheeks reddened from the heat and dressed in a white cap and full-body white apron, is stirring a large pot or, with lightning speed and flashing steel, chopping a mound of fragrant basil in a narrow kitchen.

Perhaps it's the idea, a golden image in the visitor's mind, of such a scene in a small family-run place that makes the food taste so good. But it is more likely the leg of lamb, cooked to tender perfection so that the meat, simmered for hours in a rich sauce, is hard to keep on the fork; or the pasta, cooked al dente in a way that most non-Italians or non-Sicilians can never match; or the fresh vegetables steamed to just the right crunchiness.

There is never a sense that you need to hurry through your meal in these places. They exist in neighborhoods of large cities, such as Palermo, Siracusa, or Noto, or in smaller villages, such as Racalmuto or Castrofilippo. Some are clean, well-lighted places. Others, like the Shanghai in Palermo's Vucciria, might give you concern as you walk up a narrow stairway badly in need of paint and plaster.

However, when you twist your fork around those strands of pasta, lightly coated with an unpresumptuous sauce, and pop it in your mouth, followed by a gulp of mineral water *con gas* and then a bit of crisp bread, you forget about that stairway and luxuriate in the aromas of the place and the smile of the family member serving you. They are everywhere in Sicily. You just have to search them out. Most of the time, you won't be disappointed.

To name them, as *The New York Times'* travel section or popular guidebooks do, is to change them.

Food writer and historian Clifford A. Wright, in his sweeping work *A Mediterranean Feast*, writes that Sicily's richest agricultural period was during the Arab years of the ninth and tenth centuries. The Arabs had introduced, along with an extensive irrigation system, many of the crops and fruits the island is famous for today. A significant number of the varieties of vegetables grown there under the Muslims were not known in Europe at that time. And I found in another book, *Food: The*

History of Taste, that we have the Arabs to thank for that marvelous Sicilian dessert *cannolo.* H. D. Miller, who wrote an article in that book, said the dish, called *qanawāt,* involved "pieces of dough made into tubes, deep fried and filled with a variety of sweets."

In November 2009, I was treated to one of these Arab-based confections in Noto, where the owner of Pasticceria Mandorlafiore (almond flower), Marco Braneti, took a few moments to demonstrate his skills. He handed a small individual *cassata,* made that morning, to my son Brad, and disappeared into his kitchen. Moments later he emerged with a just-made *cannolo.* The ricotta filling was light, the freshly made tube was just-right crunchy, and the ends of the ricotta emerging from the tube were each dipped in crushed Bronte pistachios from the slopes of Etna. The *cannolo* certainly derives from the Arab influence, Marco believes.

While that theory may not be questioned by food historians, I found in a bit of research that the origins of the *cassata* are in dispute. It can be as big as a cake or, like the one Brad had delightfully devoured, made for the individual.

Italian studies professor John Dickie, in his book *Delizia! The Epic History of Italians and Their Food,* proposes that *cassata* "does not derive from the name for a bowl in Arabic, as is often claimed. Much more prosaically, it originates in the Latin for cheese." He's not sure it has Arabic origins, and it wasn't until the 1700s that the green-and-white color combination was used. The way it appears today, with candied-fruit slivers arrayed on top of the ricotta coating over sponge cake, is an even more recent invention.

I took a small bite of the confection Brad was eating. It was teeth-achingly sweet, the thin, green marzipan border almost impossible to finish. But the ricotta–sponge cake combination was the best I had ever tasted. Perhaps there is a place elsewhere in the world where you can get *cassata* or a *cannolo* this good, but I doubt it.

John Dickie, ever the realist and not prone to sentimentality, warns us not to have romantic notions about the origins of Sicilian cuisine. "Whatever flavors and smells characterized Islamic Sicily's civilization of the table, most of them, like the planisphere, [an eleventh-century Persian star chart] have been irretrievably lost."

This skepticism aside, Noto's pastry master Marco believes in Islamic origins for many of the pastries that come out of his shop. He points to the pistachio and almond cookies found only in the province of Siracusa.

"These are from recipes of our grandparents," he said. Knowing their origins "tells you about poverty, about a people who survived on bread, cheese, and olives, who enjoyed sweetness wherever they could find it" in these simple honey, flour, and egg-white concoctions.

He adds, proudly, that he does not use anything "industrial" in the making of his pastries, pointing out that Noto is known for its artisan pastry tradition. He is not about to break with that tradition.

When Muslim rulers displaced the Greek Byzantines in the late ninth century, they reversed the Roman and Byzantine practice of amassing large swaths of land by breaking up the *latifundia,* or expansive estates. Smaller parcels were handed out to the Muslim immigrants, and villages were created to house them.

When the Normans arrived, a new social structure focusing on barons developed. They, said Clifford Wright, were allowed to "rape the land" by re-creating the Roman and Byzantine idea of "large and inefficient agricultural estates." Many rebellious Muslims were eventually chased out of Sicily; whole villages disappeared. Of course, by this time, Arab blood was flowing freely through the veins of the islanders, mingling with the blood of ancient Greeks, Carthaginians, and a few Normans. Many Islamic traditions, including styles of dress for Christian Sicilian women, remained for years after the Normans arrived.

As far as the island's cuisine was concerned, it likely bore no resemblance to the cuisine we celebrate. In fact, Wright tells us bluntly that "the very poor of Sicily had no cuisine." He looked at inventories of household goods from the medieval period that showed most peasant homes had no *foculàri*, or slow braziers. Also, prepared food that was sold for consumption included a large tax, making it impossible for the poor to purchase it. Their homes did have *"batteria da cucina—* spits, fryers, and pans—[that indicate] the simplest of cooking methods."

Today, in a land famous for its olive oil, it is tough to imagine a time when it was too expensive for most people to use. Wright says that from the fourteenth to the eighteenth centuries "animal fats such as butter, bacon, lard, mutton fat . . . and beef suet were used in Sicilian cooking."

"In fact," he writes, "the preferred cooking fat in fifteenth-century Sicily was butter." It was common practice, he said, for farmworkers to carry butter, not cheese, into the fields to eat with their scraps of bread.

Olive oil has been a product of the Sicilian landscape since the beginning of recorded time. The colonizing Greeks, three thousand years ago, planted trees in abundance. But "it [olive oil] was rare and expensive until recently," says Wright. Jews on the island during the Middle Ages started buying oil in quantity "as pork fat was forbidden to them," and Jewish merchants sold the product. Such a modest production during those centuries means that oil "was used on bread or for seasoning dried vegetable soups."

Another point Wright makes is that chickens were not included in the historical Sicilian cuisine. Chickens were expensive, compared to pork and veal, as were their eggs. "This accounts in part for why there is almost no chicken cookery in Sicily." But there are plenty of recipes for the cooking of other animals, especially the organs, a custom coming from Tunisia's influence on the island during the Arab period.

Noto, that unique baroque city in the southeast of Sicily near Siracusa, is a culinary heaven. I discovered it through the recommendation of a new friend, Renée Restivo, a Sicilian-American New Yorker. She spends part of each year in Sicily conducting cooking programs through her organization, Soul of Sicily. Its mission: to educate people not only about Sicilian food, particularly the cuisine found in the southeastern part of the island, but also about that food's connection with local agriculture. Apart from the food angle, she and a group of

Notinesi are working to save much of the wide-open spaces around the city from development.

This educator and writer about Sicilian culinary traditions made it possible for my son Brad and me to spend several nights in the house of Noto's favorite son, the late journalist and poet Corrado Sofia (1906–1997). It is here, in the stunning countryside, that many of Renée's cooking demonstrations and hands-on events for culinary tourists take place. Her students work with Notinesi cooks to learn how to make the pasta that is unique to this area of Sicily and to cook traditional meals.

We have the large house to ourselves. No one lives here on a regular basis. It sits on a hill overlooking the eastern end of the Val di Noto and, beyond, the Golfo di Noto.

The tree-studded property is flanked on its uphill side by a group of older, and a growing number of newly planted, olive trees, one hundred twenty in all. Just outside of the kitchen door is an herb garden full of sweet-smelling clusters of green that triggered a memory of something I once read that was attributed to the ninth-century Holy Roman Emperor Charlemagne, a Frenchman. When asked if he knew what an herb was, he supposedly replied, "A physician's friend and the praise of cooks!"

On the south side of the house is a terrace with the view all the way to the sea, perhaps four or five miles distant. At some point during the American and British invasion of Sicily in the summer of 1943, the British general Sir Harold Alexander, commander of Britain's Fifteenth Army Group, dropped by this house to visit an old friend, Corrado Sofia's father. They sat on this same terrace where my son and I sat late one night smoking two stubby cigars and contemplating the evening beneath a starry sky. Possibly they were smoking cigars themselves and drinking golden-yellow *moscato di Noto*, a delicacy in these parts and said to be superior to its forebear, *moscato di Siracusa*. Alexander wrote somewhere that sharing that *moscato* was a sweet gesture unlike any that he could have gotten in all of war-torn Europe.

Corrado Sofia had already made a name for himself in journalism and in Sicilian and Italian literary circles. He reportedly was the first journalist to break the news of the death of Luigi Pirandello in 1936; in addition to his poetry, he wrote about the cuisine of his beloved city. The house, after Sofia's 1997 death, was designated the "House of the Poet."

For our first night, sixty-six years after Sir Harold's visit, we discovered a remarkable meal laid out for us in the kitchen.

The antipasto, prepared by our host cook, Tinuccia, featured *polpette di finocchietto*, a mixture of rice, ricotta cheese, wild fennel, and eggs. Tinuccia said this was a traditional dish her grandmother would have made. The antipasto was followed by the *primo*, on this occasion a small penne pasta with a combination of yellow squash (*zucca gialla*), toasted slivered almonds, a hint of anchovies, and a sprinkling of hot peppers. Then the *secondo,* or as Sicilians would say, *secunnu,* arrived: a fish called *lampuga* in Sicilian. It most easily translates in English into "dolphin fish." This is not the air-breathing dolphin mammal.

The *lampuga* is a seasonal fish, Tinuccia tells us via Renée, and is caught off the coast of nearby Siracusa. The dish is thought to have originated as seagoing fare because it keeps well in vinegar. In Tinuccia's creation, it uses grated bread crumbs—"very traditional," she says—along with slivered almonds and parsley. It is cooked *"a sfincione,"* or where the fish is dredged through the bread crumbs and fried. Served with it is a mixture of olives, peppers, eggplant, pine nuts, carrots, celery, and raisins—a playful combination of flavors.

Tinuccia says that the dish's origins with fish as the main ingredient are from noble Sicilian families. Renée later said that the fish used in aristocratic family recipes was *polipo,* or octopus. And in *Siracusano* style, "a spoonful of finely grated bitter chocolate is sometimes added at the end."

Without the fish it would be "peasant style," with eggplant as a primary ingredient, a sort of *caponata.* Renée puts on her educator's hat. Every province has its own version of the dish since the ingredients depend on what's on hand at the time, she says. But every vegetable must be fried separately, with each kind taking a different length of time to cook. A basic tomato sauce becomes the base of the dish. A bit of sugar is added along with white wine vinegar.

"It's a combination of salty and sweet. That's very Arabic in origin."

Now the dessert is presented, a *cassatine di Pasqua,* or Easter cake. This is not cake in the traditional American style. The "cake" is sweetened ricotta cheese, flavored with cinnamon and lemon zest and baked in a raised, pie-shaped pastry shell. The crust is made using only water, yeast, and pastry flour, without sugar.

Renée explained that the dish is traditionally made around Easter because ricotta is at its best then, and there is an abundance of fresh eggs. Of course, each village and perhaps each family has its own version. In Modica, for example, it is served with no crust and with copious amounts of cinnamon on top. In Tinuccia's version, the cinnamon is lightly sprinkled, the color a beautiful contrast to the white of the ricotta.

I was particularly dazzled by this light confection. Renée kindly figured out the recipe and sent it weeks later.

Sicilian Easter Cake
Cassatine di Pasqua
(Serves 4)

Ingredients
14 ounces pastry flour, plus more for dusting
1 tablespoon of extra-virgin olive oil
salt
1 package of yeast
14 ounces of fresh ricotta sweetened with sugar, to taste
lemon zest of 1 lemon
2 egg yolks, divided
cinnamon

In a bowl mix the flour and a pinch of salt. Make a well in the middle of the flour mixture and add the yeast and then, gradually, a little warm water. Once you've mixed the yeast and warm water, add one egg yolk and olive oil and gradually mix into the flour to form a dough. Knead for a few minutes until soft.

Put the dough in a warm place and let it rise until it

doubles in size. It should rise for about an hour, but the exact time will depend on many factors, including the warmth of your home.

Heat the oven to 400°.

Sprinkle some flour on a dry surface and, using a rolling pin, roll out the dough so that it is very thin and fits the pan you are using.

Place the pastry shell in a round pan (you can use a rolling pin to roll the dough up onto it and then place it in the pan).

In a small bowl, mix the remaining egg yolk with the sweetened ricotta and lemon zest.

Spread the ricotta mixture into the shell.

Make a nice crust around the edge by folding it down over the side, and sprinkle the top generously with cinnamon.

Bake the cassatine for 15 minutes. It should remain slightly moist and not dry out.

The shape of the crust varied from family to family, says Tinuccia. When I made it, I used a regular pie tin. My crust turned out a bit thick. It expands during baking, so when the recipe says to roll it out into a "thin, delicate sheet," it means *thin*.

Dessert in general was served only in wealthy households. Everyone else used fruit or nuts. Due to the extreme poverty of the war and postwar years, desserts did not become a regular staple in most households until the 1960s, Tinuccia says.

Following this remarkable, satisfying dinner, we go into the living room and are warmed by a fire in a large, stone fireplace. Here, through Renée's interpreting skills, I learn how Sicilians feel about their wines.

Tinuccia's husband, Paolo, is with us, and he points out, for example, that the province of Trapani, on the island's west coast, has more vineyards than Tuscany. Commonly grown across the island are whites such as Ansonica, Catarratto, and Chardonnay. Reds include varieties such as Cabernet Franc, lighter than its cousin Cabernet Sauvignon, which also is grown in Sicily, along with the Calabrese grape, or Nero d'Avola, common to both the island and the mainland. There also is the slightly bitter Sicilian variety known as Perricone, which is commonly used as a blending grape with other varieties. Other common Sicilian reds include Frappato di Vittoria, thought to have been cultivated for at least three hundred years around the province of Ragusa, near Noto.

Sicilian grapes not used on the island are sent north to Italy and France, where vintners blend it with their own grapes, says Paolo. This is clear recognition, he says proudly and with enthusiasm, of the high quality of Sicilian grapes. This has led to foreigners coming to Sicily and purchasing vineyards.

"The Swiss and Tuscans can now produce their own Sicilian varieties," Paolo says. Winemaking in Sicily has gone global.

I ask Renée for another recipe, one featuring eggplant. This is a vegetable that always causes me trouble. There must be a way that I can enjoy this plant that, in its purple-black magnificence, looks as if it should taste wonderful. It always tastes bitter to me, no matter who cooks it. I have stayed away from it, even in Italian and Sicilian restaurants, because *Pasta alla Norma,* for example, seems to call for the eggplant to be cut into cubes and then cooked in the tomato sauce. The cubes seem overcooked, mushy, and bitter in my opinion—not crunchy like vegetables should be.

Renée comes up with a "true" Sicilian recipe that she figures will overcome my objections. Sicilian-American friends back home scoff. They claim that *Pasta alla Norma* always includes cubed eggplant simmered in the sauce. When they eat the one I cook, courtesy of Renée's faithful transcription, they become believers. It shows that often what families cook from one province or village to the next can, even using the same ingredients, differ dramatically.

⌒·⌒

Pasta alla Norma
Sicilian style
(Serves 6)

Ingredients
2 medium eggplants
sea salt (Sicilian, if possible)
extra-virgin olive oil (Sicilian, please!)
4 cloves of garlic, divided
1 can of whole tomatoes, preferably San Marzano, crushed
   by hand
pepper, to taste
dried oregano, to taste
1 teaspoon sugar

1½ pounds *pennette rigate*

peperoncino chile peppers, sliced (or dried red-pepper flakes)

fresh basil leaves, torn by hand

1 cup freshly grated *ricotta salata*

1 small onion, finely chopped

Cut the eggplant lengthwise into thin slices. Do not peel. Remove the bitterness from the eggplant by placing the slices on a plate and sprinkling them with salt. Place another plate on top of the layer of eggplant and then put something heavy, such as a large pot or a cutting board, on top. Let the eggplant sit for at least twenty-five minutes. It is ready when you see brown bitter liquid on the bottom of the dish. Pat the eggplant dry with a paper towel or rinse quickly with water and then blot dry. The amount of time you should press eggplant depends on how bitter it is.

Meanwhile, cover the bottom of a large skillet with extra-virgin olive oil and add two cloves of garlic, each sliced in half to release the garlic's essential oils. Simmer over medium heat until the garlic is golden; do not let it turn brown. Add the crushed tomatoes. Add salt, pepper, and dried oregano to taste. If the tomato sauce is not sweet enough, add sugar a few minutes before ladling the sauce over the pasta.

Bring a large pot of salted water to boil, making sure you have enough water to cover the pasta. Follow the instructions on the package for cooking times.

In a large skillet over medium heat, fry the remaining

two cloves of garlic in olive oil until they are golden, then remove them from the pan. Fry the eggplant slices in the olive oil until they are golden and then drain them on a paper towel–covered plate to remove the excess oil.

When the water comes to a boil, cook the *pennette rigate* until just al dente. Drain the pasta and transfer it to a large ceramic serving bowl.

Ladle the sauce onto the pasta, sprinkling *peperoncino* flakes over it, and arrange a layer of fried eggplant slices atop that. Decorate the family-style serving plate with a border of basil leaves, and sprinkle a generous amount of *ricotta salata* on top. You can never have too much, so be generous and remember to have extra sauce, cheese, *peperoncino,* and basil on the table for your guests. Enjoy!

Food is such a part of Sicilian life that some island-born writers weave the subject into their work. Andrea Camilleri has his detective, Montalbano, frequent his favorite restaurant and eat dinners of fresh-caught fish or, at home, enjoy fantastic meals made for him by his housekeeper. The character becomes lost in a state of ecstasy during these scenes, picking up a plate of mullets, holding it an inch from his nose, and inhaling the fragrance. He often fails to notice the passage of time, and only when he gets a phone call wondering where he is does he remember that he was supposed to pick up Livia, his girlfriend, at the airport—an hour ago, and it's a two-hour drive away.

In *The Snack Thief,* Montalbano is eating in a newly discovered restaurant in Màzara, where he "gobbled up a sauté of clams in bread crumbs, a heaping dish of spaghetti with white clam sauce, a roast turbot with oregano and caramelized lemon, and he topped it off with bitter chocolate timbale in orange sauce. When it was all over he stood up, went into the kitchen, and shook the chef's hand without saying a word, deeply moved."

In a collection of culinary writing about food from Provincia di Siracusa, the Italian periodical *Del mangiar siracusano,* editor Antonino Uccello uses excerpts from both the writer Leonardo Sciascia and the poet/journalist Corrado Sofia about their experiences with food.

Sciascia noted the "rich island of orchards" in the area around the coastal village of Avola, just a bit west and north of Noto. He particularly singled out the almond trees there that produce some of the finest almonds in the world. They bear the name of the village and are "less dry than the others, fuller, better in weight and a perfect oval shape that makes one recall the female faces of Antonello."

His reference to Antonello is poignant. Sicilian Antonello da Messina (1430–1479) was a fifteenth-century Italian Renaissance artist who painted the portrait of one of the most iconic figures in Italian art, the *Virgin Annunciate.* It shows Mary being interrupted at her reading by an unseen angel who informs her of her Immaculate Conception. The painting shows her expression the instant she is told she is pregnant. Mary's face, framed by the blue headscarf that drapes down around her shoulders and is clasped at her breast, is an almond shape.

Sciascia waxes poetic about what can be done with these sublime almonds. He refers to *confetti,* the Sicilian word for candy-coated almonds, and two types of *torrone,* or slivered almonds mixed in either white- or caramel-colored nougat.

An ingredient in this confection that, to Sciascia, is as important as the almonds is the honey from the bees of Avola. This honey comes from the area encompassing the Iblei Mountains. Sciascia writes that it "is the best and in such quantities that some scholars want to give the bees the name of the town. In both types then, the *torrone* is particularly good: fragrant, full of aromas, and at times coated with chocolate."

His obsession with Avola almonds and honey is similar to the obsession Sicilians have for the Bronte pistachio, grown near the village of Bronte in Provincia di Catania in the rich volcanic soil of Etna. This is the same soil that produces the remarkable lemons and blood oranges islanders hold in reverence.

Sofia, meanwhile, delves into the world of roasted peppers and other delicacies cooked over an outdoor fire. He tells how the "common people" of his youth would gather around the fire and tell their stories. "Over charcoal fry the snails, the pot bubbling on the stove with the beans. . . .

The smell of the soup with the oil, the breaded fried onions and stuffed with dried tomatoes, these scents remain in the memory of my childhood with the smell of sage, wild herbs, branches of orange or from vines that are to increase the flames. . . . The [storytellers'] chatter is the sauce, better than the bread they eat.

The roasted peppers were the most frequent and hardy dish. We toasted the peppers on the grill, peel them, cut in thin slices, leaving a few pieces of skin blackened by fire.

For the flavor and the sauce you add tomatoes and roasted them with a lot of olive oil—dense, green, full of aroma, which served mainly to temper the fire of the burning peppers. [We didn't have forks.] Each used a knife or made a fork out of a two-branch cane with which to "fish" in the great common dish.

Lynne Rossetto Kasper, in her book *The Italian Country Table,* mentions Corrado Sofia. In his memoir, she says, he described how Sicilians made what we refer to as sun-dried tomatoes. Rossetto Kasper calls them "oven-candied summer tomatoes." She says Sofia "remembers how the women on his father's farm used to make them in the leftover heat of the bread oven after the loaves came out." The heat would gradually decline in the charcoal or wood-fired ovens. She writes that the tomato slices are "slow-roasted with olive oil until their edges have a lacy golden crust and the tomatoes taste like candy."

Sounds marvelous? They are. Her book has a recipe for accomplishing this dish using a modern, temperature-controlled oven.

FIFTEEN

Un Giro

To have seen Italy without having seen Sicily is not to
have seen Italy at all, for Sicily is the clue to everything.
—Johann Wolfgang von
Goethe, *Italian Journey*
(1786–1788)

Goethe, Germany's foremost writer of the eighteenth century, made this oft-quoted statement in his well-known
eighteenth-century travelogue. It is no doubt true on many
levels, but Goethe never explains what he means by it. Does
he mean that he believed Sicily to be, in his time, well behind
the Italian peninsula in its development? Perhaps he felt that
the mainland, particularly the north, once was like what Sicily
represented to him during his visit: backward, still medieval.

Keep in mind that in the eighteenth century, Sicily and
much of southern Italy were ruled from Naples by the Bourbons of Spain; Unification with the more developed north didn't
happen until 1861, three-quarters of a century after his visit.

Sicilians, who spoke a distinct language, had virtually nothing in common with northerners.

Goethe's section on Sicily is nearly devoid of any reference to the everyday people of the island. He makes an allusion, while describing his travels north of Agrigento toward Caltanissetta, to seeing, at a distance, peasants working in a field. He observes that "women live in these hamlets all the year round, spinning and weaving." The men, meanwhile, live in the fields during the week "and sleep at night in reed huts."

Leonardo Sciascia's beloved Racalmuto is along this route; Goethe may have passed through. But wherever it was that he was observing the peasants at work, Goethe wishes "for the winged chariot of Triptolemus to bear us away out of this monotony." (For the record, the Greek goddess Demeter taught the demigod Triptolemus the secrets of agriculture, and she gave him a chariot to go around the world spreading this knowledge.)

Goethe writes extensively about the geography and geology of the island, even praising the work of a fellow German who came before and studied the island's minerals. And he takes note of the various ruins of ancient Greek temples. He generally likes the food. "The vegetables are delicious," he declares, singling out lettuce as particularly delightful. The oil and wine are okay; he likes the fish, but says of the beef, without further explanation, that "most people do not recommend it." He gives us descriptions about how "they" plant cabbages and how "they" rotate crops, once again giving us very little information about who "they" are.

Of course, he spent weeks on the backs of horses and mules making his *giro,* or tour of the island. It took place in 1787 throughout April and into May, wonderful seasons in the southern Mediterranean. It is not too hot or cold. The rolling hills are green and wildflowers are everywhere.

Goethe's accommodations were typical of the time: small dirty rooms in houses or the infrequent inn, where "[c]hairs, benches, and even tables do not exist; one sits on low blocks of solid wood." When he leaves the island in mid-May and arrives in Naples, he declares, "My journey across Sicily was quick and easy . . . My old habit of sticking to the objective and concrete has given me an ability to read things at sight, so to speak, and I am happy to think that I now carry in my soul a picture of Sicily, that unique and beautiful island, which is clear, authentic and complete." Again, there is nothing in that statement that refers to the islanders. But his is one of the few descriptions by an outsider that far back in time. His translators, W. H. Auden and Elizabeth Mayer, obviously enamored of their subject, say only, "If Goethe did not tell everything, what he did tell was true enough."

The early European travelers, such as Goethe and de Maupassant, often cross my mind as I go for long drives around the island. It took Goethe, for example, a month and a half to travel, in a V-like slash, south from Palermo down to the coast at Agrigento and then to the northeast toward Messina, where he departed by sea for Naples. In our time, of course, you can drive, in a horrifically long day, I suppose, around the entire island, staying on main roads that occasionally leave the coast and dart inland for brief stretches. Or you can crisscross it via a web of well-marked secondary roads—foot- and mule paths

in the days of the early European travelers—connecting isolated villages.

Traveling on these narrow roads, I believe, makes for more
pleasant journeys—journeys of unexpected discoveries—than
following the autostrada or the truck-jammed main highways.
All you need is a good map and a sense of adventure.

More realistically, it might take three to four hours to go
from a remote point in the southeast, say Noto or Ragusa, to
the west coast at Scopello, just west of Castellammare del
Golfo. Or, over a few days from a base in a small village, say
from Racalmuto, you can head in different directions each
morning and easily explore a third of the island without having to move your luggage from inn to inn.

One such place was in Scopello. The first visit was in November 2009. My son and I arrived late in the evening, around
nine. We had crossed the island east to west from just north of
Catania in a rambling trip that took an entire day due to a
handful of impetuous stops. One was to the hilltop town of
Agira, birthplace of Diodorus Siculus, the first-century B.C.
Greek-Sicilian historian. It is a town—its ancient Greek name
was Agyrium—with a tenuous grip on the mountainside and
prone to underground rumblings from Etna to the east. And we
also stopped at Enna, situated in Sicily's dead center and placed
strategically on a high, almost-impregnable plateau that had
mightily resisted countless assaults over the centuries by swarm
after swarm of invaders.

Usually Enna was taken only after someone in it had be-
trayed the defenders and opened the gates in the dark of night.
Here, I got horribly lost trying to find the historic center. (It

took three visits before I finally got the confusing layout under control.)

On this particular journey, it was November and dark when we pulled off the main west-coast highway at Castellammare and turned toward Scopello, a tiny village with only twenty-five permanent residents. It had three hundred at the end of World War II, but most immigrated to the United States. The bed-and-breakfast I had spotted weeks earlier on the Internet, Pensione Tranchina, was easy to find. Marisin Tranchina greeted us, showed us our comfortable room on the third floor of the remarkably restored structure that likely dates back three or four centuries, and then fixed a dinner of pasta and swordfish, prepared, she said, in the style of Trapani, the port city a few miles to the south.

The olive oil that went with the bread was particularly tasty. Marisin said their harvest had just ended; the olives from their five hundred trees had just been pressed. Moments later, she handed me a sealed can containing a liter of the oil. I've never used it for cooking; the cheaper, store-bought oil works fine for that. Tranchina's oil goes on salads, over pasta flaked with basil, or is mopped up with chunks of crusty bread.

It was late. We ate and then settled our bill because we would leave for the airport before sunrise the next morning. So it was dark when we arrived and dark when we left. I immediately made another reservation, this one for three nights, for my next trip five months away.

The following morning, we came downstairs to a wonderful breakfast spread out for us during the night. We ate, sitting in the semidarkness of Tranchina's front room, croissants with marmalade and salami with slices of cheese, and drank steaming, rich, black coffee American-style. Forty-five minutes later, we were at Falcone-Borsellino Airport for our flight to Rome.

When another traveling companion, Steve McCurdy, and I arrived at Pensione Tranchina for my second visit, in March 2010, I had this one timed right. We drove up the coast during a bright afternoon that gave us impressive views of this rugged coastline. Perched on a hill, the town oversees the Gulf of Castellammare and, beyond, the Tyrrhenian Sea as it spills counterclockwise around Sicily's western edge. This whole peninsula, with Capo San Vito at the point, obviously is a tourist haven. It once was a smuggler's paradise because of its remoteness: isolated beaches against steep, rocky cliffs, few roads, and fewer houses. The road leading to Scopello and the nature preserve next door is lined with houses and signs to dozens of hotels and *pensioni,* all blessed with dazzling views of the Mediterranean.

This time, we meet Salvatore, Marisin's Sicilian husband whose family has been here for several generations. Marisin is Chinese. Because her birth name is difficult for Italians and Sicilians to pronounce, she breaks with tradition here and uses her husband's surname, Tranchina, pronounced in the Italian manner, "Tran-key-na." Women in Italy and Sicily generally carry their birth surnames while children take the father's name. She laughs at the coincidence of her ethnicity, Chinese, and Salvatore's Tranchina—"across China," she says with a smile.

The pair met in Panama, where she lived with her parents; he worked on construction projects with other family members. Salvatore came back to Scopello to take over his share of the family property in 1976; Marisin followed in 1982. They remodeled the family home, adding a couple of new floors, completely modernized the structure, and turned it into Pensione Tranchina.

There is a faded, blurry black-and-white photograph on the wall of the reception/dining area dating back to 1954. It shows Salvatore and his family posing in front of the house. Salvatore is a small child, barefoot and sitting in a doorway just east of the pensione's entrance. The photograph, taken from a low angle, shows the rough, rocky surface of the tiny piazza in front of the house, built in the 1800s.

Today, the square with a large fountain is beautifully paved. The picture shows how most piazzas looked in southern Italy and Sicily long before villages became scrubbed and modernized during the advent of mass tourism.

The Scopello of Salvatore's childhood was a fishing village; now there is a closed tuna-processing plant, a *tonnaro,* with origins deep into Muslim times, down the hill on the gulf's shoreline. It, too, has been restored and is now used for conferences and weddings. Two castle towers, dating back to the thirteenth century, are nearby. One is abandoned; the other has been converted into a home.

Paths lead down to three beaches sought after by sun-loving tourists who pack the *pensioni* in this tiny town from late spring to early fall. One of those beaches, Baia Guidaloca, located nearly two miles to the east, is where Odysseus, his clothes ripped off by a roiling sea, found himself after he was shipwrecked during an event engineered by, as Homer's poem says, "Poseidon god of earthquake." The local king's daughter Nausicaa—who "shone among her maids, a virgin, still unwed"—found him and took him to her father's court, where Odysseus told the stories of his adventures that make up much of Homer's epic poem.

Sicilians, it seems, claim that many of Odysseus's adventures occurred on or around this island: the man-eating monster Scylla at the Strait of Messina; the Aeolian islands, home of the master of the winds, Aeolus; the cyclops Polyphemus at Aci Trezza. Now he meets the lovely Nausicaa along the rocky shore in the Gulf of Castellammare. Of course, long before tourism became important here, Sicilians of all stripes in this mixed land of myth and reality knew these stories.

Marisin and Salvatore offer a tour of their olive grove, which has some of the most stunning views from the rolling hills overlooking the rich blue waters of the Gulf of Castellammare. Originally purchased by Salvatore's grandparents, this land represents his share and the shares various uncles sold to him. For the Tranchinas, it is both a place of great joy and of great disappointment.

In 1977, Salvatore, fresh from Panama, launched a building project here. He wanted to build several small, detached resort-type units and array them around the hillside, popped here and there amid clusters of the family's almond and olive trees. The land represents about one hundred thousand square meters, or nearly twenty-five acres. The skeletal frames, perhaps a half dozen or so, of those small, squat structures with their concrete floors and pillars, are still standing. But work halted before they could be completed.

The units are low-slung and were designed to blend unob-

trusively into the tree-covered hillside, not shoot up like gar-
ish multistory, view-blocking hotels of the kind that obliterate
glorious views throughout this island.

"We had all the permits, and we started building what you
see now," Salvatore tells us, speaking Italian with Marisin interpreting. The pillars went up, the floors were poured, and
then "they stopped us." "They" were regional officials based in
Palermo, who wanted the land as an undeveloped buffer to
the adjoining Lo Zingaro Nature Reserve, nearly four thousand acres of protected flora and fauna typical of Sicily.

The couple cannot get an explanation for the order to stop.
They said that even reserve officials were not opposed to their
plans because the reserve boundary begins on the ridgeline, a
significant distance uphill and out of sight from where they
wanted to place the units.

Some local officials, many years ago, told the couple the
government was wrong in its order, but nothing has changed.
It would take a great deal of money to fight it, and the Tranchinas made the decision to pour funds into their pensione rather
than fight what could be an expensive losing cause.

"Maybe we have to look for some good 'connections,' but if
you have to get involved with that . . ." Salvatore's voice trails
off, knowing he doesn't want to play the Sicilian game of pay-
offs to get officials to act in his behalf.

So the partially completed units sit there amid, in March, a
dazzling array of wildflowers, such as the yellow margarita
daisy, and abundant olive and walnut trees just now beginning to blossom. Soon, Marisin says, the wildflowers will begin to wither and dry out.

"The sirocco winds, you know. And this land will be in

danger of catching fire and burning." To prevent this, at least on their land, the couple hires workers to weed-whack the soon-to-be-brown foliage.

And, by October or November, the olive harvest begins. In 2009, the year of the oil she handed to me during my first trip, the Tranchinas harvested four hundred liters. A stronger year might yield six hundred.

We drive down the mountain on the winding dirt road and into Scopello past a large, half-completed hotel project—it would be huge in this town of small *pensioni*. Its construction has halted, like so many projects in Sicily and southern Italy over the decades, because developers ran out of funds.

It is dinnertime at Pensione Tranchina. On the table before me rests a sea bass. I wasn't a fan of seafood until Marisin served me that cut of swordfish Trapanese style five months earlier. She stands at my side and patiently shows me how to debone it. I bite into the fish, caught in the early hours of that same day, and decide that she has made me into an eater of seafood.

Four trips over a year's time, all drives around the island, spontaneous as well as planned, have been enjoyable and in-vigorating. But one in particular, to visit an area that figures mightily in twentieth-century Sicilian history but remains a tragedy cloaked in mystery, had me concerned. My emotions always run high when I walk across old battlefields, whether in the eastern United States or in Europe. On this journey, I felt a need to visit the scene of an event that most Sicilians would like to forget.

Steve McCurdy and I are off main roads and scuttling our way up and around hills and plunging down through deep valleys toward the isolated village of Piana degli Albanesi. It dates back to the fifteenth century and was one of a handful of towns established for Albanian colonists. Much of that eastern European language is still part of the local dialect.

It was from here, in 1947, that a traditional May 1 procession—led by Sicilian communists along a narrow country road a few miles to the southwest—ended in tragedy. Leftists had scored a major victory at the ballot box a few weeks earlier, electing to the Sicilian Parliament politicians who enacted laws allowing peasants to take over uncultivated land controlled by Sicily's more privileged barons.

The May 1 procession, which traditionally ended at a place known as Portella della Ginestra—it's called Portelja e Gijinestrës in the Albanian-infused local dialect—was to celebrate that victory. Dozens of flag-waving residents joined the procession.

Bands played, speakers, standing on the Sasso di Barbato, the large, flat stone that since the late 1800s had served as the stage for these celebrations, shouted into megaphones. It was named for Nicola Barbato, a physician from the area involved in the *fasci Siciliani*. This was a 1890s post-Unification socialist movement that began among artisans in cities such as Palermo. It later spread to the countryside to include the peasant class, which sought land reform and opposed what it considered oppressive taxation.

The best description I have read about what took place that day was reported by British travel writer Norman Lewis in his book *In Sicily*. It also is documented in *Salvatore Giuliano*, a

1962 Italian film directed by Francesco Rosi, whose unvarnished, truthful recounting makes it a much better film than Hollywood's 1987 version, *The Sicilian*. That film made the badly compromised Giuliano, the last remaining bandit in western Sicily, into a romantic hero, a sort of Sicilian Robin Hood.

The reality was that right-wing landowners, upset over the vote granting land to impoverished peasants, and in collusion with the Mafia, convinced Giuliano to attack the celebrants, Lewis reports, "as an example to the recalcitrant peasantry in general."

Giuliano and his men, using machine guns and other equipment left behind—or somehow, mysteriously, acquired from the American military—at the close of the war two years earlier, set up on the hillside above the open area. In the midst of speeches, cheering, bands playing, and red flags waving, the guns rained death down onto the people. The numbers are not consistent, but some sources indicate that eleven, perhaps fourteen, people, including three children, were killed and thirty wounded.

Giuliano later claimed that he ordered his men to fire over the heads of the people; some sources postulate that the Mafia infiltrated his band of bandits and fired directly at the people.

Eventually, the bandits were tracked down and many were convicted at trials that began in 1950, the same year Giuliano died at the hand of one of his trusted lieutenants. By then, Lewis says, Giuliano had been isolated; his only contact to his former band was "his cousin and originally his second in command. A secret deal was arranged whereby both men would be allowed to leave Sicily and fly to the U.S.A. in a military plane."

But the Mafia had other ideas. Mafiosi put Giuliano up in a house in the town of Castelvetrano, far to the south. Then the double-cross played out. Rosi's film, which seems fairly accurate for the few facts known in the early 1960s, shows Giuliano being visited by his cousin, Gaspare Pisciotta, who suddenly shoots the bandit leader lying in bed. He does this in collusion with the police who wanted the bandit taken alive. But hearing the shots, officials enter the room and decide the events must be rigged to show Giuliano died in a shootout with authorities.

These officials carry the body downstairs and outside into the tiny piazza in front of a small cluster of houses. There isn't enough blood, so an officer shoots him a few more times. But blood doesn't flow from the now lifeless body. So someone grabs a chicken, cuts off its head, and sprays blood over the body and onto the cobblestones.

There is a photograph on the cover of a book, *Mafia and Outlaw Stories from Italian Life and Literature,* showing this key scene from the movie: the bandit's body sprawled facedown on the stones, a pistol and a rifle nearby, and a group of Sicilian men gathered against a stone wall, looking down at the body.

The movie was filmed in all the actual locations: Giuliano's village of Montelepre and the mountains surrounding it; Portella della Ginestra, where the massacre took place; in Castelvetrano in the room where he was murdered by his cousin; and in the tiny square outside.

One side note: Many of the people from Piana degli Albanesi who had survived the May Day massacre fifteen years earlier appeared in this same scene in the film. When the cameras started rolling and the recorded shots rang out, it became too much to bear for some of the participants. Many felt as though they were reliving the actual event and became hysterical. They panicked and scattered, giving the director far more realism captured on film than he had bargained for.

I visited Portella della Ginestra on a warm March afternoon, following the short drive from Piana degli Albanesi. Today, there are stone walkways through the site. Large rocks carved with the names of some of those who died there and other stones carved into with the brief outline of the story, stand like monoliths across the space. There is no mention of either Giuliano and his men or the Mafia.

The stones list names like Mergheritacles Ceri, Giorgiocu Senza, Dimaggio Giuseppe, La Fata Vincenza, Intravaia Castense—all names still common to the area, many reflecting Albanian origins. On another stone is this inscription, in Sicilian, translated by Alissandru (Alex) Caldiero:

> *U me cori*
> *doppu tant'anni*
> *e' a Purtedda*
> *e nte petri*
> *e nto sangu*
> *di' cumpagni*
> *ammazzati*
>
> My heart
> after so many years
> is in *Purtedda*

and in the stones
and in the blood
of murdered
comrades

Purtedda is the Sicilian name for the Italian word *"Portello"* and it represents the area where the massacre took place. There are low stone walls around the site. Across the narrow highway is a huge parking area. In 1947, none of this was here. There were fallen rocks embedded in the fields of *ginestra,* or broom plants, that naturally come out in spring.

It is quiet here. I don't believe a single vehicle comes along the roadway in the hour or so Steve McCurdy and I walk around the area. Slight breezes come off the flanks of the Pizzuta, the mountain that hangs over the small valley, on whose flanks the bandits were arrayed with their American machine guns. I've never gotten a satisfactory answer to why American weapons were used. Some say they were supplied to the bandits by U.S. Army officials. No one seems to know what motive the Americans would have to do that, other than perhaps the typical U.S. opposition in that era to anything that smacks of communism. I do know that Salvatore Giuliano reportedly had written a letter to President Harry S. Truman asking that the United States annex Sicily much as it had done with Puerto Rico. I don't know if Truman responded.

The reality of what happened here may be deeply embedded in the failed separatist movement that was so strong immediately following the war. Giuliano, at war's end, was made a colonel in the separatist militia. What likely happened was that when he was no longer needed—the separatist movement essentially died when Rome gave Sicily regional autonomy in 1946—and following the disaster at Portella, his Mafia and political handlers had to do something about him.

And they had to do something about his cousin, who knew too much. Four years after Giuliano's death, Gaspare Pisciotta died in his Palermo prison cell when he drank his morning coffee, which had been laced with strychnine. The key players are dead; none gave enough information during their trials and incarcerations to explain the backstory of the bandit's motives during those postwar years. More than half a century later, much of the mystery still simmers.

The tiny courtyard in Castelvetrano is still there. The gate so clearly shown in the movie is closed the day we arrived. A small garage has been built over the spot where Giuliano's body was displayed; the doorway into the house where he was staying—it had belonged to a mafioso of the time—is shut tight; it doesn't look like anyone is living there. Farther back, on the opposite side of the tiny square, stands a two-story apartment house. A young woman is on the balcony hanging laundry. Visitors to this spot, I am sure, are not infrequent, and she took no notice.

On the left side of the gate a marker notes that this is the spot where the bandit Salvatore Giuliano was gunned down. The myth survives. Again, there is no mention of the Mafia involvement or complicity by police.

Just seven months after our visit, on October 28, 2010, ANSA, the Italian news service, reported that Palermo prosecutors had ordered the exhumation of Giuliano's body from the Montelepre cemetery. They wanted to check his DNA to be sure that the body was really his. A new report had showed contradictions in official reports about the death, and authorities wanted to be sure the bandit was not spirited away to live out his life elsewhere. It would take several months, they said, for the test results to be known. In April 2011, the online edition of *Corriere del Mezzogiorno* reported that there was a "degree of compatibility" between the body's DNA and that of a nephew of the bandit.

In four trips to the island within a year's time, I've experienced early spring twice, a blistering summer, and a comfortable, golden fall with the air heavy with grapes. No matter the season, something is always growing here or always ready for harvest. I watched olives tumble from the trees in the fall; saw ripening almonds clustered on dark branches in advance of their August harvest; walked by fields of tomatoes in various shades of red, hanging heavily on vines and awaiting pickers during the year's hottest months; dodged swaying trucks with high, slatted sides delivering mounds of black and deep purple eggplant; and glided through, in a small boat on the Ciane River near Siracusa, vast lemon groves awaiting harvest. Along eastern Sicily highways in the late fall and early winter were thousands of acres of various varieties of heavily laden orange trees, including Etna's famed blood oranges.

Around Piazza Armerina, in the island's south-central quadrant, I drove for miles through vast fields of cactus plants being grown as a fruit crop. In perfect rows, the plants looked to be at least fifteen feet tall. They bear fruit that Americans know as the prickly pear. This has a taste similar, I discovered, to watermelon. Served cold and with the tough outer

skin removed, the fruit is refreshing. In some places in southern Sicily, Sicilians use it to make liqueur called *ficodi*. At a
small, roadside stand, a young man made a face as he told me
about it. "It tastes like medicine," he said with a grimace. I didn't
try it.

Obviously, Sicily's identity is tied to the land. There are vast
fields covered in plastic sheeting by giant corporate growers to
push growing seasons earlier and earlier. There are small plots
managed by individual families who haul their vegetables,
fruits, lemons, and oranges to the daily markets in villages of
all sizes.

Even when one is locked within urban concrete and far
from the fragrant land, fresh produce is available daily. I recall
being lost while driving through a heavily built-up section of
Mazara del Vallo, near Marsala on the southwest coast. As I sat
in my rental car pondering my next move, a slow-moving
truck playing loud chimes turned the corner and stopped in
front of a building. Women appeared on a half dozen balconies
across the length of the building two and three floors above the
street. They lowered baskets on ropes to the man, who opened
the back of the truck to expose rows of vegetables: eggplants,
Sicilian squash, lettuce, potatoes, and several varieties of leafy
crops I didn't recognize.

The women shouted down their orders, the man piled the
baskets high, and they were then hauled up, hand over hand.
He shouted something to each woman, and the baskets came
back down again with euro bills and change inside. I suspect
milk is delivered in the same way to these urban neighborhoods, built far from the open market areas that abound elsewhere.

The southwestern corner of Sicily has seen much over the centuries. Its prehistory may be hidden to us, but from the archaic era through medieval times the area has been integral in how this island developed. Mazara del Vallo is where the Arabs landed in A.D. 827 to begin their conquest of the island. And just southeast from that modern city, at a place the Greeks called Selinous (the Romans called it Selinus; today it is listed on maps as Selinunte), sits a massive archaeological site that dazzles the mind. Its acropolis is situated on a promontory between two rivers—the Modione to the west, called in ancient times the Selinous, and the Belice on the east. In those days, these rivers were much larger and offered bays that clearly defined the promontory. Now, a few houses are built on land that has filled in the bays, and the rivers trickle their way past, snaking across narrow beaches into the sea.

This Greek city was established the farthest west of any other Greek cities on the island. It was founded in the seventh century B.C. during a migration involving colonists from Sicily's east coast who found themselves too close to Siracusa, then called Syracusae, to the south and other colonists to the west and north. Because the Greeks were never politically unified as a nation and despite their common language and shared culture, Greek city-states fought one another throughout ancient times. The same held true for the Greek-Sicilian colonists.

In Selinous, at the bow of the promontory jutting into the narrow Strait of Sicily that separates the island from Tunisia, they built the acropolis. Massive temples dedicated to various

gods were arrayed across the landscape. One, a temple dedicated to Zeus's wife, Hera, and known as Temple E, is the only
one that has been partially reconstructed. Today the foundations of hundreds, if not thousands, of ancient homes, built in
neighborhood grids, are spread out across the landscape.

An aerial photograph shows much more open land yet to
be uncovered and explored. Clearly marked streets, some narrow, some wide boulevards leading to city gates, remain.

Its residents fought many skirmishes with Segesta to the
northeast, only one of Selinous's enemies. By the second century B.C., the once magnificent city was fairly well abandoned.
Built on land composed primarily of sand and sandy clay, Selinous was devastated by earthquakes, not to mention the wars
its citizens fought and lost.

The death blow came during the First Punic War at the
hands of the Carthaginians. Most of its twenty-five thousand
citizens were moved to Lilybaion, today's Marsala, on the far
southwest coast. Rome left then empty Selinous alone when
Romans defeated Carthage and took over the island, and the
place crumbled into piles of golden stones, probably wracked
over the centuries by earthquakes and now overgrown by
low-lying brush and wild celery plants that still flourish on the
plain and gave the city its name.

I drove to Selinous/Selinunte one glorious March 2009
morning, just an hour or so after leaving the lone temple at
Segesta. The archaeological park is huge, covering nearly 667
acres. Guy de Maupassant, the French writer who traveled
here during his Sicilian odyssey in the late 1880s, gave this
place a four-sentence description in his book *Sicily*. In it, he
raved about Segesta and its solitary unfinished temple and

amphitheater. But he mocked Selinous, this once magnificent Greek city, as "a heap of collapsed columns" and a "shapeless heap of stones" that could appeal only to "archaeologists or poetic souls."

It took a long time for those archaeologists to make sense of the rubble. They waited until the 1950s, I am told, to begin restoring the temple to Hera, Temple E. Ironically, the single temple at the more famous Segesta, which likely draws more tourists, is much smaller than any of the individual temple sites at Selinous.

Today, Temple E and the acropolis are the only places in the vast Selinous plain with columns resurrected. But brush has been cleared from some of the areas where houses once stood three thousand years ago. As far as the eye can see, it is obvious that many of these now leveled dwelling sites remain hidden by nearly impenetrable thorny brush.

For a few extra euros beyond the admission price, a visitor can get a ride in a golf cart from one edge of the park, say from the visitor's center to the area around Temple E, and then to the acropolis. On the day I was there, and then again in the following July, many hikers eschewed the carts, and with backpacks full of their picnic lunches, set off on foot.

That seemed to me the right way to do it—if you have time to spend a day. But just walking across the tumbled stones of the acropolis, with its gate to the north and its scaffold-covered columns lined up in a west-east layout, got me in touch with the place.

On the western edge of the acropolis, overlooking the Modione River and a beach community far in the distance, I discovered I was standing in the midst of ruins that either once

were houses or, given their proximity to the acropolis, perhaps a cemetery. It was here that I realized what a paradise
this island was to the Greeks and all the successive conquerors
that made their way here. But it was a paradise wracked by
brutal times.

On this stunning promontory, surrounded by golden columns and a city full of life, its citizens could be defeated, forcibly
transported to strange locations, and these temples and hundreds of homes abandoned. We, of course, know parallels in
our modern era.

It was a rare moment that March; I felt the emotion, sat
down on a stone chiseled millennia ago for the wall of someone's house, and rode it out.

I first visited Siracusa in 1986. I was there for a few hours as a
reservist, traveling with a group of U.S. Navy people based at
Sigonella Naval Air Station near Catania. We were visiting the
grave in that city of an American sailor who had died in 1803
while aboard the USS *Constitution,* Old Ironsides, anchored in
the harbor. This was during the First Barbary War against the
pirates based in Tripoli.

I remember little of that visit. Our van passed the cata-
combs where someone mentioned Archimedes had been en-
tombed. In a subsequent trip many years later, I tried to find
the place where the sailor's grave was located but failed. Then,
in the late 1990s, I returned for five days and had ample opportunity to explore the city, particularly the original city on the
island where the Greeks first settled and built their temples,
and that became a magnificent center rivaling Athens.

I made a handful of other trips over the years to Siracusa. On one, I went for a middle-of-the-night walk from my pensione across the short bridge connecting the mainland to the ancient island of Ortygia, where the 2,700-year-old city began.

It was near midnight. Only a thin scattering of electric lights highlighted small patches of the medieval buildings packed onto the tiny island that once held, centuries before Christ, the Greeks of Syracusae. A full moon overwhelmed the sky above, its light subduing the stars that on a darker night would set the heavens ablaze above the Ionian Sea.

Sitting on a low stone wall, I watched the natural light filter down, kissing the honey-colored buildings. There was no suggestion of motors this late at night, only the hint of air moving through the canopies of trees lining the water's edge, the sound of water gently slapping against stones, and the bump of wooden boat hulls against their restraints and the stone wall of the tiny harbor.

This scene out of the late twentieth century could have been unchanged from one viewed from this spot on a similarly dark, almost silent night hundreds of years earlier. It was a comfortable few hours away from the clamor of the city.

Siracusa is a walkable city, particularly on the island and even in the congestion of daytime traffic. The most stunning sight is the duomo, built in the first half of the eighteenth century on top of a Greek temple dedicated to the goddess Athena. The Greek pillars are still there, blended into the walls and supporting the massive roof. It is quiet in that church; as soon as the door closed behind me, the sounds from the busy square in front disappeared. I had the same sensation in Milan when I strolled into the duomo there: absolute silence within a vastness incomprehensible to the American psyche. The world, in all its noise and grime, is completely shut out. Such a setting is a wonderful place to sit, observe the commingling of ancient and medieval, and take stock after a long and tiring day.

But on my last trip, in March 2010, the best part was out of the city on the mainland side of the bay directly across from the island's docking areas. Here flow small spring-fed rivers: the famous Ciane and the nondescript Saline.

My photographer friend and fellow traveler on this particular trip, Steve McCurdy, and I drive to where I have been told we can get a boat ride on the Ciane. I am eager to do this for two reasons: The river is steeped in myth—it got its name from the nymph who tried to stop Hades from carrying Persephone into the underworld—and it is the only place in Europe where papyrus grows. Years before, I had watched an artist paint a Siracusian landscape showing ruined Greek or Roman columns, a cactus with two ripe prickly pears, and a pond with a pair of ducks on a sheet of papyrus, likely ordered from Egypt; it now hangs in my office and, along with my replica bust of the goddess Hera, each takes me back to long-ago times.

The myth that is part of this short river's heritage is only some of what it is known for. It is the site where Greeks harvested papyrus, also known as *byblos,* for writing. Sicilian historians believe it most likely was brought to Sicily from Alexandria when ties between that Egyptian city and Siracusa were very close.

Today, the tall, rangy plants, some reaching as high as nineteen feet, are clustered around a small area along Ciane's banks, today protected as a nature reserve. The river is accessible only by boat, and only operators with special permits can navigate the waters. The plants, with the billowy, balls-of-fluff tops, cannot be harvested.

We pay our fee and hop into Vella Corrado's brightly painted, well-maintained boat. It is docked in a canal that runs adjacent to the Ciane. Vella takes us downstream where we grab a quick view of Siracusa's boat harbor across the bay.

It is early afternoon; the light is perfect, and the view stunning. Vella, hand on the tiller of a nearly silent motor, maneuvers us around and into the mouth of the Ciane. It is narrow. Tree limbs overhang the water, giving it almost a feel of gliding along a bayou in the southern United States. The river is three to four miles long; we will go only halfway in a journey of less than an hour.

We move slowly, exulting in the calm, clear, fragrant air. To our right is a lemon orchard. Vella gives us the etymology of lemons. The trees produce a very sweet, barely tart variety known as *Femminello* that produces four times a year, compared to orange trees that only produce once a year. A Web site administered by the University of California–Riverside, quoting *The Citrus Industry*, reveals: "The autumn [lemon] crop is called *Primofiore,* the winter-to-spring crop is called *Limoni,* the spring crop is called *Bianchetti,* and the summer crop is called *Verdelli.*"

I had discovered this lack of tartness in Sicilian lemons on an earlier trip. A bowl of fruit had been placed for us at a house I was staying in near Noto, a thirty-five-minute drive west of Siracusa. I was advised to eat the lemons in that bowl as I would eat an orange. I cut it into quarters and slurped each slice from the rind. The taste was remarkable. There was only a hint of tartness; otherwise it was just pure lemony sweetness, like an orange in its mild assault on the taste buds, but different from the orange in flavor.

Vella is the third-generation boatman in his family and has been taking people along the Ciane for thirty years. "It is the only work I have ever done," he says. He is a lucky man, I think, in this land of chronic double-digit unemployment. He and his brother, Rossario, who also travels the Ciane with tourists, make their own boats. Vella discounts buying one readymade. "Progress is good," he says, "except when it comes to making a boat."

We reach an area where the river borders a large tree-shaded pond fueled by groundwater. I wonder, in a brief flight of fantasy, if this is where Hades turned the nymph into the spring.

Vella points to a narrow trail along the riverbank and says that a few dozen feet beyond are the papyrus plants. We find the giant clusters. The stems are woody but pliable. Turn the green outer stem inside out and you find a white interior. I can see how the ancients gathered these reedlike stems together, split them open, and pounded them into a material strong and permanent enough to write on.

Vella, the man with the perfect job, is in no hurry. We linger, listen to the birds and the trees trembling in the light breeze. It's a paradise here; there are so many paradises in Sicily. Reluctantly, we make our way back to the boat.

"Are you sure you want to go now?" Vella asks, offering to linger with us. Unfortunately, we have to be miles up the coast by late afternoon, past more lemon and orange groves in this wonderfully sweet-smelling land. Even the oil refineries and chemical-plant complexes a few miles up the road in Augusta can't spoil that.

The goal of our late-March 2010 trip is, finally, to experience Easter in Sicily. A year earlier, I had left too soon for the annual weeklong holiday. Many years before that, when I was touring southern Italy along the Ionian Sea, I had left before the holiday as well. Easter is a major event, especially in southern Italy and Sicily; it needs to be experienced.

My sense is that this time of the year, a time that is deeply embedded in the Sicilian soul, outpaces Christmas. The July festival in Palermo honoring that city's patron saint is massive, to be sure. Tens of thousands turn out for the spectacle and then get the next day off. The March 19 altar-bread festival on San Giuseppe's feast day in Racalmuto brings out the villagers en masse, and the July festival there with men on horseback charging up steep stone steps into a church ends three days of good, raucous fun drawing thousands.

But Easter is sacred, it's emotional, and the festivities in many towns and villages last the whole of Easter Week, from Good Monday through Good Friday and then the climax, Easter Sunday.

For this experience, Steve McCurdy and I are drawn to the central Sicily city of Enna because its celebration of the sacred week is known worldwide. There are nearly one hundred churches, all Catholic, of course, in this city of thirty thousand souls. When Easter is talked about on international news programs, it seems each broadcast features a clip of the solemn processions that define this city. The Good Friday procession here, perhaps the best-known outside of Sicily, is done in a Spanish style that goes back a few hundred years to the time of Spanish domination. It is done in near silence; after all, the faithful here are marking the most tragic day in Christendom: Christ's crucifixion.

We arrive on Thursday of Easter Week and check into the B-and-B Proserpina—the Roman name for the Greek goddess Persephone—in the heart of the old city. The location places us along the route of the processions that move up and down Via Roma just a few dozen feet away. The di Miceli family warmly greets us and helps with luggage. The next morning, brother and sister Dario and Laura di Miceli offer to take us on a tour in their specially designed three-wheel motorized Ape.

We discover one of the city's two remaining ancient gates—La Porta di Janniscuru—high on a hillside honeycombed by caves and grottoes that once were prehistoric tombs. This gate, Dario and Laura tell us, is almost always missed by tourists. Featuring a small Roman arch and built in the seventeenth century, it is one of the "newer" gates of the seven or nine or twelve that once were arrayed around Enna's walls.

Different sources give different numbers. Dario and Laura believe that the number is twelve, and included four big gates, four smaller ones like the Janniscuru, and four "doors." This one is barely noticeable from one of the modern roads into the city where traffic rumbles by perhaps one hundred feet below. The only other surviving gate is the Porta di Palermo, a narrow walkway off Via Roma near the cathedral and adjacent to one of the finest ceramic shops I have ever come across: Gaetano Mirisciotti's Ceramiche Artistiche. During two different trips to visit Gaetano, I had missed the significance of this gate, set back on the side of his small shop. It looks northwest in the direction, of course, of Palermo.

The brother-and-sister duo then show us the castle that dominates one end of Enna's old city center, but what catches my attention is the high rock at the plateau's end. Laura explains that this spot, Rocca di Cerere, is where Enna's teenagers hang out at night to survey the lights of the massive Dittaino Valley spread out far below.

More important, she says, it once was the site of a Greek shrine to Demeter, Persephone's mother. It is from the top of this rock that Mary Taylor Simeti stood and imagined Demeter in this same place losing sight of her daughter along the shore of Lago di Pergusa in the valley far, far below. Where teenagers now frolic, sacrifices to appease the goddess of agriculture were carried out.

The remains of another ancient Greek temple to Demeter have been uncovered as well. Across Enna, on a higher part of the plateau, stands the Church of Montesalvo, built on top of an ancient temple to Persephone. Next to it stands a column on the spot that is supposed to be the precise center of Sicily.

Across from Demeter's rock sits a massive walled Lombardstyle castle where, in the fourteenth century, Frederick III, the brother of the king of Spanish Aragon, was crowned king of Trinacria, the name the French demanded as part of the Treaty of Caltabellotta to end the war of the Sicilian Vespers.

There are those who believe that the castle rests on the remains of Arab fortifications and, perhaps, below that are foundations from a Roman-era fort. We enter the castle grounds and climb one of the remaining towers. The view after a long, circular, strenuous climb up narrow stone steps is spectacular and worth the effort.

The observance of Good Friday begins in the old town around two o'clock. That is when police start to ban parking along Via Roma and the other streets where the procession, which begins at the top of the hill around the cathedral, will flow. Vehicle owners have been warned: No cars allowed after two. Still, tow trucks are busy.

Visitors have started arriving, working their way on foot along Via Roma toward the cathedral. Sometime around four o'clock—times on printed schedules are never precise; this is Sicily, where things happen on their own time—a procession from one church, San Leandro, travels to another church, the Addolorata, where various confraternities are gathered. It is here that the statue of the grieving Madonna is kept. They are met by the confraternity from the Church of Santa Santissima Salvatore, where the statue of the dead Christ is lodged.

Confraternities are groups of laymen who do special work of piety and service for their particular churches. In Enna, the oldest of the fifteen still active, the Confraternita del S.S. Salvatore, was established in 1261. Its cape color is deep yellow and has the Maltese cross on the left side. The newest, the Confraternita del S.S. Crocifisso di Pergusa, was founded in 1973. Its members wear an old Spanish habit. The hood is pointed. Their church is San Leonardo.

In some cases, the groups were formed out of those practicing a specific trade and who went to a specific church for such practitioners. For example, the Confraternita del Sacro Cuore di Gesù, established in 1839, was primarily comprised of sulfur miners. The Confraternita dello Spirito Santo, organized in 1800, was made up of farmers from a district of Enna known as the Funnurò.

The confraternities, each with members distinguished by various colorful robes, walk in the procession in a specific order that, for centuries, has never varied. They are made up of Catholic men of all ages and boys from about age five upward. Each group has a specific function. Within the clusters of male-dominated confraternities, young girls ranging in age from six or seven to early teens are dressed in nuns' habits or white silk robes, and they walk with the men and boys.

Two confraternities carry the *simulacri,* or statues, of the crucified Christ and the grieving Madonna. This Madonna has a sword through her breast, representing her pain at the death of her son. The adult men, perhaps as many as seventy-five to a statue, who carry the monstrously heavy loads do not wear hoods over their faces as others in the procession do. The cloth is pulled back over their heads to keep their vision clear.

These are huge statues: The Madonna is standing upright, towering over the city street; the bloody Christ is prone and is laid out in a glass-walled casket. Both are larger than life. Like soldiers and sailors, the adult robed men carrying the statues on their shoulders walk jammed tightly together, swaying slightly in unison. They don't stride, they shuffle. A small group of men walk backward at the front, guiding the ends of the heavy beams supporting the *simulacro,* their eyes fixed on the statues to detect any problem. As I did in Racalmuto during the feast of Saint Giuseppe, I wonder if any of the giant figures ever topple. No one I ask can, or will tell. "No, no, no. Unthinkable!" one says.

At the rear, other men guide the beams' ends using ropes that aid in guiding the carriers as they swing the whole contraption around corners. It all runs with precision. The guides keep the men shouldering the heavy statues in unison and on track with quiet commands.

Other members of confraternities—wearing hoods with tiny holes cut out for the eyes—carry other symbols that relate to the story of the Passion. One group carries items on red satin pillows, such as Christ's crown of thorns, or the nails that held Christ's hands and feet to the cross, or the hammer that drove those nails. Others carry candles, some real, some powered by batteries. Other groups carry torches. Small boys, dressed identically to their elders and with hoods in place, walk in the procession with adults in their midst to keep them in proper order.

The route is long, perhaps two miles. It begins at the cathedral amid pealing bells and firecrackers, and then the procession and spectators plunge into near silence. The route winds down through the ancient city streets to the cemetery. There the marchers pause and rest up for the journey back. It begins around six o'clock and ends close to midnight.

I am amazed at the endurance represented here, especially the children, whether bedecked in robes of the confraternities, or nuns' habits, or white silk dresses. They carry candles shrouded in brown paper. The girls walk with solemn expressions, their hands clasped in prayer. For five or six hours this goes on. No one drops out; no one quits. Back at the cathedral, they are finally joined by their families.

In times past, I was told, some members of the crowd would follow the procession barefoot as a sign of their devotion. I did not see any of that this Easter, but the crowd of observers, thousands of them, seemed nearly as big at the end of the night as it was at the beginning.

The old town is jammed for this spectacle. With automobiles out of sight and, except for the murmuring of the crowds and the flash of light from hundreds of cameras and the modern dress of the observers, it could be Enna of a hundred years ago.

Good Friday's procession is somber. The Banda Cittadina de Enna, its members interspersed throughout the procession, plays the same dirgelike music over and over and over. There is no joy here. Christ has been crucified, his mother is grieving. Despite the presence of thousands of humans, the silence is almost deafening.

Two days later, in the late afternoon of Easter Sunday, everything changes. The confraternities are back; more thousands of observers start gathering around the cathedral. Something new and remarkable is about to happen. I stand near the cathedral's top steps. For about two hours, the crowd builds. Then, suddenly, a cheer breaks out. At the top of Via Roma, a confraternity turns a corner from a side street bearing a new statue. This is the risen Christ standing tall; a hand, its palm spotted with red, is raised in peace. He becomes like a living organism: His movements are subtle and under control by the dozens of men shouldering the beams that hold him in place. He moves a bit, swaying slightly, as if he is impatiently waiting for someone.

He is. There is a rumbling of the crowd lining the street a

hundred or so feet downhill on Via Roma. Just as suddenly as the statue of Christ appears, a statue of the Madonna turns a corner at the bottom of the street, looking up.

What happens next, to my uninitiated eyes, is remarkable. This is not the statue of the grieving Madonna of two nights earlier. This one is without the sword through the breast. On her face is a full smile. This is a joyful Madonna.

The men carrying her make movements in unison that seem to bring her to life. She looks up the hill; it dawns on her that what she is seeing is her son, raised from the dead. She is in shock, she takes a step backward and then she moves forward a few feet. As it sinks in on her what has happened, she sways from side to side, her disbelief dissolving into belief that her son is alive. Then, suddenly, she sprints toward her son; the sweating men carrying this massive statue are actually running up the hill in strict choppy-step unison.

Christ, by now, is moving down the hill toward his mother. She reaches him next to the cathedral, and the confraternity members carrying her execute an amazing 180-degree maneuver. They turn her around completely and, in seconds, she is standing next to her son, moving down Via Roma. The pair then turns into the piazza in front of the cathedral, where more than 150 men jockey their way up the steep steps and inside.

The crowd is cheering; the municipal band is playing bright, happy tunes. We push our way inside the great church and look up at the two statues side by side. Weary robed men, their hoods pulled back to show smiling, sweat-glistened faces, are leaning against pillars or straddling chairs, exhausted.

AFTERWORD

Iᴛ ᴡᴀs early one evening in either 1998 or 1999—my memory
is faulty here—when I boarded a train in Siracusa after a five-
day visit to that most wonderful, most walkable, and friendly
Sicilian city. I was ensconced in a semiprivate cabin on a sleeper
car heading to Bologna in northern Italy. Later, I discovered
that I had not only the cabin but the entire car to myself. No
one boarded this sleeper during the night as the train passed
through Catania, Taormina, Messina, crossed the strait by
ferry, and dropped onto the toe of Italy's boot before heading
north to Naples, Rome, and then, by midmorning the next
day, into Bologna, the end of the line.

That first evening, as we were slowly leaving Siracusa, I
briefly had as a companion the train's first-class porter who
made up my tiny room, explaining that he had to make up
the second bed in case someone boarded during the night with
a similar reservation. After all, I had not paid for complete
privacy.

His job, without other passengers, was going to be easy
during that trip, and we stood out in the passageway with train

windows lowered halfway, feeling the warm, lemon-scented breeze of early spring, and speaking a basic mixture of English and Italian. He was telling me about his job and how often he saw his family. I told him where I was from and about my family. His interest seemed genuine and warm.

As we talked, the train slowed a bit and stopped on what appeared to be a siding. We hadn't quite reached Augusta, the highly industrialized area twelve miles north of Siracusa. "Another train is coming," he said. *"Aspettiamo."* (We wait.) It was a long wait. As I looked out toward the Ionian Sea across the southern edge of the Golfo di Augusta and to our right, I realized that within my line of sight was the archaeological site of Thapsos on a small island tied to the coast by a narrow causeway. I had just read about it, perhaps in a tourist guidebook, and knew only that this settlement of indigenous Sicilians greatly predated by several hundred years the arrival of the Greeks.

Thapsos was only a short distance to the south, and just out of our line of sight from the train, from the ancient Greek-Sicilian city of Megara Hyblaia, colonized by a group from Megara in Greece, perhaps fifteen years before a group of Corinthian Greeks ever set foot on what became Siracusa.

I turned to my new traveling companion and started to tell him what I knew was on the tiny island just a few hundred feet offshore. Immediately I could see he understood what I was referring to, and when I asked him what he knew about it, he shrugged slightly and said, *"Oh, solo un po.'"* (Just a little). Then he proceeded to tell me, in a unique combination of simple Italian and basic English so that I could follow, about when it was first inhabited, perhaps around 1400 B.C. He described how pots and other items recovered showed that the people of the Thapsos culture had traded with the people of what became Greece and perhaps the people of what is today Malta. He talked about the Greeks and how they came to Sicily to find homes in a New World. "Like America was at one time," he said with a smile.

This man clearly knew the history of his island and was pleased that I wanted to learn more about it.

The evening was now in twilight. My friend had things to do, and I returned to my small room and read until quite late, enjoying the rocking of the train and the soft, muffled clacking sound of wheels against tracks. In the morning, I thanked the porter for our conversation, we shook hands, and I stepped off the train in Bologna for a twenty-four-hour visit before heading back to Rome and my airplane home.

This encounter on the train and subsequent conversations I have had with dozens of Sicilians of various ages have shown that these Mediterranean islanders are attuned to their three-thousand-year history.

These visits and the reading of Sicilian literature have given me a better understanding about the impact on a people of one conqueror after another sweeping across their island. An identity cannot be formed. Self-determination cannot occur in the wake of all-powerful foreign invaders. No wonder their society was closed for so long; no wonder they could really trust only those within their own families. Silence with strangers and authority figures was commonplace.

While the Normans, French, and Spanish certainly exerted their influence on this island—its buildings, street names, churches, dominant religion—it is the Greeks and the Arabs from whom most Sicilians descend and identify with. Sicilian surnames and the names of their towns and villages come from those languages. While a small part of their cuisine has French and Spanish touches, it is made up of ingredients the Greeks and Arabs brought there, such as olives, lemons, almonds, and certain spices.

As outsiders, we will never comprehend the Sicilian psyche; perhaps many Sicilians don't fully understand it, either. So again, I turn to the Sicilian poet Ignazio Buttitta (1899–1997), to help explain Sicily to me. These are the last five stanzas from a poem entitled *"Lingua e dialettu"* ("Language and Dialect"). It was written in 1970 and translated by Alissandru (Alex) Caldiero, a onetime student and friend of Buttitta.

Lingua e dialettu

Un poviru,
c'addatta nte minni strippi
da matri putativa,
chi u chiama 'figghiu'
pi nciuria.

Nuàtri l'avevamu a matri,
nni l'arrubbaru;
aveva i minni a
funtani di latti
e ci vìppiru tutti,
ora ci sputanu.

Nni ristò a vuci d'idda,
a cadenza,
a nota vascia
du sonu e du
lamentu:
chissi non nni
ponnu rubari.

Nni ristò a
sumigghianza,
l'annatura,
i gesti, i lampi nta
l'occhi: chissi non nni
ponnu rubari.

Non nni ponnu
rubari,
ma ristamu poviri
e orfani u stissu.

Language and Dialect

I'm a poor man,
who suckles the barren breast
of a so-called mother
who calls him 'son'
as an insult.

Once we had a mother,
they stole her from us;
her breasts were fountains of
     milk,
and everyone drank from
     them,
now they spit on them.

For us her voice remains,
the cadence
the low note
of its music and the sorrow:
they couldn't rob us of these.

They couldn't rob us of these,
but we're poor
and orphaned just the same.

ACKNOWLEDGMENTS

To be able to do what I do and to see the things I get to see is, I think, remarkable. Better still is the opportunity to meet fascinating people willing to share their lives, stories, and, in the case of this book, their views of this world just "north of Africa" that I am struggling to understand.

Countless books have been written about Sicily. My challenge was to make this one different from the typical travel narrative. I wanted to put the island and its people in proper perspective to show why they are Sicilians before they are Italians, and why no amount of time under the control of Rome will ever change that.

I had a lot of help.

Perhaps one of the most fortunate friendships I made was with Conchita Vecchio, a Brooklyn-born Sicilian-American who has spent several years on her ancestral island teaching, writing, serving as a tour guide, and interpreting for businesspeople and government officials. When I needed help in Palermo with interviews, she would rearrange her schedule to accommodate me and act as intermediary when my poor language skills let me down as I attempted to schedule interviews. Her interpreting abilities made it possible for me to have extended, quick-paced conversations with key individuals. And one of my fondest memories is her generous invitation to join her group of friends for Palermo's festival of Santa Rosalia. It was a wonderful evening of food, conversation, and spectacle.

Good fortune struck when Linda Graci, librarian at the Leonardo Sciascia Foundation in Racalmuto, put me in touch with Vito Catalano, grandson of the famous author who figures so prominently in this book. Vito, a published writer, and his wife, Anna Kowalska, drove me one hot July afternoon to the Sciascia family home at Noce a few miles out of Racalmuto and introduced me to Maria Sciascia (who is Vito's mother and Sciascia's daughter), and her husband, Nino Catalano.

Vito, over a period of a few days, led me on tours of Sciascia's two homes: the one at Noce and his apartment in Palermo. While there, Vito also orchestrated a tour, led by his father, of the Inquisitor's Prison in a wing of the Steri Palace, also known as Palazzo Chiaramonte.

I owe gratitude to a number of bed-and-breakfast folks who sent me off in directions that yielded gold for this book. I particularly am in debt to Marisin and Salvatore Tranchina of Scopello, who showed generous hospitality during two of my trips while I lodged in their Pensione Tranchina. They spent the better part of an afternoon on their nearby property that overlooks the Mediterranean Sea explaining the ins and outs of Sicilian bureaucracy and how it has affected them and their land.

Most particularly, I thank Giuseppe Andini and Paola Prandi, who became among my closest friends in Sicily and with whom I stayed, during four trips, at their bed-and-breakfast Tra i frutti (Among the Fruit), on the outskirts of Racalmuto. They are transplanted northern Italians who have absorbed much of their adopted village's lore and legends. Paola stayed in close contact during the writing of this book, finding answers to questions about the village. Giuseppe offered thoughtful suggestions and information about places around the countryside that would add to my understanding of Sicilian country life.

Preparing to write this book began with conversations with university professors in Vancouver, British Columbia: Dr. Franco de Angelis of the University of British Columbia and a historian of Sicily's archaic period under the Greeks, and Dr. Sam Migliore, an anthropologist at Kwantlen Polytechnic University. They spent an afternoon discussing Sicily from a historical and cultural perspective. Sam claims Racalmuto as his ancestral home, and he encouraged me to devote a lot of time in that southern Sicilian village to get a sense of place and a feel for the *Sicilitudine* expressed by the village's favorite son, Leonardo Sciascia.

And I give special thanks to two women who helped me navigate the world of Sicilian food: Renée Restivo of Soul of Sicily, who arranged five days of tours in Noto and Siracusa and demonstrations of actual Sicilian cooking and pastry making; and Polly Franchini, who was involved with the New York City publishing house Oronzo Editions. It produces beautifully written and illustrated books on regional Italian cooking. Renée and Polly gave permission for me to use carefully selected recipes that accurately portray authentic Sicilian cuisine.

And I owe thanks to colleague Lesli Nielson who helped edit the recipes.

Steve McCurdy, one of the most sensitive travel photographers and film documentarians I know, was a wonderful companion during my fourth trip. He showed me how to be a traveler and not a tourist. His language skills served us well during our two-week drive around the island; his affability softened my sometimes edginess about meeting schedules, and his willingness to approach people in small towns made many scenes in the book possible.

Still to thank are two of my dearest and most loyal friends, both Sicilian-Americans, without whom this book would have been a very difficult task: Alissandru (Alex) Caldiero, poet, performer, linguist, social critic, and teacher; and Dr. Leonard Chiarelli, a historian and specialist in Sicily's Arab period. Brooklyn-born Leonard, whose roots go deep into the soil of southwestern Sicily, considers his lineage Arabic; Alex, born in the southeastern quarter of the island, claims Greek DNA.

Alex was the first person I talked to about how to approach this book, and his insight was invaluable. He shared mysteries and other information about the Sicilian language and offered thought-provoking theories about Greek myths as they pertain to the island of his birth. It was he who opened my eyes to the realization that Sicilians view themselves as living north of Africa rather than south of Italy.

That realization is a major step on the path to understanding Sicily and its people.

Leonard helped shape this book more than anyone else. For years, we have met nearly every Saturday morning for breakfast, and then for cigars on my front porch or on his grapevine-covered terrace. Like Sam Migliore, Leonard's ancestral village is Racalmuto. I had heard stories about his visits there, about his conversations as a young man with Leonardo Sciascia, and his kinship with his cousin Laura Sciascia. He also told me what it was like growing up Sicilian and described the impact of the Arabs on Sicilian culture.

When I started, Leonard scoured the Marriott Library at the University of Utah, where he works as Middle East librarian, for books, articles, dissertations, and various tracts and pamphlets to help light my way. He took time from finishing his own definitive history about the Arabs in Sicily to read my final manuscript and to save me from numerous embarrassing mistakes.

I also thank my editor at Thomas Dunne Books/St. Martin's Press, Kathleen Gilligan, whose insight and gentle suggestions did much to improve this book. My manuscript editor, Frances C. Sayers, also has my deepest gratitude. And I recognize the friendship of my friends Bette Joe Caldwell Clapp and Jerry Clapp. They made their Lake Cascade home in central Idaho available to me during one particularly productive writing period.

Once again, I know for a certainty that none of this could have been accomplished without the continued support of my wife and partner, Connie-Lou Disney, also a lover of books and one who has the enviable job of designing them. She understands that doing what I love involves long weeks of sometimes-solo travel and endless hours of research and writing. She accommodates and supports me, keeping outside distractions

at bay. Her constructive insight as a final reader of my manuscript proved invaluable.

—John Keahey
Salt Lake City, Utah
July 2011

SELECTED BIBLIOGRAPHY

Abulafia, David, ed. *The Mediterranean in History*. London: Thames and Hudson, 2003.

ANSA. "DNA of Fugitive Mafia Boss Reconstructed." July 1, 2010.

Apollodorus. *The Library of Greek Mythology*. Translated by Robin Hard. Oxford: Oxford University Press, 1997.

Astarita, Tommaso. *Between Salt Water and Holy Water: A History of Southern Italy*. London: W. W. Norton, 2005.

Barzini, Luigi. *The Italians*. New York: Atheneum, 1964.

Braudel, Fernand. *The Mediterranean in the Ancient World*. Translated by Siân Reynolds. London: Penguin Books, 2001.

Buttitta, Ignacio. *Io faccio il poeta*. Milan: Feltrinelli Editore, 1972.

Caldiero, Alissandru (Alex) F. *Grammar of the Sicilian Language*. Unpublished manuscript, 2008.

Camilleri, Andrea. *The Paper Moon*. Translated by Stephen Sartarelli. New York: Penguin Books, 2008.

———. *The Shape of Water*. Translated by Stephen Sartarelli. New York: Penguin Books, 2005.

———. *The Smell of the Night*. Translated by Stephen Sartarelli. New York: Penguin Books, 2005.

———. *The Wings of the Sphinx*. Translated by Stephen Sartarelli. New York: Penguin Books, 2009.

Chiarelli, Leonard. *A History of Muslim Sicily*. Sta Venera, Malta: Midsea Books, 2011.

Cicero. *The Verrine Orations*, volumes I and II. Translated by L. H. G. Greenwood. Cambridge, Mass.: Harvard University Press, 1953.

Coria, Giuseppe. *Sicily: Culinary Crossroads*. Translated by Gaetano Cipolla. New York: Oronzo Editions, 2008.

Croce, Marcella, and Moira F. Harris. *History on the Road: The Painted Carts of Sicily*. Saint Paul, Minn.: Pogo Press, 2006.

De Angelis, Franco. *Megara Hyblaia and Selinous: The Development of Two Greek City-States in Archaic Sicily*. Oxford: Oxford University School of Archaeology, 2003.

De Maupassant, Guy. *Sicily*. Edited and translated by Robert W. Berger. New York: Italica Press, 2007.

Dickie, John. *Delizia! The Epic History of the Italians and Their Food*. New York: Free Press, 2008.

Dunbabin, Jean. *Charles I of Anjou: Power, Kingship and State-Making in Thirteenth-Century Europe*. Harlow, United Kingdom: Addison-Wesley Longman, 1998.

Fiorentino, Paolo. *Sicily Through Symbolism and Myth: Gates to Heaven and the Underworld*. Mineola, N.Y.: Legas, 2006.

Freedman, Paul, ed. *Food: The History of Taste*. Berkeley: University of California Press, 2007.

Grady, Ellen. *Blue Guide Sicily*, seventh edition. New York: W. W. Norton, 2006.

Green, Toby. *Inquisition: The Reign of Fear*. New York: St. Martin's Press, 2007.

Gutkowski, Emanuela. *Does the Night Smell the Same in Italy and in English Speaking Countries? An Essay on Translation: Camilleri in English*. Enna, Sicily: Ilion Books, 2009.

Jensen, Frede, ed. and trans. *The Poetry of the Sicilian School.* New York and London: Garland Publishing, Inc., 1986.

Kagan, Donald. *Thucydides: The Reinvention of History.* New York: Viking, 2009.

Kay, George R., ed. *The Penguin Book of Italian Verse.* Baltimore: Penguin Books, 1958.

Lampedusa, Giuseppe di. *The Leopard.* Translated by Archibald Colquhoun. New York: Time Reading Program, 1966.

———. *The Siren and Selected Writings.* Translated by Archibald Colquhoun, David Gilmour, and Guido Waldman. London: The Harvill Press, 1995.

Leighton, Robert. *Sicily Before History: An Archaeological Survey from the Paleolithic to the Iron Age.* Ithaca, N.Y.: Cornell University Press, 1999.

Lewis, Norman. *In Sicily.* New York: St. Martin's Press, 2000.

Loud, G. A. *The Age of Robert Guiscard: Southern Italy and the Norman Conquest.* Harlow, United Kingdom: Longman/Pearson Education, 2000.

Marani, Dacia. *Bagheria.* Translated by Dick Kitto and Elspeth Spottiswood. London: Peter Owen Publishers, 1994.

———. *The Silent Duchess.* Translated by Dick Kitto and Elspeth Spottiswood. New York: The Feminist Press, 1998.

Mazzucchelli, Chiara. "Ethnic Regionalism in American Literature: The Case of Sicilian/American Writers." *Tamkang Review,* vol. 38, no. 1.

Menocal, María Rosa. *The Arabic Role in Medieval Literary History: A Forgotten History.* Philadelphia: University of Pennsylvania Press, 1987.

Messina, Annie (Gamlîa Ghâli). *The Myrtle & the Rose.* New York: Italica Press, 1997.

Messina, Maria. *Behind Closed Doors: Her Father's House and Other Stories of Sicily.* Translated by Elise Magistro. New York: The Feminist Press, 2007.

Migliore, Sam. *Mal'uocchiu: Ambiguity, Evil Eye, and the Language of Distress.* Toronto: University of Toronto Press, 1997.

Norwich, John Julius. *The Middle Sea: A History of the Mediterranean.* New York: Doubleday, 2006.

Pickering-Iazzi, Robin. *Mafia and Outlaw Stories from Italian Life and Literature.* Toronto: University of Toronto Press, 2007.

Pillitteri, Peppi. *Traditions of Our Fathers: The True Sicilians.* Hamilton, Ontario: Seldon Printing, 1992.

Pirandello, Luigi. *The Late Mattia Pascal.* Translated by William Weaver. New York: New York Review Books, 1964.

———. *The Notebooks of Serafino Gubbio or (Shoot!).* Translated by C. K. Scott Moncrieff. Sawtry, United Kingdom: Dedalus, 1919.

———. *The Oil Jar and Other Stories.* Translated by Stanley Appelbaum. New York: Dover Publications, 1995.

———. *Tales of Madness.* Translated by Giovanni R. Bussino. Wellesley, Mass.: Dante University of America Press, 1984.

———. *Tales of Suicide.* Translated by Giovanni R. Bussino. Wellesley, Mass.: Dante University of America Press, 1988.

Privitera, Joseph F. *Sicilian: The Oldest Romance Language.* Brooklyn, N.Y.: Legas, 2004.

———. *Sicily: An Illustrated History.* New York: Hippocrene Books, 2002.

Rigoglioso, Marguerite. "Mysticism, Mother Worship, and Misogyny in the Navel of Sicily: A Spiritual History of Enna, Lake Pergusa, Demeter, and Persephone." Master's thesis, California Institute of Integral Studies, 2001.

Runciman, Steven. *The Sicilian Vespers: A History of the Mediterranean World in the Later Thirteenth Century.* Cambridge: Cambridge University Press, 1992.

Scarth, Alwyn, and Jean-Claude Tanguy. *Volcanoes of Europe.* Oxford: Oxford University Press, 2001.

Schneider, Jane C., and Peter T. Schneider. *Reversible Destiny: Mafia, Antimafia, and the Struggle for Palermo.* Berkeley: University of California Press, 2003.

Schneider, Peter, and Jane C. Schneider. "Giovanni Falcone, Paolo Borsellino and the Procura of Palermo," *OC Newsletter*, ECPR Standing Group Organized Crime, May 2002.

Sciascia, Leonardo. *Candido: Or a Dream Dreamed in Sicily*. Translated by Adrienne Foulke. New York: Harcourt Brace Jovanovich, 1979.

———. *The Council of Egypt*. Translated by Adrienne Foulke. London: HarperCollins Publishers, 1993.

———. *The Day of the Owl*. Translated by Archibald Colquhoun and Arthur Oliver. New York: New York Review Books, 2003.

———. *Equal Danger*. Translated by Adrienne Foulke. New York: New York Review Books, 2003.

———. *The Moro Affair*. Translated by Sacha Rabinovitch. London: Granta Books, 2002.

———. *One Way or Another*. Translated by Adrienne Foulke. New York: Harper and Row, Publishers, 1977.

———. *Open Doors and Three Novellas*. Translated by Marie Evans, Joseph Farrell, and Sacha Rabinovitch. New York: Alfred A. Knopf, 1992.

———. *Salt in the Wound*, followed by *The Death of the Inquisitor*. Translated by Judith Green. New York: Orion Press, 1969.

———. *Sicilian Uncles*. Translated by N. S. Thompson. London: Granta Books, 2001.

———. *Sicily as Metaphor*. Conversations presented by Marcelle Padovani. Translated by James Marcus. Marlboro, Vt.: Marlboro Press, 1994.

———. *To Each His Own*. Translated by Adrienne Foulke. New York: New York Review Books, 2000.

———. *The Wine-Dark Sea*. Translated by Avril Bardoni. New York: New York Review Books, 2000.

Siculus, Diodorus. Translated by C. H. Oldfather. The Library of History. Cambridge, Mass.: Loeb Classical Library, Harvard University Press, 1939.

Simeti, Mary Taylor. "At the Prince's Table." *Gastronomica: The Journal of Food and Culture,* vol. 7, no. 2, pp. 64–70, 2007.

———. *On Persephone's Island: A Sicilian Journal.* New York: Vintage Books, 1995.

Snodgrass, Mary Ellen. *Encyclopedia of Kitchen History,* New York: Taylor and Francis Books, 2004.

Stille, Alexander. *Excellent Cadavers: The Mafia and the Death of the First Italian Republic.* New York: Vintage Books, 1996.

Timpanelli, Gioia. *Sometimes the Soul: Two Novellas of Sicily.* New York: Vintage Books, 1998.

———. *What Makes a Child Lucky.* New York: W. W. Norton, 2008.

Uccello, Antonino. *Del mangiar siracusano.* Noto, Sicily: Azienda Provinciale Turismo di Siracusa, 2000.

Verga, Giovanni. *Cavalleria Rusticana and Other Stories.* Translated by G. H. McWilliam. New York: Penguin Books, 1999.

———. *I Malavoglia: The House by the Medlar Tree.* Translated by Judith Landry. Sawtry, United Kingdom: Dedalus, 2008.

———. *Little Novels of Sicily.* Translated by D. H. Lawrence. South Royalton, Vt.: Steerforth Italia, 2000.

———. *Mastro Don Gesualdo.* Translated by D. H. Lawrence. London: Dedalus, 1984.

———. *Sparrow.* Translated by Lucy Gordan and Frances Frenaye. New York: Italica Press, 1997.

Washington, Booker T., with Robert E. Park. *The Man Farthest Down.* New Brunswick, N.J.: Transaction Books, 1984.

Wilson, R. J. A. *Sicily Under the Roman Empire.* Warminster, England: Aris and Phillips, 1991.

Wright, Clifford A. *A Mediterranean Feast: The Story of the Birth of the Celebrated Cuisines of the Mediterranean, from the Merchants of Venice to the Barbary Corsairs, with More Than 500 Recipes.* New York: William Morrow, 1999.

INDEX

PERMISSIONS

Caldiero, along with the translation of a stanza carved in stone by an anonymous carver: "U me cori/doppu tant' anni . . ." (My heart/after so many years . . .).

Photographs: Permissions granted to use photographs by, or owned by, Steven R. McCurdy, Bradley W. Keahey, Francesca Corrao, architects Gabriele Graziano and Alice Franzitta, and Gerard Fouet-AFP-Getty Images.